Science Fiction and Political Philosophy

Politics, Literature, and Film

Series Editor: Lee Trepanier, Saginaw Valley State University

The Politics, Literature & Film series is an interdisciplinary examination of the intersection of politics with literature and/or film. The series is receptive to works that use a variety of methodological approaches, focus on any period from antiquity to the present, and situate their analysis in national, comparative, or global contexts. Politics, Literature, & Film seeks to be truly interdisciplinary by including authors from all the social sciences and humanities, such as political science, sociology, psychology, literature, philosophy, history, religious studies, and law. The series is open to both American and non-American literature and film. By putting forth bold and innovative ideas that appeal to a broad range of interests, the series aims to enrich our conversations about literature, film, and their relationship to politics.

Recent Titles

The Politics of Twin Peaks, edited by Amanda DiPaolo and James Clark Gillies
AIDS-Trauma and Politics: American Literature and the Search for a Witness, by Aimee Pozorski
Baudelaire Contra Benjamin: A Critique of Politicized Aesthetics and Cul-tural Marxism, by Beibei Guan and Wayne Cristaudo
Updike and Politics: New Considerations, edited by Matthew Shipe and Scott Dill
Lights, Camera, Execution!: Cinematic Portrayals of Capital Punishment, by Helen J. Knowles, Bruce E. Altschuler, and Jaclyn Schildkraut
Possibility's Parents: Stories at the End of Liberalism, by Margaret Seyford Hrezo and Nicolas Pappas
Game of Thrones and the Theories of International Relations, by Ñusta Carranza Ko and Laura D. Young
Age of Anxiety: Meaning, Identity, and Politics, in 21st Century Film and Literature, by Anthony M. Wachs and Jon D. Schaff
Science Fiction and Political Philosophy: From Bacon to Black Mirror, by Timothy McCranor and Steven Michels

Science Fiction and Political Philosophy

From Bacon to Black Mirror

Timothy McCranor and Steven Michels

LEXINGTON BOOKS

Lanham • Boulder • New York • London

Published by Lexington Books
An imprint of The Rowman & Littlefield Publishing Group, Inc.
4501 Forbes Boulevard, Suite 200, Lanham, Maryland 20706
www.rowman.com

6 Tinworth Street, London SE11 5AL

British Library Cataloguing in Publication Information Available

Library of Congress Cataloging-in-Publication Data

Library of Congress Control Number:2019957120

ISBN 978-1-4985-8643-6 (cloth)
ISBN 978-1-4985-8645-0 (paperback)
ISBN 978-1-4985-8644-3 (electronic)

for S.D.

Contents

An Introduction to Science Fiction and Political Philosophy

Timothy McCranor

In a February 2017 report, a science advisory committee lent its support to clinical trials for "genome editing of the human germline—adding, removing, or replacing DNA base pairs in gametes or early embryos."[1] The committee provided a narrow set of criteria for the treatment and prevention of diseases and disabilities but recommended the prohibition of genome editing for enhancement purposes. While the decision hastens the possibility of curing the incurable, such as Huntington's, Tay-Sachs, and Cystic Fibrosis, it may also suggest a posthuman future.[2] For such processes, together with the development of gene-editing technologies like CRISPR-Cas9, constitute significant steps toward our ability to genetically engineer intelligence, beauty, and strength. As the *New York Times* wrote: the "new report heralds a day scientists have long warned is coming. After decades of science-fiction movies, cocktail party chatter and college seminars in which people have idly debated the ethics of humanity intervening in its own evolution, advancing technology dictates that the public now make some hard choices."[3]

There can be little doubt that the biotechnology revolution poses profound challenges to our political, economic, and social order. What are the implications for human dignity and human rights once we are confronted with conclusive proof of our indefinite malleability? Or for liberal democracy when there is a growing divide between those who can afford genetically enhanced children (and grandchildren) and those who cannot? Or for human greatness when neither life is tragically short nor death anxiously near? The biotechnology revolution will soon render us inhuman, unequal, or uninteresting—perhaps.

At the height of the Cold War, and largely for military purposes, the United States and the Soviet Union launched mankind's journey into space. But much like other technological breakthroughs, such as the personal computer or GPS, the race into space has increasingly become a private endeavor. In late 2017, Asgardia-1 was launched into space—a satellite containing data from the citizens of Asgardia, a group of people trying to create "the first ever space nation" to realize "man's eternal dream to leave his cradle on Earth and expand into the Universe."[4] Igor Ashurbeyli, the founder of Asgardia, is not exactly one of a kind. Whether for the sake of curiosity, humanity, or vanity, wealthy business magnates and entrepreneurs, including Elon Musk, Jeff Bezos, and Eric Schmidt, are promoting and shaping the future of space exploration.[5] Apart from satisfying mankind's abiding desire to explore, discover, and encounter, the growing pace and diversity of space enterprises may serve mankind's increasingly apparent and dire need to find, settle, and populate another planet.

If only age-old fears of newfangled ways to exploit planetary resources and private communications marked the water's edge—not to be outdone, or left behind, the United States officially expanded its commitment to space in August 2018, when U.S. Vice President Mike Pence announced a plan to establish the U.S. Space Force. Setting aside whether genetically-enhanced clones would be involved, newly discovered domains shall soon exist from which, and within which, great powers will exert influence, declare sovereignty, and wage war. At the same time, the cultivation of such capabilities may prove fortuitous for our species if we encounter other intelligent life. As Stephen Hawking has pointed out, "We only have to look at ourselves to see how intelligent life might develop into something we wouldn't want to meet."[6] But again, perhaps.

Genetic engineering may relieve us from painful disease, or even postpone death, significantly if not permanently. A distant planet may excite us, or even save our species. But what good is life if we are still compelled to work? What good is species-survival if we still must labor individually? What good is biotechnology and space travel without the machines that provide my abundance of food; that build my formidable home; that efficiently and cheaply deliver my online orders; that drive cars more safely; that guide missiles more precisely; that make and sync appointments; that track our movements and recognize our faces; that automatically record our conversations; that look and sound like us; that think like humans?

On December 12, 2017, a group of bipartisan U.S. senators and representatives introduced the Future of Artificial Intelligence Act, a "first-of-its-kind legislation that would promote an enabling environment for the continued development of artificial intelligence (AI) technology."[7] The new bill came in the wake of increasing debates about, and calls for, the regulation of AI, whose potential rewards and risks arguably far outweigh those of biotechnology and space travel. AI is likely to touch upon, if not transform, almost every aspect of human life, from health care and education to public debate and defense. As Bill Gates observed, AI is like "nuclear weapons and nuclear energy" in terms of what it might do for humanity but also for the danger it poses.[8] Elon Musk and Stephen Hawking are two of the most prominent and fervent advocates of space travel—AI alarms both of them. Musk has described AI as an "existential threat to humanity."[9] Whether it be for the sake of our preservation or theirs, there seems to be good reason as to why we should all end up in pleasure machines built by robots.

Biotechnology, space travel, and AI are arguably the three most promising and portentous scientific developments confronting humanity in the twenty-first century. They are hardly the only ones, however, and the list of technology-related concerns, problems, or threats only seems to be growing by the day. Big data threatens our privacy and autonomy, and it only grows bigger, in apparent disproportion to the number of tech giants that want to own it, store it, and sell it. Social media, and our addiction to it, facilitates our atomization and undermines our social capital. It provides a platform for hate and discrimination, to say nothing of bullying and taunting. Online disinformation campaigns, aided and abetted by bots, trolls, and deepfakes, seek to subvert and disrupt liberal democracy, first by exploiting our credulity and then by encouraging our apathy—the only thing worse than a populace that believes anything is a populace that believes nothing.[10] Facial recognition and location services improve the depth and scope of state surveillance. Our identities can be stolen and sold, our desktops hijacked and ransomed. Automation will cause tectonic shifts in the job market, destroying jobs at a rate nigh impossible to keep pace with. As global travel becomes cheaper and easier, global pandemics become more likely and less containable. The list could go on. But if all that were not enough—bookstores may soon become obsolete.

The degree to which any of these concerns truly constitute a Pandora's box is an open question. Fears and warnings concerning technology have proven to be misplaced or overstated in the past. Nevertheless, the fact that these concerns should be topics of public debate is beyond dispute. And, yet, the extent to which these concerns are seizing the attention of America (let alone the world) is likewise a question. At best (or maybe worst), such stories go unnoticed because the country is distracted by the sensational or sexy. More defensibly, the urgent stifles the important. A president who might have obstructed justice; a crisis of the American middle-class; an erosion of American identity; the revival of great power rivalry; falling sea levels and rising temperatures—in light of all this, and so much more, why would, or should, American citizens clamor for a debate about what *could* adversely affect their children's grandchildren? It seems equally probable, however, though far more alarming, that such stories are ignored, or quickly forgotten, because we do not see cause for concern. CRISPR and Alexa fuel our hopes more than our fears. Worse yet, in other words, these stories are not ignored or forgotten at all; they are embraced. Serious discussion of technological change is thus confronted with a twofold challenge: on the one hand, to resist the human, all-too-human tendency to disregard the important for the sake of the urgent; and, on the other, to expose possible perils where we are inclined to see imminent paradise—all without succumbing to apathetic despair.

In the weeks following Donald Trump's 2016 presidential victory, sales for George Orwell's *1984* steadily rose, especially after Kellyanne Conway's remarks about "alternative facts."[11] Orwell's dystopian novel presciently warned us about the political dangers of information technology and its ability to enable a centralized state to threaten, if not eliminate, personal privacy and preserve its own power. True, the Berlin Wall fell, and the Soviet Union collapsed, but Orwell's warnings have hardly been discredited or rendered irrelevant. China's growing use of high-tech surveillance, such as facial recognition and massive database records, has helped to fuel growing concerns over the rising tide of technology-based authoritarianism poised to define the twenty-first century.

But at the same time, information technology has also empowered those who wish to undermine entrenched political power—just ask Ben Ali, Hosni Mubarak, and Muammar al-Gaddafi. But more importantly, nobody who reads *1984* is left wondering whether something is wrong with the picture just painted. Questions regarding prevention and resistance come to mind. The same cannot be said about Aldous Huxley's *Brave New World*, whose sales also rose after President Trump's victory, though not as sharply.[12] In contrast to *1984*, the power of *Brave New World* comes from the unease, rather than the horror, the novel provokes. Resisting perpetual war, secret police, and state-sponsored violence is, for the most part, a no-brainer. But what's wrong with perpetual peace, open promiscuity, and state-sponsored pleasure? And yet few who read *Brave New World* fail to sense that something is seriously amiss here, even if one cannot quite figure out what it is— "like a splinter in your mind."[13]

Science fiction writing is particularly well-suited to explore the challenges and possibilities that are posed by the ever-accelerating advance of science and technology in the twenty-first century. According to Yuval Noah Harai, in fact, "In the early twenty-first century, perhaps the most important artistic genre is science fiction."[14] Such literature can surely express the extremes of what may lie ahead; it can depict those idyllic hopes and far-fetched fears alluded to above. But perhaps more instructively, science fiction can depict, neither the quixotic nor apocalyptic, but the purely ominous. It can help us to disregard the sensational and sexy, and to contextualize the urgent. The economic threat posed by artificially intelligent automation, or the potential abuse of classified databases enhanced by neural networks and biometrics, for example, is more important than Stormy Daniels's legal dispute but more plausible, certainly in the next century, than Skynet's Judgment Day.

Better still, science fiction can address that challenge of confusing perils with paradise, which is probably why Americans should be rushing to read the dystopian warnings of *Brave New World* rather than *1984*.[15] However pivotal they may be, neither presidents nor judges (let alone special counsels) are destiny. Fast fading are the days when the same can be said of technology. Insofar as it can reach a larger audience, especially one that does not read the latest scientific journals, science fiction can raise questions, not about the how, when, or if of technological innovation in the twenty-first century, but of the whether and why.[16] As Dr. Ian Malcolm succinctly puts it in the science fiction classic *Jurassic Park*: "Scientists are actually preoccupied with accomplishment. So they are focused on whether they can do something. They never stop to ask if they should do something."[17]

Yet these technological advances, and the challenges they pose, may hardly be as novel, or transformational, as we presume. It is not implausible to consider developments in biotechnology as nothing more than the most recent advances in health and medicine, in the characteristic modern attempt to prevent premature death, alleviate pain, and extend life. Likewise, one might ask, what is the fundamental difference between the exploration of outer space in the twenty-first century by means of the VSS Unity and the exploration of the entire globe in the sixteenth century by means of the Santa María? Is not space just that—the next frontier, as opposed to a wholly new one? And aren't machines that talk, look, and think like us simply the next, rather logical, stage in other modern processes, such as industrialization and mechanization? In short, then, these developments constitute nothing more than quantitative rather than qualitative differences—medicine is medicine, ships are ships.

Accordingly, the questions or concerns raised by biotechnology, space travel, and AI in the twenty-first century are comparable to, if not identical with, the questions or concerns raised by science and technology as such, which have played a prominent and defining role in the entire modern project since about the sixteen century, a project launched by philosophers such as Niccolò Machiavelli, Francis Bacon, and Thomas Hobbes, as well as scientists such as Galileo Galilei and Isaac Newton. Indeed, these philosophers and scientists themselves expressed a variety of concerns over their own endeavors. In general, however, they thought that the promise of science and technology outweighed their perils.

The balance between hope and despair, however, began to tip in the other direction with the advent of the intellectual tradition subsequently known as modern discontent, or as the Counter-Enlightenment, or by other such appellations. It is a tradition arguably started by Jean-Jacques Rousseau in 1750 with his prize-winning essay, *Discourse on the Sciences and Arts*. It was continued by other thinkers and writers of the 19th and 20th centuries, such as Alexis de Tocqueville, Gustave Flaubert, Friedrich Nietzsche, and Martin Heidegger. To be sure, this tradition of modern discontent is very diverse, partly because the modern project itself is not monolithic. Whether it be in Rousseau's *le bourgeois*, Tocqueville's *l'individualisme,* Nietzsche's *der letzte Mensch*, or Heidegger's *das Man*, critics of modernity disagree over the sources, substance, and severity of their discontent. [18]

Nevertheless, there is a broad realm of comparable and over-lapping concerns among these thinkers. They might question the restless and exacerbating pursuit of comfort and security that drives technological innovation. Or they might challenge the materialism and commercialism that constitute the foundation, or exacerbate the underlying impulse, of scientific research. Or they might reject the application of scientific principles to the realm of human affairs. Or they might even question the value or credibility of the faculty that underlies science and technology: reason itself. Reflecting on the scientific proposals and projects of her own day, Hannah Arendt, one of Heidegger's most important students, did not doubt the possibility of realizing them. "The question," however, anticipating Dr. Malcolm's very concern from above, "is only whether we wish to use our new scientific and technical knowledge in this direction, and this question cannot be decided by scientific means; it is a political question of the first order and therefore can hardly be left to the decision of professional scientists or professional politicians." [19]

But this line of inquiry can be pushed even further, for the questions posed by science and technology are hardly the prerogative of late modern thought. Such problems were alive and well for Plato and Aristotle as much as they were for Rousseau and Nietzsche. In Book I of the *Politics*, for example, Aristotle envisions shuttles that "would weave themselves," or picks that would "play the lyre," such that "craftsmen would no longer have a need for subordinates, or masters for slaves." [20] Aristotle seems to have envisioned man's liberation from the necessity of labor, though without it apparently piquing his interest. In Book II, in reference to Hippodamus of Miletus, he raises the question of whether the city should have laws that honor those "who discover something advantageous for the city." [21] His answer is rather firmly in the negative. Such innovation would slowly yet surely subvert the authority of the city's *nomos*—the conventions, customs, or traditions necessary for a healthy and stable political community. Tech icons such as Mark Zuckerberg and Steve Jobs would likely be ostracized rather than idolized in Aristotle's ideal *polis*.

In point of fact, the subservient role that Aristotle assigns to applied science and technology is clearly indicated in his definition of political science (or art) as "the most authoritative and most architectonic one." Because political science (or art) "makes use of the remaining sciences and, further, because it legislates what one ought to do and what to abstain from, its end would encompass those of the others, with the result that this would be *the* human good."[22] No less than modern discontent, and perhaps even more so, classical political thought inquired into the purpose and goodness of science and technology. From the perspective of human happiness, of *eudaemonia*, science and technology were comparable to other individual goods, such as wealth, health, and martial victory, which are, at best, partial goods. Speaking, in effect, for this entire tradition, Nietzsche proclaims that "*genuine philosophers*," not scientists, "determine the Whither and For What of man."[23]

Yet one could easily raise at least two objections at this point. On the one hand, the technological changes set to characterize, if not define, the twenty-first century do, in fact, amount to qualitative transformations. Let's set aside the arguably trifling example of Aristotle and his little loom, and consider the more illuminating case of Karl Marx, who revealed with novel clarity and insight the manner in which automation threatens the stability and even viability of capitalism, but who also failed to consider adequately whether that same automation would create as many jobs as it destroyed, as well as whether the government could soften the blows of the market. These considerations, however, are rendered irrelevant by the rate at which AI threatens to displace human labor in the twenty-first and twenty-second centuries. Across the globe, advanced, technology-based economies driven and dependent on constant innovation may be confronted—in the span of years rather than decades—with unemployment numbers, not in the tens of thousands, but the tens of millions. No entrepreneur is likely to be creative enough, and no government-sponsored safety net big enough, to cope with such systemic stress.

On the other hand, one could deny the transformational character of biotechnology and AI, but nonetheless maintain that Aristotle's case for controlling science is no less chimerical—and hence no more helpful—than Rousseau's or Nietzsche's. Machiavelli's critique of the ancients was right all along: technology is destiny—insofar as foreign relations, and hence war, inescapably fuel technological innovation. Debate what we will about the meaning of equality, freedom, and virtue in America, and the delicate balance we wish to maintain between them, and decide what we will concerning biotechnology, space exploration, and AI, and the constraints we wish to impose on their development, the coming confrontation with Russia and China will render all of it meaningless, or cast the American project into the ash heap of history. Speaking to a group of Russian schoolchildren, Vladimir Putin recently said that "the future belongs to artificial intelligence" and that "whoever becomes the leader in this sphere will become the ruler of the world."[24] Good cities, by necessity, must take their bearings from bad ones.[25]

Adopting any one of these positions, however, does not detract from the pertinent and primary point here: that science fiction is particularly well-suited to explore any and all of these questions. That is to say, science fiction can indeed explore the dangers and opportunities of biotechnology, space exploration, AI, and any number of other technology-related issues of the contemporary world. But science fiction can also explore the reservations and critiques that have been raised against the attempt to conquer nature throughout the entire history of political philosophy, particularly those that were raised by the Counter-Enlightenment in response to the meteoric and assertive rise of the modern world. It can also force us to reconsider whether that leap from Musk to Marx, or from Jobs to Hippodamus, is truly tenable. It can make us wonder whether, or to what extent, that tradition of political philosophy continues to ask the right questions, to say nothing of whether it still provides useful answers, when confronted with the prospect of the singularity, whose significance does seem to slightly overshadow the invention of the telescope. Last but not least, science fiction can compel us to consider whether it is worth our time to question the juggernaut that is technology at all. Ironically, technology is no longer the dike or dam originally meant to control the violent river that is *fortuna*—it's become the river itself, and no amount of *virtù* will be able to contain it.[26] Joining the Way of the Future—the first religion of artificial intelligence—might just be the least bad way to outrun the coming flood,[27] or to place a bet on the twenty-first-century version of Pascal's wager. None of this is to suggest that works of science fiction can replace careful readings of the Great Books, nor that works of science fiction frequently reach the same level of depth. But it can pursue these lines of inquiry with an approach that is more accessible and more available, to say nothing of more entertaining.

A whole series of other objections at this point could be raised over the very questionable assumption of our discussion so far: that science fiction is primarily, perhaps even exclusively, concerned with science and technology. Worse still, science fiction has been portrayed for the most part so far as nothing but a Cassandra of science and technology. To be sure, science fiction often takes place in the future, aboard space ships, or within laboratories; it often makes use of non-human lifeforms, whether they be genetically-engineered, extraterrestrial, or robotic; and its message is often alarmist. But this hardly means that science fiction is limited to the problems posed by the apparent or imminent hegemony of Salomon's House.

At the end of the day, like any good literary genre, science fiction is a form of literature that raises questions about a broad spectrum of issues that typically fall within the gamut of political philosophy. Science fiction can, and does, raise questions about justice, equality, the best political order, and so on—all the while without ever concerning itself with the pursuits and experiments of Laputa. It simply does so, and presumably for a variety of reasons, through a particular setting or context that can be classified as science fiction. Perhaps better still, science fiction can make use of new technologies in order to sharpen questions about justice and equality, much like Plato uses the Ring of Gyges to sharpen Thrasymachus's claim about injustice.[28] Furthermore, science fiction can aspire to have the same salutary effects as any good literary genre, such as improving our creativity or increasing our empathy. With its frequent use of diverse and unfamiliar lifeforms, science fiction seems to be particularly well-situated to treat growing concerns over racial animus, xenophobia, even hyper-partisanship. Finally, the great bulk of science fiction writers are hardly paranoid Luddites. Just as frequently, they are Fordians, spanning the spectrum from the merely hopeful to the irredeemably delusional. Accordingly, its readers can turn to the genre, not in order to despair of the world, but to re-enchant it.[29]

This volume is a modest attempt to support the key claims that have so far been made on behalf of science fiction. Each chapter presents a careful analysis of a classic or contemporary work in the genre to illustrate and explore the themes and concepts discussed above. It is arranged chronologically, according to the release date of the book, story, film, or show, beginning with Francis Bacon's *New Atlantis* (1626), a novella that depicts a society guided by science and governed by scientists, and concluding with the Netflix anthology *Black Mirror* (2011), a highly popular television series that offers disturbing vignettes of Bacon's original vision. The latter, created by Charlie Brooker, and examined by David N. Whitney and Steven Michels below, is the piece most closely concerned with the likely gizmos and gadgets of the twenty-first century. Drawing upon the thought of Bacon, Nietzsche, and contemporary transhumanists, Whitney and Michels take a look at two of the show's episodes, one of which depicts the ramifications of having a device surgically-implanted behind the ear that records every moment of our (mistake-laden) lives; the other considers the possibility of transferring our consciousness, either temporarily or indefinitely, to a proverbial "cloud." The first is dark and unsettling; the second is more likely to leave a splinter in the viewer's mind. Juxtaposed, they nicely reflect two opposing orientations that science fiction can adopt. Nivedita Bagchi explores the dangers and drawbacks of bureaucratic despotism backed by test-tube babies, pleasure-focused pharmacology, and highly-tuned hypnopaedia techniques. But Bagchi also shows how *Brave New World* (1932) points to the natural limitations of any attempt to condition human behavior, regardless of how sophisticated and pervasive the science behind it is.

Several chapters are more focused on some of the themes underlying the attempt to conquer fortune and chance. Rather than dwell on its utopian hopes (or perhaps its dystopian warnings), Erin A. Dolgoy and Kimberly Hurd Hale consider *New Atlantis* through the lens of Bacon's "Idols of the Mind" in order to encourage readers to reflect upon their own intellectual predispositions concerning science. In their interpretation of the *Tempest* (1611), Paul T. Wilford and Nicholas Anderson present Shakespeare as an early foil to Bacon's utopian project, which comes to light as impossible, since even the wisest of rulers are dependent on calm waters and favorable winds, but also ignoble, since it cultivates neither wonder nor moderation. They do not, however, pigeonhole the play as a critique of the new science; instead, they explore the risks and costs of various forms of utopian idealism and cynical realism, such as More's *Utopia* and Machiavelli's machinations. Jeff J. S. Black challenges the long-standing position that Mary Shelley's *Frankenstein* (1818) is a cautionary tale about the dangers of modern technology. By casting light on the numerous allusions to Rousseau throughout the novel, Black shows how each of the five stories nested within *Frankenstein* questions the very goodness of enlightenment, which makes monsters, not out of machines, but out of men, by undermining family, friendship, and virtue itself. Likewise, through an unorthodox reading of Herman Melville's "Lightning-Rod Man" (1854), Tobin L. Craig illustrates how technology frustrates our search for happiness by enhancing our awareness of the very thing we seek to alleviate: our insecurity. Rather than putting us at ease, technology makes us question whether any particular device is sufficient and reliable. The device is a reminder of the danger being kept at bay. It makes us brood over the lurking dangers yet to be contained. Finally, Damien K. Picariello takes a look a Fritz Lang's silent film, *Metropolis* (1927), bringing to life the heartless, arrogant, and ultimately futile enterprise of political rationalism, epitomized by Frederick Taylor's *The Principles of Scientific Management.*

Other chapters substantiate the claim that science fiction can address an array of concerns embedded in the tradition of political philosophy itself. Eschewing a single-issue interpretative lens, Steven Michels and Danielle Sottosanti make wide-ranging use of the interspecies war and zero-gravity battle simulations depicted in Orson Scott Card's *Ender's Game* (1985) to discuss questions concerning human nature, equality, education, just war theory, and democratic deliberation, all with the help of Plato, Machiavelli, and Nietzsche. Taking a somewhat different approach, Daniel J. Kapust examines the efficacy of Immanuel Kant's categorical imperative with the help of a single episode from *Star Trek: The Next Generation*, "I, Borg" (1992). Relying in particular on the cinematography of the episode, Kapust argues that Adam Smith's moral psychology as described in *The Theory of Moral Sentiments* better explains the crew's behavior than recourse to Kantian human rights. Taking her cue from Kazuo Ishiguro himself, Constance C. T. Hunt explores, not the implications of biotechnological innovation, but rather the experience of being confronted with knowledge of one's own imminent death, in a reading of *Never Let Me Go* (2005). Finally, drawing upon the thought of Aristotle, Thomas Hobbes, and Machiavelli, Erin A. Dolgoy and

Kimberly Hurd Hale return to discuss what the apocalyptic end of humanity in M. R. Carey's *The Girl with All the Gifts* (2014) can teach us about the significance of the state of nature, the essence of political foundings, and the importance of the liberal arts.

Whatever be the laudable merit of each individual chapter, the volume as a whole is modest, intentionally and inescapably so, because the chapters included herein do not substantiate every claim that was made above on behalf of science fiction. Indeed, it would be rather presumptuous to presume that the discussion above exhausts the avenues of analysis available to science fiction. Similarly, and not surprisingly, there are countless worthy works of science fiction that were not included. Jules Verne's *Twenty Thousand Leagues Under the Sea* (1870), Isaac Asimov's Foundation series (1942–1950), Frank Herbert's *Dune* (1965), Douglas Adams's *The Hitchhiker's Guide to the Galaxy* (1979)—this list, too, goes on. Furthermore, and with equal regret, some of the most pertinent political philosophers were not included, or perhaps not given their due. Marx and Nietzsche make only brief appearances, and the penetrating critiques of technology by Heidegger, Herbert Marcuse, and Arendt, for example, appear not at all. Perhaps even more problematic and disappointing, a definition of what constitutes science fiction has not yet been included either, let alone one that does justice to the epochs that have defined it, to the growing diversity of subgenres that comprise it, and to the conceptual debates that have shaped it.

We did not consider it necessary to operate on the basis of a rigorous, promulgated definition of what constitutes a work of science fiction, partly because we wanted to avoid being vague or banal, but also because the volume was driven more by a set of questions we sought answers to, rather than a particular genre we sought to explain, defend, or promote. Decisions regarding what to include were based on an understanding of science fiction that was broad and more or less lenient; it was also not overly concerned with attempting to determine which works of science fiction were the most philosophically profound. Nevertheless, there were a few guidelines we tried to follow. We sought to incorporate classical as well as contemporary pieces. Non-literary forms of science fiction were included, such as film and television, as well as literary ones. Although the two genres are not mutually exclusive, and the lines between them rather fuzzy, we chose to exclude works that would be more readily identified as fantasy—with the possible exception of the *Tempest*, whose thematic treatment of Baconian science seemed to justify the inclusion. We were also somewhat deliberate in selecting the analytical lenses through which these works are viewed. Partly because a dozen chapters criticizing science by way of Nietzsche and Heidegger seemed ill-advised, if not tiresome, but also because we think science fiction can do more than criticize science, we sought to include a variety of other important theorists from the tradition.

In a word, this volume is modest because we consider it, at best, nothing more than an introductory volume, of sorts, to science fiction and political philosophy. Like many of the contributors to this volume, we are not experts in science fiction, but rather students of political philosophy, especially that of Rousseau, Nietzsche, and Arendt. Accordingly, our ability is fairly limited when it comes to putting together a volume that uses science fiction to explore questions regarding tomorrow's technology, today's science, and yesterday's justice; a volume that would use science fiction to explore nothing but the prospects of biotechnology, space exploration, *or* AI, everything from the apocalyptic to the quixotic; that would make use of science fiction to explore nothing but the pending political threats of tomorrow's technology; that would explore, say, science fiction and Nietzsche, or science fiction and the Frankfurt school; that would make use of the finer distinctions within sci-fi; or that would disregard questions concerning science and technology altogether. We sincerely hope that others have the ability and will to pursue these projects. The genre of science fiction is too rich, and its customary concerns too pressing, for there not to be additional, and better, volumes.

NOTES

Thanks to Jeff J. S. Black, Tobin L. Craig, Christopher Kelly, Steven Michels, and Paul Wilford for their comments on earlier versions of this chapter.

1. "With Stringent Oversight, Heritable Germline Editing Clinical Trials Could One Day Be Permitted for Serious Conditions; Non-Heritable Clinical Trials Should Be Limited to Treating or Preventing Disease or Disability at This Time," *The National Academies Sciences, Engineering, Medicine*, February 14, 2017, https://nam.edu/with-stringent-oversight-heritable-germline-editing-clinical-trials-could-one-day-be-permitted-for-serious-conditions-non-heritable-clinical-trials-should-be-limited-to-treating-or-preventing-diseas/.

2. Francis Fukuyama, *Our Posthuman Future: Consequences of the Biotechnology Revolution* (New York: Farrar, Straus and Giroux, 2002).

3. Amy Harmon, "Human Gene Editing Receives Science Panel's Support," *New York Times*, February 14, 2017, https://www.nytimes.com/2017/02/14/health/human-gene-editing-panel.html.

4. Igor Ashurbeyli, "Concept 'Asgardia—The Space Nation,'" *Asgardia: The Kingdom*, https://asgardia.space/en/page/concept.

5. Emily Tamkin, "Billionaires May Be the Future of Space Policy. Here's What They Want," *Foreign Policy*, December 18, 2017, https://foreignpolicy.com/2017/12/18/billionaires-may-be-the-future-of-space-policy-heres-what-they-want/.

6. Tad Friend, "How Frightened Should We Be of A.I.?", *The New Yorker*, May 7, 2018, https://www.newyorker.com/magazine/2018/05/14/how-frightened-should-we-be-of-ai.

7. "Cantwell, Bipartisan Colleagues Introduce Bill to Further Understand and Promote Development of Artificial Intelligence, Drive Economic Opportunity," *Maria Cantwell: United States Senator for Washington*, December 12, 2017, https://www.cantwell.senate.gov/news/press-releases/cantwell-bipartisan-colleagues-introduce-bill-to-further-understand-and-promote-development-of-artificial-intelligence-drive-economic-opportunity.

8. Paxton Scott and William Yin, "Bill Gates, Gov. Gavin Newsom speak at Unveiling of New Human-centered Artificial Intelligence Institute," *The Stanford Daily*, March 19, 2019, https://www.stanforddaily.com/2019/03/19/bill-gates-gov-gavin-newsom-speak-at-unveiling-of-new-human-centered-artificial-intelligence-institute/.

9. Oren Etzioni, "How to Regulate Artificial Intelligence," *The New York Times*, September 1, 2017, https://www.nytimes.com/2017/09/01/opinion/artificial-intelligence-regulations-rules.html.

10. Charlie Warzel, "He Predicted the 2016 Fake News Crisis. Now He's Worried about an Information Apocalypse," *BuzzFeed.News*, February 11, 2018, https://www.buzzfeed news.com/article/charliewarzel/the-terrifying-future-of-fake-news.

11. Travis M. Andrews, "Sales of Orwell's '1984' spike after Kellyanne Conway's 'alternative facts'," Washington Post, January 25, 2017, https://www.washingtonpost.com/news/morning-mix/wp/2017/01/25/sales-of-orwells-1984-spike-after-kellyanne-conways-alternative-facts/?utm_term=.a4a73f771306.

12. Brad Tuttle, "Sales of Dystopian Novels Have Been Spiking on Amazon Since the Election," *Yahoo! Finance*, January 25, 2017, https://finance.yahoo.com/news/sales-dystopian-novels-spiking-amazon-172912415.html.

13. Laurence Wachowski and Andrew Paul Wachowski, *The Matrix*, directed by Laurence Wachowski and Andrew Paul Wachowski (Burbank, CA: Warner Home Video, 1999), DVD.

14. Yuval Noah Harari, *21 Lessons for the 21st Century* (New York: Spiegel & Grau, 2018), 250.

15. Consider Fukuyama, *Our Posthuman Future*, 3–8, and Harari, *21 Lessons*, 257.

16. Harari, *21 Lessons*, 250.

17. Michael Crichton, *Jurassic Park* (New York: Ballantine, 2012), 318.

18. Consider Steve B. Smith, *Modernity and Its Discontent: Making and Unmaking the Bourgeois from Machiavelli to Bellow* (New Haven: Yale University Press, 2016).

19. Hannah Arendt, *The Human Condition*, 2nd Edition (Chicago: The University of Chicago Press, 1998), 3.

20. Aristotle, *Politics*, trans. Carnes Lord (Chicago: Chicago University Press, 2013), 1253b38–1254a1.

21. Aristotle, *Politics*, 1268b24–25.

22. Aristotle, *Nicomachean Ethics*, trans. Robert C. Bartlett and Susan D. Collins (Chicago: Chicago University Press, 2011), 1094a27–1094b7. Emphasis added.

23. Frederick Nietzsche, *Beyond Good and Evil: Prelude to a Philosophy of the Future*, trans. Walter Kaufmann (New York: Vintage Books, 1989), 136.

24. Friend, "How Frightened Should We Be of AI?"

25. Consider the closing passages of Leo Strauss, *Thoughts on Machiavelli* (Chicago: University of Chicago Press, 1958), 295ff.

26. Niccolò Machiavelli, *The Prince*, 2nd ed., trans. Harvey Mansfield (Chicago: The Chicago University Press, 1988), Chapter XXV.

27. Mark Harris, "Inside the First Church of Artificial Intelligence," *Wired*, November 15, 2017, https://www.wired.com/story/anthony-levandowski-artificial-intelligence-religion/.

28. I am indebted to Jeff J. S. Black for this point and example.

29. Christine Folch, "Why the West Loves Sci-Fi and Fantasy: A Cultural Explanation," *The Atlantic*, June 13, 2013, https://www.theatlantic.com/entertainment/archive/2013/06/why-the-west-loves-sci-fi-and-fantasy-a-cultural-explanation/276816/.

BIBLIOGRAPHY

Arendt, Hannah. *The Human Condition*, 2nd ed. Introduction by Margaret Canovan. Chicago: The University of Chicago Press, 1958.

Aristotle. *Nicomachean Ethics*. Translated, with an Interpretative Essay, Notes, and Glossary by Robert C. Bartlett and Susan D. Collins. Chicago: The University of Chicago Press, 2011.

———. *Politics*. Translated and with an Introduction, Notes and Glossary by Carnes Lord. 2nd ed. Chicago: The University of Chicago Press, 2013.

Crichton, Michael. *Jurassic Park*. New York: Ballantine, 2012.

Fukuyama, Francis. *Our Posthuman Future: Consequences of the Biotechnology Revolution*. New York: Farrar, Straus and Giroux, 2002.

Harari, Yuval Noah. *21 Lessons for the 21st Century*. New York: Spiegel & Grau, 2018.

Machiavelli, Niccolò. *The Prince*. 2nd Edition. Translated and with an Introduction by Harvey C. Mansfield. Chicago: The University of Chicago Press, 1998.

Nietzsche, Frederick. *Beyond Good and Evil: Prelude to a Philosophy of the Future*. Translated by Walter Kaufmann. New York: Vintage Books, 1989.

Smith, Steven B. *Modernity and Its Discontents: Making and Unmaking the Bourgeois from Machiavelli to Bellow*. New Haven, CT: Yale University Press, 2016.

Strauss, Leo. *Thoughts on Machiavelli*. Chicago: The University of Chicago Press, 1958.

Chapter One

Fiction and the Science of Self-Reflection

Francis Bacon's New Atlantis *and the Idols of the Mind*

Erin A. Dolgoy and Kimberly Hurd Hale

It is anachronistic yet entirely appropriate to apply the term "science fiction" to Francis Bacon's *New Atlantis*. When posthumously published in 1627,[1] *New Atlantis* was a new model of literature concerned with science, human progress,[2] and society. While the fable does not involve "alien life, space or time travel," it does "feature hypothetical scientific [and] technological advances."[3] Yet, Bacon does not understand these advances as fictions; rather, he believes that the advances depicted in *New Atlantis* are both entirely possible and fundamentally desirable. These focal aspects of *New Atlantis*— scientific advancement and technological creation, social order yet no clear model of government, and religious adherence with emphasis on tolerant moderation—parallel features of Bacon's Instauration, his proposed refounding of modern society on principles of scientific inquiry, which promises to improve the human experience through the use of scientific methodology and the pursuit of technological and philosophical innovations.

In his grand project, Bacon endeavors "to try the whole thing anew upon a better plan, and to commence a total reconstruction of sciences, arts, and all human knowledge, raised upon the proper foundations."[4] The Instauration is utopian insofar as it promises to remake the world in order to improve the human condition. Neither fictional nor hypothetical, the Instauration is decidedly practical and exceedingly ambitious. The natural world, using Bacon's method, can be more effectively altered to accommodate the needs of human beings. Human beings can also be modified through education, inculcation, and medical intervention to meet desired specifications. Bacon repeatedly argues that he is capable of improving the human experience by increasing human knowledge and inspiring increased technological innovations.[5] His project's title, Instauration, signals both a restoration or renewal of that which already exists and an institution or founding of something new. In *New Atlantis*, we see these complementary aspects of Bacon's project that are fundamental to subsequent examples of science fiction: a programmatic approach to scientific and technological advancement; and the yearning for utopia, manifest in the insatiable desire for a better, more comfortable existence.

New Atlantis inspires extreme and irreconcilable interpretations. Some have read *New Atlantis* as a utopian call to arms for the new, practical republic of science, which Bacon hopes to inaugurate through his Instauration.[6] Jerry Weinberger goes further, arguing that *New Atlantis* is the unacknowledged sixth part of the *Great Instauration*, intended to show how Bacon's proposed plan would function in a completely realized society.[7] Others understand the fable as Bacon's dystopian warning about the dangers of science and unregulated scientists.[8] In his other works, Bacon's silence regarding *New Atlantis* increases its mystery and intrigue.

Unlike previous analyses of *New Atlantis*, in this chapter we apply Bacon's Idols of the Mind, his well-known, quadripartite formulation of the intellectual predispositions common to human beings, as an interpretive lens through which to view *New Atlantis*. First, in order to establish a foundation from which to evaluate our argument in this chapter, we highlight key aspects of *New Atlantis* as they relate to Bacon's Instauration. Second, we explicate Bacon's four Idols of the Mind; we explain the ways in which each Idol is depicted in *New Atlantis* and, as a consequence, how *New Atlantis* provides an opportunity to reflect on our own intellectual predispositions. In the final section, we turn to the importance of fiction and poetry as they relate to Bacon's Instauration. We suggest that Bacon's *New Atlantis*, as an early work of science fiction, offers an opportunity for self-reflection and evaluation of one's perspectives on science and politics. We argue that Bacon has designed *New Atlantis* as a fable in order to help his readers examine their own Idols of the Mind, and thereby encourage them to be more receptive to the aims of his Instauration.

NEW ATLANTIS AND THE INSTAURATION: SAILORS, SECRECY, AND SCIENCE

New Atlantis signals the spirit of advancement or renewal prominent in the sixteenth and seventeenth centuries. Bacon's time is marked by significant social, political, and scientific change. Increased emphases on global trade, political liberty, and scientific advancement give rise to many unprecedented possibilities for human flourishing.[9] Concurrently, Europe is politically unstable, and tensions are increasing between religious leaders and men of science. Thomas More, a staunch Catholic and the author of *Utopia*, published in 1516, is convicted of treason and executed in 1535 for refusing to accept King Henry VIII's marriage annulment from Catherine of Aragon or the Oath of Supremacy. Bacon draws a comparison between the marriage customs in Sir Thomas More's *Utopia* and the "more civil" practices in the commonwealth depicted in *New Atlantis*.[10] Tycho Brahe, the Danish astronomer who posits a geocentric account of the universe, receives state sponsorship by the king of Denmark, yet is exiled by his patron's successor in 1597. Giordano Bruno, who affirms Copernicus's heliocentric account of the world, is charged with heresy and burned at the stake in 1600 by Catholic authorities. That same year, Tomasso Campanella, the Italian astrologer, philosopher, and author of the theocratic utopia, *The City of the Sun*, is imprisoned for twenty-six years for attempting to establish a communist republic. Bacon is not immune to these political machinations. Burgeoning political, religious, and scientific advances during his time offer new opportunities for improving mankind's conditions, but also the potential for accompanying dangers, as these innovations threaten to upend existing powers. Aware of such dangers, Bacon couches his new, revolutionary, scientific, and political ideas in an imaginary commonwealth that feels familiar to, yet is simultaneously radically different from, the social and political world of his readers. Bacon's fiction about science provides a literary form in which to explore the possibilities of a social and political world shaped by the Instauration. Since he depicts imaginary events and people creating space for divergent interpretations and personal reflection, Bacon is able to simultaneously protect himself from potential persecution and inspire his readers to consider their perspectives on science, technology, politics, and religion. Bacon leads us on an intellectual adventure that tests our preparedness for scientific advancement and technological innovation. *New Atlantis* is purposefully educative.

Understood most simply, *New Atlantis* is a nautical exploration gone wrong.[11] It is "a taut fantasy in a short but crammed adventure story."[12] As the narrator (one of the sailors) relates, their ship, *en route* from Peru to China and Japan, becomes lost at sea. Devoid of hope and as a last resort, the sailors pray for salvation. The next day, through the mist, the sailors unexpectedly see an island—Bensalem, so called by its inhabitants. The narrative introduces this "fabulous island in the Pacific whose possession of Baconian science made possible its long history of peaceful progress and its harmony of science and religion."[13] Strangely, the sailors have heard no previous account of the island's existence, which has remained hidden from the rest of the world for nineteen hundred years. The islanders, to the contrary, know much about the sailors, including their languages, religions, and customs, as well as about global politics, religions, technological innovations, scientific discoveries, and mechanical arts. While housed (and perhaps observed) in the Strangers' House, the public institution where foreigners are lodged at the expense of the state, the sailors are taught Bensalem's unique account of world politics, which is significantly different from the history with which they are familiar, or the history that any reader of *New Atlantis* would have learned. According to the Governor-Priest of the Strangers' House, "Three thousand years ago, or somewhat more,"[14] nautical travel and technological expertise were more extensive than they are in Bacon's own time. In those years, the island was not hidden; rather, Bensalem was part of a vast, global trade network. The islanders traveled freely, and "almost all nations of might and fame resorted" to Bensalem.[15] Then, a global war erupts. Bensalem is attacked by "the great Atlantis (that [we] call America)."[16] Bensalem's historical account of the Great Atlantis expands upon and corrects the "poetical and fabulous" account that is recorded in two Platonic dialogues, the *Timaeus* and the *Critias*.[17] Atlantis, according to the Governor-Priest, is an autonomous world superpower that is defeated by the then reigning Bensalemite King, Altabin, "a wise man and a great warrior."[18] Within a hundred years, Atlantis is "utterly lost and destroyed . . . by a particular deluge."[19] In the centuries that follow the destruction of the Great Atlantis, the rest of the world declines and regresses.

As the outside world reverts to a pre-cosmopolitan, pre-scientific, pre-navigational way of life, Bensalemites avoid these "accident[s] of time."[20] Not only do they retain their historical knowledge and technological prowess, but they expand their international awareness. These islanders enforce their choice to remain hidden from the rest of the world through Laws of Secrecy, established nineteen hundred years ago by King Solamona, "the lawgiver of [their] nation."[21] These Laws forbid Bensalemites from traveling abroad and "prohibi[t the] entrance of strangers."[22] King Solamona also founds Salomon's House, which "is dedicated to the study of the Works and Creatures of God."[23] The Fathers of Salomon's House are scientists, hierarchically ordered according to a strict division of labor based on task and seniority. These men who devote their lives to the study of nature and the acquisition of knowledge choose to live in an isolated compound with those who serve them, dedicating their lives to "knowledge of the Causes, and secret motions of things; and the enlarging of the bounds of Human Empire, to the effecting of all things possible."[24] In a private meeting with the narrator, the Father of Salomon's House reveals the scientists' secret workings. Much of their research, experimentation, and engineering concerns the well-being of the human body, including the preservation,[25] prolongation,[26] and even resuscitation of bodies.[27] They study, control, and reproduce natural phenomena—including winds and water, color and light, sound and tone, temperature and force, size and material[28]—in order to delight and delude the senses.[29] They use "engines and instruments for all sorts of motions,"[30] including "perpetual motions."[31] They travel in the air, emulating birds, and deep underwater, emulating fish and whales. Their engineers have constructed elaborate war machines, including "cannons and basilisks,"[32] as well as formulations for "gunpowder, wildfires burning in water," and "fire-works of all variety"[33] that exceed those with which the narrator is familiar. In case the narrator is concerned about the misuse of these technologies by Salomon's House, the Father assures him that they "do hate all impostures and lies: insomuch as [they] have severely forbidden to all [their] fellows, under pain of ignomiry and fines, that they do not shew any natural work or thing, adorned or swelling; but only pure as it is, without all affectation of strangeness."[34] The detailed knowledge that the Bensalemites possess about the rest of the world has been acquired secretly and skillfully through espionage. Merchants of Light, a subset of the Fathers of Salomon's House, "sail into foreign countries, under the names of other nations, (for [their] own [they] conceal)."[35] These scientist-spies covertly travel the world, collecting information about the latest international developments, scientific discoveries, and technological innovations. They do not share their own knowledge with foreign scientists, philosophers, or statesmen, nor do they reveal their true identities or country of origin.

At the request of the sailors, the Governor-Priest of the Strangers' House also recounts the island's conversion to Christianity, which occurs "[a]bout twenty years after the ascension of" Jesus.[36] A Father of Salomon's House testifies that the event of their conversion is "a true miracle."[37] Since the scientists in Salomon's House have mastered nature,[38] they choose "which of the inventions and experiences which [they] have discovered shall be published, and which not."[39] The Laws of Secrecy include keeping secrets from the islanders and seem, therefore, to imbue the Fathers of Salomon's House with religious and political authority.

After their three-day seclusion, the sailors are invited to explore the city. As they observe the local customs and culture, they learn that the people of Bensalem believe themselves to be the happiest people in history. Two of the sailors are invited to witness the Feast of the Family, a ritual that honors those who have fathered many children. According to the narrator's observations, the lives of the Bensalemites are comfortable, safe, and free from worry. They seem to practice religious toleration and moderation. As Joabin, a local man who is described as a Jew and a merchant, wise in matters of policy, argues, the people of Bensalem are happier and more virtuous than Europeans in every way. Guided and protected by the Fathers of Salomon's House, the lives of the people of Bensalem appear utopian to the beleaguered sailors.

At the end of the text, the Father of Salomon's House gives the narrator "leave to publish [this relation which he has made] for the good of other nations,"[40] thereby rescinding the Laws of Secrecy, ending the policy of

isolationism, and lifting the veil of concealment from the island. Throughout
the text, Bacon's narrator establishes an explicit contrast between Europe and
the sailors (as part of the old world) and Bensalem and the islanders (as part
of the new world). On the island, not only are there "many things right
worthy of observation and relation," but "if there be a mirror in the world
worthy to hold men's eyes, it is that country" of Bensalem.[41] Repeatedly, the
narrator reminds his readers how happy are the people of Bensalem. Bensalem is, in all ways, superior to the rest of the world. As is the case with
subsequent works of science fiction, Bacon and his enigmatic narrator leave
us with many questions.

IDOLS OF THE MIND: THINKING ABOUT *NEW ATLANTIS*

The Instauration is contingent on the willingness both of Bacon's contemporaries and his successors to support the possibilities offered by scientific and
technological advancement. In order to convince his contemporaries to join
his endeavor, Bacon must persuade them to accept the potential for advancement as more than simply fiction, and instead as a programmatic possibility
for the betterment of the future. Bacon believes that human beings possess a
"natural curiosity and desire to know,"[42] which forms the foundation of his
well-known and enduring critique of human understanding, presented in *New
Organon* and *Great Instauration,* both published in 1620. He classifies the
facets of human intellection into four illusions—Idols of the Tribe, Cave,
Marketplace, and Theatre—that help to explain one's intellectual predispositions and idiosyncrasies. The Idols of the Mind are a rubric by which to
analyze our individual intellectual impediments and propensities.[43] We can
study the Idols and in some cases even excise them. But, as Bacon understands them, the Idols are necessary for our cognition and make each of us
unique. In order to be receptive to the possibilities of science and accept *New
Atlantis* as more than mere fiction, we must be willing to step outside our
own experiences, evaluate our knowledge of the world, and imagine beyond
what we think possible.[44]

Experience teaches us, Bacon notes, that human understanding is infinite-
ly fallible and patently subjective.[45] One risk for the Instauration is that
people will not be amenable to the idea of science. We need to be prepared in
order to be receptive to human progress. Human beings should, as Bacon
explains, be "forewarned of the danger [of these idols and false notions and]
fortify themselves as far as may be against their assaults."[46] Human beings
must, he argues, "force themselves for a while to lay their notions by and
begin to familiarise themselves with facts."[47] In order to accept Bacon's
Instauration, we must first understand our own Idols of the Mind. We must

accept that there are things that we may not know, but that we can learn through properly applied reason and method. Fiction about science thus allows us to practice fortifying ourselves against the assaults of the Idols.

When Bacon describes the Idols, he suggests that they are "several and distinct sorts, every sort comprehending many subdivisions."[48] Yet, in practice, these Idols are overlapping. They manifest simultaneously and in various ways. We can appreciate the complexity in these Idols when we apply this framework to *New Atlantis*. Human interactions and human thoughts are rarely neatly categorized: "The human understanding is like a false mirror, which, receiving rays irregularly, distorts and discolors the nature of things by mingling its own nature with it."[49] Bacon's account of the Idols clearly reveals the variation in humankind. He recognizes the complexities in human beings and realizes that different types of individuals experience the world in very different ways.

IDOLS OF THE TRIBE: ORDER AND REGULARITY

The Idols of the Tribe "have their foundation in human nature itself, and in the tribe or race of men."[50] Bacon's Idols of the Tribe are evident in our desire to see regularity where it may not exist; in our recalcitrant adherence to our opinions once they have been established; in our susceptibility to immediate information, experiences, or emotions; in our restless desire to seek information when doing so is no longer necessary; in the dominance of our emotions at the expense of our reason; in the limited power of our senses; and in our predisposition toward abstraction.

Problematically, "[t]he human understanding is of its own nature prone to suppose the existence of more order and regularity in the world than it finds."[51] As a consequence, we discern patterns where there may not be patterns. These Idols demonstrate our tendencies toward abstraction, even when the particulars do not accord with our theories; they shape our predispositions to believe the things that we already believe—because we have created or invented them, devoted time to them, or are attached to them— even when we are presented with evidence to the contrary; they explain that our immediate inclination to accept information, experiences, and emotions is driven by our passions at the expense of our reason; and they account for our willingness to seek additional information, even when sufficient evidence has been gathered.[52] While there is much to the human experience that we do not understand,[53] in order to participate in political society we must have expectations concerning the ways in which events will unfold and individuals will behave. We seek patterns that allow us to engage in scientific and philosophic reasoning to determine the best ways to organize and govern human society.

New Atlantis begins with an invitation to identify ourselves with these adventuring mariners as "[w]e sai[l] from Peru."[54] Not only the sailors, but also *we* become lost at sea, "g[i]ve ourselves up for lost . . . prepar[e] for death,"[55] and pray for salvation. We become part of the crew who follow the clouds, see land, and "enter into a good haven, being the port of a fair city."[56] We can choose, as readers, whether to include ourselves in this group of sailors, or to become dispassionate observers of this tale. Bacon is relying on our natural curiosity. Adventure is not without danger. It is a step into the unknown, a willingness to forgo the comforts of home, familiarity, certainty, and safety. Individuals who forge an unknown path risk the potential for either disaster or excellence.[57] Those who undertake great acts of scientific discovery or political upheaval risk not only failure, but also their own bodily safety. It is often in the unforeseen consequences that human knowledge and human power significantly advance.[58] *New Atlantis* presents us with familiar patterns in an unfamiliar context.

Throughout the text, the narrator references the orderliness of the Bensalemites, noting perceived patterns in their behavior. When the sailors first arrive in port, that narrator explains that "we entered into a good haven, being the port of a fair city; not great indeed, but well built, and that gave a pleasant view from the sea."[59] The narrator assumes that the island is "a good haven" because the city is fair and pleasant. Fair and pleasant cities offer safety and refuge. When the sailors are denied landing but granted supplies, the narrator claims that the sailors are "much perplexed."[60] In their experience of maritime behavior, the sailors expect that they will either be denied landing and denied supplies, or permitted landing and permitted supplies.

The narrator's desire to see orderliness in the Bensalemites is evidenced by his description of the islanders. The sailors first encounter civilian Bensalemites after they disembark from their ship and are led to the Strangers' House. As the sailors proceed through the streets of the city, the narrator describes that "there were gathered some people on both sides, standing in a row; but in so civil a fashion, as if it had been, not to wonder at us, but to welcome us: and divers of them, as we passed by them, put their arms a little abroad; which is their gesture, when they did bid any welcome."[61] The narrator assumes, presumably based on his previous understanding of human behavior, that the islanders have gathered of their own volition to greet the sailors, not to observe them. He believes that they are civil and welcoming and free to gather as they see fit.

Bacon's sailors and his readers are encouraged to reorient their understanding of their own political history as they learn about the island from the Father of the Strangers' House, who does not think the sailors will believe him since his account of the island's history is contrary to what the sailors believe that they already know.[62] The history, as presented by the Governor-Priest, exhibits Bacon's understanding of the Idols of the Mind: "One method of delivery alone remains to us; which is simply this: we must lead men to the particulars themselves, and their series and order; while men on their side must force themselves for a while to lay their notions by and begin to familiarise themselves with facts."[63]

IDOLS OF THE CAVE:
OUR PROPER AND PECULIAR NATURES

The Idols of the Cave are unique to one's nature, mind, and body, and are influenced by one's education and life experiences.[64] As Bacon explains, "every one has a cave or den of his [or her] own, which refracts and discolours the light of nature."[65] Discernment of one's unique manifestation of the Idols of the Cave requires one to consider one's own intellectual habits. Some individuals notice similarities, while others notice differences; some individuals love new things, while others love old things; and some individuals focus on details, while others concentrate on generalities. Each person experiences the world from an isolated and unique vantage. According to Bacon, these Idols of the Cave are our "proper and peculiar nature."[66] These Idols are simply part of all individuals and, in many respects, influence our dispositions. These qualities not only determine our characters and predispositions, but also influence the basic possibilities that are available to us and the ways in which other individuals interact with us. Health, intelligence, physical prowess, and even physical attractiveness significantly affect the possible trajectories of our lives. The Idols of the Cave, which each human being experiences uniquely and subjectively, essentially isolate each of us in a cave of our own body and our own experiences. As is the case with the Idols of the Tribe, the Idols of the Cave are innate. They are imbedded within our constitutions and our humanness.

Bacon argues that understanding our own intellectual predispositions and aversions allows us to assess the condition of our learning.[67] Part of coming to understand those things that we think that we know requires knowledge of an individual's self. Much like the Delphic imperative to know ourselves,[68] Bacon encourages us to "rightly understand . . . [our] store or [our] strength."[69] While sequestered in the Strangers' House, the narrator reminds the sailors of the need to "know ourselves, and how it standeth with us."[70] In order to explore our preconceptions about what is possible, by becoming increasingly objective and cognizant of our intellectual predispositions, we must be pushed beyond our comfort zones,[71] thereby clearing the way for a sharper understanding of the benefits and challenges of a scientific society.

We learn about the island from Bacon's enigmatic narrator, who never discloses his name, age, country of origin, marital status, education, likes, or dislikes. Yet, we do learn details about him throughout the fable. He speaks

Spanish and may also have knowledge of Hebrew, Greek, and Latin. [72] He, along with the rest of the sailors, identifies as Christian, has biblical knowledge, and is comforted by the Christian symbols on the island. [73] He appears to consider Europe his home and is familiar with the "collegiate diet." [74] The narrator also holds a place of privilege within the crew: he is among the six sailors who first go ashore to examine the Strangers' House; [75] he calls the sailors together in the Strangers' House, reminding them of the uncertainty of their position and encouraging them to behave well; [76] he stays with the six men who speak to the Governor of the Strangers' House after their three-day sequester, learning about the history of the island; [77] and he is chosen by his fellow sailors for a private audience with the Father of Salomon's House. [78] The narrator is relatable to the reader. Like many of Bacon's readers, he is educated, Christian, and reasonable. He is a plausible representative of the type of European man who is desirable in and valuable to Bacon's scientific society. He is unafraid of and open to new ideas, people, and possibilities.

Throughout the fable, many of the accounts are secondhand. The narrator relies on the explanations of other individuals, who also experience the Idols of the Mind in unique and subjective ways, rather than his own experiences. He does not personally witness either the Feast of the Family, which is attended by two members of the crew, or Bensalem's marriage rites, about which the narrator learns from "some of the company" and Joabin. [79] While the narrator's account *seems* reliable, the sailors never have unrestricted access to the island. They are forbidden to travel beyond "a mile and a half" from the city's wall. [80] In relating the political history of the island, the Governor-Priest of the Strangers' House also clarifies that he "must reserve some particulars, which it is not lawful for [him] to reveal," [81] including how the envoys from the island are able to remain hidden from the rest of the world. [82] Both the Governor-Priest and Joabin are called away by mysterious messengers when topics of politics and policy arise. [83] Since we know that the island is governed by Laws of Secrecy, it is unclear whether the Governor-Priest and Joabin know all the secrets of the island and are withholding some from foreign sailors, or whether they, too, are kept in the dark.

Made wary, perhaps, by the text's hazy narrative structure, omissions, and secrets, readers are also repeatedly reminded that the account itself may not be believable, or is unlikely to be believed. When the Governor of the Strangers' House relates the history of the island to the sailors, he adds "perhaps [they] will scarce think [it] credible." [84] He further avers that any internationally proliferated accounts of the island "could be taken . . . but for a dream." [85] The narrator refers to Joabin's account of religion as "Jewish dreams." [86] The island is first revealed to the sailors—who are "lost men" at sea, starving, and hopeless—after they follow "thick clouds." [87] The dreamlike quality of the text and the fact that the story begins with the sailors consuming strange fruit and "small grey or whitish pills," [88] invoking

Homer's "lotus-eaters,"[89] call the perceptions of the narrator into question. The "ambiguous and open-ended" nature of the text "ensures that the reader remains active and alert, being encouraged to examine the different positions from which knowledge is presented, rather than simply accepting them."[90] As we each consider our own evaluation of the text in light of the Idols of the Cave, we can discern whether we tend to focus attention on the particular details of the text, even if they are often unclear, or the general narrative. Our predispositions toward specific narrative details or the broader narrative structure, helps us learn about the Idols of the Cave as they manifest in each of us.

In his discussion of the Idols of the Cave, Bacon encourages us to consider whether we prefer novelty or antiquity.[91] This question—the new or the old—is of fundamental import to how we understand both Bensalem and the possibilities offered by the Instauration. The sailors in *New Atlantis*, when contrasting their own societies with Bensalem, clearly prefer novelty. Throughout his works, Bacon argues that we must begin anew.[92] He requires that his supporters accept the possibilities offered by science. Yet, barring some disaster (natural or of human construction)—such as the "particular deluge or inundation" that destroys Atlantis,[93] or an earthquake, plague, or war—true re-foundings are impossible. Human beings, Bacon believes, must practice being adaptable.

IDOLS OF THE MARKETPLACE: SOCIAL ASSOCIATION

Despite their potential to be excised, Bacon believes that the Idols of the Marketplace "are the most troublesome of all."[94] What we say, as well as how we say it, has meaning that affects understanding. These are the Idols of words and names. These "Idols for[m] by the intercourse and association of men with each other"[95] and develop through human interaction.[96] Our understanding of other individuals is contingent on our ability to communicate in speech or writing. As Bacon explains, "it is by discourse that men associate; and words are imposed according to the apprehension of the vulgar."[97] Precision in one's vocabulary is essential to ensure that one understands one's own argument and that other individuals do as well.[98] Bacon argues that these Idols may be excised by steadily rejecting obsolete theories.[99]

Language and linguistic distinctions are prominent features of *New Atlantis*. Not only do the islanders have their own language, one with which the sailors seem unfamiliar,[100] but they are also praised for knowing "the languages of Europe,"[101] including Spanish, Hebrew, Greek, and Latin, which gives the sailors comfort.[102] In the text, the name of the island—Bensalem— is identified as being "in their language,"[103] although the name of a city on the island—Renfusa—is not specifically identified as being in the local language.[104] While no further linguistic interpretation is provided, some commentators note that Bensalem may be derivative of two Hebrew words: *ben,* meaning son; and *salem,* meaning peace, completeness, or safety.[105] Following Weinberger's analysis, Renfusa is often translated as "a combination of the Greek words *rhen* and *phusis,* meaning 'sheep-natured' or 'sheep like.'"[106] These etymologies encourage the sailors and the readers to consider the peaceful nature of the island and the docile nature of the islanders. There are other instances in the text when the narrator translates the meaning of a word. For example, we learn that "a *karan* . . . is with them a mile and a half,"[107] a *Tirsan* is what they call "[t]he Father of the Family,"[108] and "a *Taratan* . . . is as much as a herald."[109] The ways in which we understand these terms—Are the Bensalemites peaceful? Are the Renfusans sheeplike? Does Taratan have any additional connotations?—necessarily influence our interpretation of the fable and our evaluation of the relationship between *New Atlantis* and Bacon's larger project.

There are key points in the text at which the meaning or origin of a turn of phrase can influence the interpretation of an entire passage. For example, a prohibited practice on Bensalem is that of being "twice paid."[110] The sailors first encounter the term after they are permitted to disembark. They offer pistolets to an islander and are told, "He must not be twice paid for one labour."[111] The narrator reflects on the practice and presumes that the injunction against being "twice paid" indicates that the Bensalemites are compensated with a "salary sufficient of the state for . . . service."[112] He later learns that "they call an officer that taketh rewards, *twice paid,*" which does not mean that the Bensalemites are necessarily adequately compensated, but simply that it is forbidden to take monetary gifts for executing one's job.[113] The narrator imputes a particular interpretation on the Bensalemite practice, based on his own experiences and expectations of acceptable behaviors. His analysis is further complicated when, at the end of the text, he is given "two thousand ducats" by the Father of Salomon's House as a "bounty for [him] and [his] fellows."[114] In the final sentence of the text, the narrator interprets this gift as an affirmation of the Bensalemites' generosity: "For they give great largesses where they come upon all occasions."[115]

Perhaps the clearest example of the purposefully ambiguous use of language in the text is the oft repeated assertion, "Happy are the people of Bensalem."[116] The Bensalemites' happiness mantra affirms their belief in the superiority of their own culture as compared to all other political organizations. This raises the question: What exactly constitutes happiness for the Bensalemites? For the members of Salomon's House, happiness is possible when they are free to pursue their scientific endeavors and are recognized and honored for their achievements by their fellow scientists.[117] This freedom depends on the autonomy of the scientists. Civilian Bensalemites are free to enjoy the safety, security, prosperity, and fecundity of a technologically advanced society in exchange for their non-interference in the rule of Salomon's House. One's perspective on the happiness of the islanders, especially the different types of islanders, is a clear indication of both the Idols of the Marketplace and the Idols of the Cave. An island is a type of cave, isolated and self-contained. Bensalem is "hidden and unseen to others," and illuminated from within.[118] This observation raises a second question: Do we believe their happiness is legitimate? As readers, we are apt to project our own conception of happiness onto the text and thus judge the relative happiness of the scientists and nonscientists according to whether we consider their lives appealing for ourselves.

IDOLS OF THE THEATRE: CREATED WORLDS

The final Idols, those of the Theatre, pervade theology, philosophy, and science.[119] We knowingly allow the Idols of the Theatre to permeate our thoughts as we adhere to specific theoretical accounts of the world. Bacon likens these Idols to "stage-plays, representing worlds of their own creation after an unreal scenic fashion."[120] There are an infinite number of possible Idols of the Theatre. Bacon explains that "the Idols of the Theatre are not innate, nor do they steal into the understanding secretly, but are plainly impressed and received into the mind from the play-books of philosophical systems and perverted rules of demonstration."[121] These are the Idols of popular opinion.

The sailors' acceptance of the Christianity of the Bensalemites is a clear example of the Idols of the Theatre. Upon first encountering the Bensalemites' welcome party, the sailors are relieved to see the sign of the cross and to learn that they have arrived in a Christian nation. Even after becoming more familiar with the rituals and customs of the ordinary people of Bensalem, all of which are rife with pagan symbols,[122] the sailors do not question the religiosity of the islanders. The narrator is unconcerned that the account of Bensalem's miraculous conversion to Christianity is moderated and affirmed by "one of the wise men of the society of Salomon's House."[123] The Governor-Priest, who describes the conversion, even likens the witnesses to the audience "in a theatre."[124] The sailors seem unperturbed by the Governor-Priest's claim that Bensalemites, at the time of the conversion, are given "all the canonical books of the Old and New Testament" as well as "some other books of the New Testament, which were not at that time written."[125] While the narrator is skeptical of neither the Christianity on the island nor the Jewish merchant Joabin's Christian affirmations—including Christ's immaculate conception[126]—he is skeptical of Joabin's account of Bensalemite Judaism, which traces its lineage to Abraham's son Nachoran, teaches that the Laws of Bensalem were ordained by Moses in a second covenant, and pre-

dicts that the Bensalemite king will sit at the feet of the Messiah.[127] Bacon's
narrator recognizes the theatrical and possibly fictional aspects of Joabin's
understanding of his own Judaism,[128] but does not extend his critique to his
own or Bensalem's understanding and practice of Christianity. It is often
easier to see the dreams and limited understandings of others than to see our
own.

The narrator relates two social practices on the island: the Feast of the
Family, which honors the Tirsan; and the marriage rituals of the people. The
Feast of the Family is described as "[a] most pious, and reverend custom . . .
shewing that nation to be compounded of all goodness."[129] The feast honors
men who have "lived to see thirty persons descended of [their] body."[130] The
three-day ritual begins with the Tirsan's two-day adjudication and appease-
ment of any familial disputes or discords. On the day of the Feast, the Tirsan
selects a favored son, referred to as "the Son of the Vine," who will "live in
house with him."[131] The Father, who is financially rewarded by the state, is
served by his children, whom he blesses. If one woman has birthed all the
children, "there is a traverse placed in a loft above the right hand of the
[Tirsan's] chair, with a privy door, a carved window of glass, leaded with
gold and blue; where she sitteth, but is not seen."[132] The narrator interprets
the Feast of the Family as an example of "a solem[n ritual] wherein nature
did so much preside."[133] Joabin concurs with the narrator's assessment of the
"excellent institution of the Feast of the Family."[134]

Joabin maintains that Bensalem's policies regarding marriage are more
virtuous than are those of Europeans, as the Bensalemites experience no
divorce, adultery, or homosexuality. He tells the narrator about the "*Adam
and Eve's pools*, where it is permitted" for a betrothed couple to have a friend
"see them severally bathe naked."[135] This policy, whereby a third party may
witness the nakedness of a betrothed couple, is a modification of policies
included in Plato's *Republic* and Thomas More's *Utopia*, which permit engaged couples to see each other naked before their marriage, so as to ensure
that no deception occurs.[136] Joabin, however, appears to believe that the
rituals described by Plato and by More are actual practices in European
marriage customs, rather than fantastical inventions. He understands the fictional accounts of Plato and More as evidence of European decadence and
corruption.[137] Although he is identified as a wise man, Joabin's inability to
distinguish between actual practice and fiction reveals his partial understanding of European society. It is unclear whether Joabin is simply misinformed,
or whether the reconnaissance of the Merchants of Light is neither as coher-
ent nor as accurate as the islanders believe.

While the Governor-Priest and Joabin praise the policies on Bensalem,
the precise political structure of the island is never explained. Although we
are told that historically there have been kings on the island and that there is a
"king of Bensalem,"[138] neither the narrator nor the sailors are introduced to

the reigning monarch. The Fathers of Salomon's House seem to be in charge. They travel the island with all the pomp and spectacle of state, interpret and affirm miracles,[139] and determine policy. Despite the importance of the Fathers to the identity of the islanders, the arrival of the Father of Salomon's House, according to Joabin, is a rare and celebratory event.[140] Joabin, who has been "commanded" by the Father of Salomon's House to arrange an audience with the sailors, explains that they should be "happy men" for receiving such an honor.[141] During their private meeting, the Father promises the narrator that the Fellows of Salomon's House "hate all impostures and lies: insomuch as [they] have severely forbidden it to all [their] fellows, under pain of ignomiy and fines."[142] Fathers of the House and other islanders employed in the House "take all an oath of secrecy, for the concealing of th[at] which [the Fathers of Salomon's House] think fit to keep secret."[143] Yet, the mandate of the "Foundation is the knowledge of Causes, and secret motions of things."[144] While the workings of the House are kept secret and their discoveries are only selectively revealed to the general public, the Father of Salomon's House relays, in great detail, "the true state of Salomon's House,"[145] including the purpose of the House, its "preparations and instruments," and its "employments and functions."[146] The account of the island's history and practices may not be complete, since the Father of Salomon's House admits that he "must reserve some particulars, which it is not lawful for [him] to reveal."[147] Further, in accordance with the Laws of Secrecy, the Fathers of Salomon's House not only conceal Bensalem from foreigners, but also control the information and discoveries that they "reveal . . . to the state."[148]

The Idols of the Theatre can be seen in the Bensalemites' faith in science and in their belief that the policies of Solamona represent the best possible regime.[149] As with the director or writer of a play, the Fathers of Salomon's House are able to orchestrate the flow of information into the society,[150] thereby ensuring that Bensalem remains regimented and controlled. The people of Bensalem are happy, dependent, and civil.[151] The policies and practices of the Bensalemites affirm their beliefs about the world and their own history, while their own history and beliefs about the world affirm their policies and practices. As we begin to see the Idols of the Theatre in Bensalem, we can apply those Idols to our own conceptions of religion, philosophy, and politics.

FICTION AND FABLES, POESY AND IMAGINATION: INCHOATE SCIENCE FICTION

Bacon is not simply a craftsman of fictional societies. His Instauration is actionable and practical. Bacon establishes a method (induction) and a rational framework for the systematic study of nature. Yet, he never abandons his concern with poetry and mythmaking. In *De Augmentis*, Bacon classifies "poesy [as] nothing else than feigned history or fables."[152] Unlike science, poesy does not require one to "obey" nature in order to "command" it.[153] Fables need not be true. In the space between truth and poesy, human beings, Bacon notes, are able to exercise their imaginations. Fables are an essential part of Bacon's educative process. Serious myths and fables discussed or presented with intention and purpose are legitimate conduits for communicating deeper truths about politics, philosophy, and science. The fables of the ancients "have in them, from the beginning," Bacon explains, "some Mystery and Allegory" that is "precepted and thought."[154] Inherent in the mystery of the fable, in the structure of the allegorical form, is an incentive to think more deeply. For readers who are so inclined, a fable that depicts alternative politics offers an opportunity to examine imagined commonwealths, possible futures, and diverse presents. By immersing ourselves in these hypothetical poetic fables, we begin to see the similarities and differences between the imagined world of the fable and our own real world. We can learn to become more critical of the present and more open to unrealized possibilities. The Idols of the Mind are Bacon's framework within which we can begin to consider the distinctions between fiction and fact, untruth and truth, as we reflect on our own intellection predispositions.

New Atlantis provides Bacon's readers with an opportunity to examine their own Idols of the Mind while they evaluate the actions and beliefs of the characters in Bensalem. As we read *New Atlantis*, we are able to test our own levels of comfort and discomfort in a particular political society organized toward the advancement of science. The fable, as a consequence, prepares us to consider the unknown; our perspectives on science; and our beliefs about religion, law, and discovery. Armed with Bacon's Idols of the Mind, readers can systematically begin to identify instances during which the sailors, scientists, and ordinary citizens of Bensalem exhibit the Idols. Once we begin to see how these Idols manifest in other individuals and other political organizations, we will, Bacon suggests, be able to see how each Idol manifests in our own lives.

As we learn to fortify ourselves against the Idols of the Mind, Francis Bacon hopes that we will become more receptive to his Instauration. *New Atlantis* allows us to evaluate our own preparedness for Bacon's proposed future. As is the case with the best works of science fiction, *New Atlantis* is a mirror that reflects (in various degrees of clarity) our intellectual predispositions and aversions, expectations for politics, and opinions concerning science and progress.

NOTES

We would like to thank Steven Michels and Timothy McCranor, who are the editors of this volume, and Frances Ratner for their detailed and very helpful notes on this chapter.

1. For considerations of the literary purpose of *New Atlantis*, see Tobin L. Craig, "On the Significance of the Literary Character of Francis Bacon's *New Atlantis* for an Understanding of his Political Thought," *The Review of Politics* 72 (2010): 226–228; Jerry Weinberger, "Science and Rule in Bacon's Utopia: An Introduction to the Reading of the *New Atlantis*," *The American Political Science Review* 70 (1976): 865; Howard B. White, *Peace among the Willows: The Political Philosophy of Francis Bacon* (The Hague: Martinus Nijhoff, 1968), 15; and Robert. K. Faulkner, "Visions and Powers: Bacon's Two-Fold Politics of Progress," *Polity* 21 (1988): 114.

2. Nichole Pohl, "Utopianism after More: the Renaissance and Enlightenment," in *The Cambridge Companion to Utopian Literature*, ed. Gregory Claeys (Cambridge: Cambridge University Press, 2010): 60.

3. Oxford English Dictionary. "Science Fiction: 'Fiction in which the setting and story feature hypothetical scientific or technological advances, the existence of alien life, space or time travel, etc., *esp.* such fiction set in the future, or an imagined alternative universe,' accessed January 27, 2019. http://www.oed.com/view/Entry/172674?redirectedFrom=science+fictions#eid.

4. Francis Bacon, *Great Instauration,* "Proceum" in *The Works of Francis Bacon*, in 14 vols., eds. James Spedding, Robert Leslie Ellis, and Douglas Denon Heath (New York: Cambridge University Press, 2011 [1858]), 4:8.

5. Francis Bacon, *Advancement of Learning*, in *The Works of Francis Bacon*, in 14 vols., eds. James Spedding, Robert Leslie Ellis, and Douglas Denon Heath (New York: Cambridge University Press, 1858), 3:294.

6. White, *Peace*, 15; Faulkner, "Visions and Powers," 11; David C. Innes, "Bacon's *New Atlantis*: The Christian Hope and the Modern Hope," *Interpretation* 22 (1994): 4; Timothy Paterson, "The Secular Control of Scientific Power," *Polity* 21 (1989): 458; Nell Urich, *Science in Utopia: A Mighty Design* (Cambridge: Harvard University Press, 1967), 140; Benjamin Farrington, *Francis Bacon: Philosopher of Industrial Science* (New York: Schuman, 1949), 76.

7. Jerry Weinberger, "Introduction," in *New Atlantis and the Great Instauration*, ed. Jerry Weinberger (Wheeling: Harlan Davidson, Inc., 1989), xi.

8. Bronwen Price, "Introduction," in *Francis Bacon's* New Atlantis*: New Interdisciplinary Essays*, ed. Bronwen Price (New York: Manchester University Press, 2002); Hiram Caton, *Politics of Progress* (Gainesville: University of Florida Press, 1988); Svetozar Minkov, *Francis Bacon's Inquiry Touching Human Nature: Virtue, Philosophy, and the Relief of Man's Estate* (Lanham: Lexington Books, 2010); Kimberly Hurd Hale, *Francis Bacon's* New Atlantis *in the Foundation of Modern Political Thought* (Lanham: Lexington Books, 2013); Jerry Weinberger, *Science, Faith, and Politics: Francis Bacon and the Utopian Roots of the Modern Age* (Ithaca, NY: Cornell University Press, 1985).

9. Pohl, "Utopianism after More," 60.

10. Francis Bacon, *New Atlantis,* in *The Works of Francis Bacon*, in 14 vols., eds. James Spedding, Robert Leslie Ellis, and Douglas Denon Heath (London, Longman & Co., 1857), 3:154.

11. For detailed discussions of the importance of seafaring in Bacon's thought, see Craig, "Literary Character," 222–225; and White, *Peace*, 93–107.

12. Faulkner, "Visions and Powers," 112.

13. Laurence Lampert, *Nietzsche and Modern Times* (New Haven, CT: Yale University Press, 1993), 18.

14. Bacon, *New Atlantis*, 3:140.

15. Bacon, *New Atlantis*, 3:141.

16. Bacon, *New Atlantis*, 3:141.

17. Bacon, *New Atlantis*, 3:142. For a comparison of these competing accounts of Atlantis, see Hale, *Foundation*, 13–32.

18. Bacon, *New Atlantis*, 3:142.

19. Bacon, *New Atlantis*, 3:142.
20. Bacon, *New Atlantis*, 3:143.
21. Bacon, *New Atlantis*, 3:144.
22. Bacon, *New Atlantis*, 3:144.
23. Bacon, *New Atlantis*, 3:145.
24. Bacon, *New Atlantis*, 3:156.
25. Bacon, *New Atlantis*, 3:156.
26. Bacon, *New Atlantis*, 3:157.
27. Bacon, *New Atlantis*, 3:160.
28. Bacon, *New Atlantis*, 3:158.
29. Bacon, *New Atlantis*, 3:161.
30. Bacon, *New Atlantis*, 3:163.
31. Bacon, *New Atlantis*, 3:164.
32. Bacon, *New Atlantis*, 3:163.
33. Bacon, *New Atlantis*, 3:163.
34. Bacon, *New Atlantis*, 3:164.
35. Bacon, *New Atlantis*, 3:164.
36. Bacon, *New Atlantis*, 3:137.
37. Bacon, *New Atlantis*, 3:137.
38. Richard Serjeanston, "Natural Knowledge in the *New Atlantis*," in *Francis Bacon's* New Atlantis: *New Interdisciplinary Essays,* ed. Bronwen Price (New York: Manchester University Press, 2002), 84–99. Serjeanston argues that many of the technologies listed by the Father of Salomon's House were already being undertaken by Bacon's contemporaries.
39. Bacon, *New Atlantis*, 3:165.
40. Bacon, *New Atlantis*, 3:166.
41. Bacon, *New Atlantis*, 3:147.
42. Francis Bacon, *Valerius Terminus, or Of the Interpretation of Nature*, in *The Works of Francis Bacon*, in 14 vols., eds. James Spedding, Robert Leslie Ellis, and Douglas Denon Heath (New York: Cambridge University Press, 1858), 3:232.
43. Francis Bacon, *New Organon*, in *The Works of Francis Bacon*, in 14 vols., eds. James Spedding, Robert Leslie Ellis, and Douglas Denon Heath (New York: Cambridge University Press, 1858). In *New Organon*, Bacon briefly mentions the Idols in Aphorism 23, and then introduces each of the four Idols in Aphorisms 38–44. He then parses each type of Idol (Tribe, Cave, Marketplace, and Theatre) between Aphorisms 45–69.
44. Bacon, *New Organon*, 4:53.
45. Psychology research shows that memories, even those we believe to be most accurate, can be implanted, and that distinct individuals experience and report on the same event in very different ways. For example, see Elizabeth Loftus, "Make-believe memories," *American Psychologist* 58 (2003): 867–873.
46. Bacon, *New Organon*, 4:53.
47. Bacon, *New Organon*, 4:53.
48. Bacon, *Valerius Terminus*, 3:242.
49. Bacon, *New Organon*, 4:54.
50. Bacon, *New Organon*, 4:54.
51. Bacon, *New Organon*, 4:55.
52. Bacon, *Great Instauration*, 4:27; and Bacon, *New Organon,* 4:55–58.
53. Francis Bacon, "Of Truth," in *The Works of Francis Bacon*, in 14 vols., eds. James Spedding, Robert Leslie Ellis, and Douglas Denon Heath (New York: Cambridge University Press, 1858), 6:377–379.
54. Bacon, *New Atlantis*, 3:129.
55. Bacon, *New Atlantis*, 3:129.
56. Bacon, *New Atlantis*, 3:129.
57. Francis Bacon, "Of Great Place," in *The Works of Francis Bacon*, in 14 vols., eds. James Spedding, Robert Leslie Ellis, and Douglas Denon Heath (New York: Cambridge University Press, 1858), 6:398–401.

58. Peter Pesic, "Francis Bacon, Violence, and the Motion of Liberty: The Aristotelian Background," *Journal of the History of Ideas* 75 (2014): 86–87.

59. Bacon, *New Atlantis*, 3:130.

60. Bacon, *New Atlantis*, 3:130.

61. Bacon, *New Atlantis*, 3:133.

62. Bacon, *New Atlantis*, 3:140.

63. Bacon, *New Organon*, 4:53.

64. Bacon, *New Organon*, 4:59–60.

65. Bacon, *New Organon*, 4:54.

66. Bacon, *New Organon*, 4:54.

67. Francis Bacon, "Of Wisdom for a Man's Self," in *The Works of Francis Bacon*, in 14 vols., eds. James Spedding, Robert Leslie Ellis, and Douglas Denon Heath (New York: Cambridge University Press, 1858), 6:431–433.

68. "Know thyself" is one of the Delphic imperatives inscribed above the entrance to the Temple of Apollo at Delphi, according to the accounts of both Pausanias and Socrates.

69. Bacon, *Great Instauration,* 4:13.

70. Bacon, *New Atlantis*, 3:134.

71. Bacon, *Great Instauration*, 4:13.

72. Bacon, *New Atlantis*, 3:130.

73. Bacon, *New Atlantis*, 3:130.

74. Bacon, *New Atlantis*, 3:134.

75. Bacon, *New Atlantis*, 3:132.

76. Bacon, *New Atlantis*, 3:134.

77. Bacon, *New Atlantis*, 3:135.

78. Bacon, *New Atlantis*, 3:135.

79. Bacon, *New Atlantis*, 3:147 and 3:152–154.

80. Bacon, *New Atlantis*, 3:135.

81. Bacon, *New Atlantis*, 3:140.

82. Bacon, *New Atlantis*, 3:146.

83. Bacon, *New Atlantis*, 3:139 and 3:154.

84. Bacon, *New Atlantis*, 3:140.

85. Bacon, *New Atlantis*, 3:145.

86. Bacon, *New Atlantis*, 3:151.

87. Bacon, *New Atlantis*, 3:129.

88. Bacon, *New Atlantis*, 3:134.

89. Homer, *Odyssey, Volume I: Books I–XII*, trans. A.T. Murray, revised by George E. Dimock, Loeb Classic Library 104 (Cambridge: Harvard University Press, 1919), Book IX.

90. Price, "Introduction," 14.

91. Bacon, *New Organon*, 4:59.

92. Bacon, *New Organon*, 4:52.

93. Bacon, *New Atlantis,* 3:142.

94. Bacon, *New Organon*, 4:60.

95. Bacon, *New Organon*, 4:54.

96. Bacon, *New Organon*, 4:55.

97. Bacon, *New Organon*, 4:55.

98. Bacon, *New Organon*, 4:55.

99. Bacon, *New Organon*, 4:55.

100. Bacon, *New Atlantis*, 3:130.

101. Bacon, *New Atlantis*, 3:139–140.

102. Bacon, *New Atlantis*, 3:130.

103. Bacon, *New Atlantis*, 3:136.

104. Bacon, *New Atlantis*, 3:137.

105. Jerry Weinberger, *New Atlantis*, in *New Atlantis and the Great Instauration*, ed. Jerry Weinberger (Wheeling, IL: Harlan Davidson, Inc., 1989), fn. 68. Also see Weinberger, "Science and Rule," 875; David Spitz, "Bacon's 'New Atlantis': A Reinterpretation," *Midwest Journal of Political Science* 4 (1960): 60.

106. Weinberger, *New Atlantis*, fn. 72.
107. Bacon, *New Atlantis*, 3:135.
108. Bacon, *New Atlantis*, 3:147.
109. Bacon, *New Atlantis*, 3:149.
110. Bacon, *New Atlantis*, 3:132.
111. Bacon, *New Atlantis*, 3:132.
112. Bacon, *New Atlantis*, 3:132.
113. Bacon, *New Atlantis*, 3:132.
114. Bacon, *New Atlantis*, 3:166.
115. Bacon, *New Atlantis*, 3:166.
116. Bacon, *New Atlantis*, 3:144, 3:147, and 3:149.
117. Salomon's House contains a hall dedicated to statues of outstanding scientists. Bacon, *New Atlantis*, 3:165–166.
118. Bacon, *New Atlantis*, 3:140.
119. Bacon, *New Organon*, 4:55.
120. Bacon, *New Organon*, 4:55.
121. Bacon, *New Organon*, 4:55.
122. For dueling discussions of the pagan imagery in *New Atlantis*, see Innes, "The Christian Hope," 22; and Steven Matthews, *Theology and Science in the Thought of Francis Bacon* (Burlington: Ashgate Publishing, 2008), 100.
123. Bacon, New Atlantis, 3:137.
124. Bacon, New Atlantis, 3:137.
125. Bacon, *New Atlantis*, 3:138.
126. Bacon, *New Atlantis*, 3:151.
127. Bacon, *New Atlantis*, 3:151.
128. Bacon, *New Atlantis*, 3:151. For a detailed discussion of the Jewish imagery in the text and its implications for our interpretation of *New Atlantis*, see Lewis S. Feuer, "Francis Bacon and the Jews: Who Was the Jew in the 'New Atlantis'?" *Jewish Historical Studies* 29 (1982): 1–25.
129. Bacon, *New Atlantis,* 3:147.
130. Bacon, *New Atlantis,* 3:147.
131. Bacon, *New Atlantis*, 3:148.
132. Bacon, *New Atlantis*, 3:148.
133. Bacon, *New Atlantis*, 3:151.
134. Bacon, *New Atlantis*, 3:152.
135. Bacon, *New Atlantis*, 3:154.
136. Plato, *Republic*, trans. Allan Bloom (New York: Basic Books, 1991), Book V; and Thomas More, *Utopia* (Cambridge: Cambridge University Press, 2016), 56 and 83–85.
137. This of course does not answer the obvious question as to why it is more corrupt for an engaged couple to see one another naked than for a third party to see the couple naked.
138. Bacon, *New Atlantis*, 3:151 and 3:149.
139. Bacon, *New Atlantis*, 3:137–138.
140. Bacon, *New Atlantis*, 3:154.
141. Bacon, *New Atlantis*, 3:155.
142. Bacon, *New Atlantis*, 3:164.
143. Bacon, *New Atlantis*, 3:165.
144. Bacon, *New Atlantis*, 3:156.
145. Bacon, *New Atlantis*, 3:156.
146. Bacon, *New Atlantis*, 3:156.
147. Bacon, *New Atlantis*, 3:140.
148. Bacon, *New Atlantis*, 3:165.
149. Bacon, *New Atlantis*, 3:144.
150. Bacon, *New Atlantis*, 3:166.
151. Bacon, *New Atlantis*, 3:132.

152. Francis Bacon, *Translation of De Augmentis*, in *The Works of Francis Bacon*, in 14 vols., eds. James Spedding, Robert Leslie Ellis, and Douglas Denon Heath (New York: Cambridge University Press, 1858), 4:292.
153. Bacon, *Great Instauration*, 4:32.
154. Francis Bacon, *On the Wisdom of the Ancients*, trans. Heidi Studer (unpublished), 7.

BIBLIOGRAPHY

Bacon, Francis. *Advancement of Learning*. In *The Works of Francis Bacon*, in 14 vols. Edited by James Spedding, Robert Leslie Ellis, and Douglas Denon Heath, 253–491. New York: Cambridge University Press, 1858, Volume 3.
———. *Great Instauration*. In *The Works of Francis Bacon*, in 14 vols. Edited by James Spedding, Robert Leslie Ellis, and Douglas Denon Heath, 4–33. New York: Cambridge University Press, 1858, Volume 4.
———. Bacon, Francis. *New Atlantis*. In *The Works of Francis Bacon*, in 14 vols. Edited by James Spedding, Robert Leslie Ellis, and Douglas Denon Heath, 123–166. New York: Cambridge University Press, 1858, Volume 3.
———. *New Organon*. In *The Works of Francis Bacon*, in 14 vols. Edited by James Spedding, Robert Leslie Ellis, and Douglas Denon Heath, 37–248. New York: Cambridge University Press, 1858, Volume 4.
———. "Of Great Place." In *The Works of Francis Bacon*, in 14 vols. Edited by James Spedding, Robert Leslie Ellis, and Douglas Denon Heath, 398–401. New York: Cambridge University Press, 1858, Volume 6.
———. "Of Truth." In *The Works of Francis Bacon*, in 14 vols. Edited by James Spedding, Robert Leslie Ellis, and Douglas Denon Heath, 377–379. New York: Cambridge University Press, 1858, Volume 6.
———. "Of Wisdom for a Man's Self." In *The Works of Francis Bacon*, in 14 vols. Edited by James Spedding, Robert Leslie Ellis, and Douglas Denon Heath, 431–433. New York: Cambridge University Press, 1858, Volume 6.
———. *Translation of De Augmentis*. In *The Works of Francis Bacon*, in 14 vols. Edited by James Spedding, Robert Leslie Ellis, and Douglas Denon Heath, 275–498. New York: Cambridge University Press, 1858, Volume 4.
———. *Valerius Terminus, or Of the Interpretation of Nature*. In *The Works of Francis Bacon*, in 14 vols. Edited by James Spedding, Robert Leslie Ellis, and Douglas Denon Heath, 215–252. New York: Cambridge University Press, 1858, Volume 3.
———. *On the Wisdom of the Ancients*. Translated by Heidi Studer (unpublished).
Caton, Hiram. *Politics of Progress*. Gainesville: University of Florida Press, 1988.
Craig, Tobin L. "On the Significance of the Literary Character of Francis Bacon's 'New Atlantis' for an Understanding of his Political Thought." *The Review of Politics* 72 (2010): 213–239.
Farrington, Benjamin. *Francis Bacon: Philosopher of Industrial Science*. New York: Schuman, 1949.
Faulkner, Robert K. "Visions and Powers: Bacon's Two-fold Politics of Progress." *Polity* 21 (1988): 111-136.
Feuer, Lewis S. "Francis Bacon and the Jews: Who Was the Jew in the 'New Atlantis'?" *Jewish Historical Studies* 29 (1982): 1–25.
Hale, Kimberly Hurd. *Francis Bacon's* New Atlantis *in the Foundation of Modern Political Thought*. Lanham: Lexington Books, 2013.
Homer. *Odyssey, Volume I: Books I–XII*. Translated by A.T. Murray. Revised by George E. Dimock. Loeb Classic Library 104. Cambridge: Harvard University Press, 1919.
Innes, David C. "Bacon's *New Atlantis*: The Christian Hope and the Modern Hope." *Interpretation* 22 (1994): 3–38.
Lampert, Laurence. *Nietzsche and Modern Times*. New Haven, CT: Yale University Press, 1993.
Loftus, Elizabeth. "Make-Believe Memories." *American Psychologist* 58 (2003): 867–873.

Matthews, Steven. *Theology and Science in the Thought of Francis Bacon.* Burlington, VT: Ashgate Publishing, 2008.

Minkov, Svetozar. *Francis Bacon's Inquiry Touching Human Nature: Virtue, Philosophy, and the Relief of Man's Estate.* Lanham, MD: Lexington Books, 2010.

More, Thomas. *Utopia.* Cambridge: Cambridge University Press, 2016.

Paterson, Timothy. "The Secular Control of Scientific Power." *Polity* 21 (1989): 457–480.

Pesic, Peter. "Francis Bacon, Violence, and the Motion of Liberty: The Aristotelian Background." *Journal of the History of Ideas* 75 (2014): 69–90.

Plato. *Republic.* Translated by Allan Bloom. New York: Basic Books, 1991.

Pohl, Nichole. "Utopianism after More: the Renaissance and Enlightenment." In *The Cambridge Companion to Utopian Literature*, 51–78. Edited by Gregory Claeys. Cambridge: Cambridge University Press, 2010.

Price, Bronwen. "Introduction." In *Francis Bacon's* New Atlantis*: New Interdisciplinary Essays.* Edited by Bronwen Price, 1–27. New York: Manchester University Press, 2002.

Serjeanston, Richard. "Natural Knowledge in the *New Atlantis*." In *Francis Bacon's* New Atlantis: *New Interdisciplinary Essays.* Edited by Bronwen Price, 84–99. New York: Manchester University Press, 2002.

Spitz, David. "Bacon's 'New Atlantis': A Reinterpretation." *Midwest Journal of Political Science* 4 (1960): 52–61.

Urich, Nell. *Science in Utopia: A Mighty Design.* Cambridge: Harvard University Press, 1967.

Weinberger, Jerry. "Introduction." In *New Atlantis and the Great Instauration.* Edited by Jerry Weinberger, vii–xxxiii. Wheeling, IL: Harlan Davidson, Inc., 1989.

———. *New Atlantis.* In *New Atlantis and the Great Instauration.* Edited by Jerry Weinberger, 35–83. Wheeling, IL: Harlan Davidson, Inc., 1989.

———. *Science, Faith, and Politics: Francis Bacon and the Utopian Roots of the Modern Age.* Ithaca, NY: Cornell University Press, 1985.

———. "Science and Rule in Bacon's Utopia: An Introduction to the Reading of the *New Atlantis*." *The American Political Science Review* 70 (1976): 865–885.

White, Howard B. *Peace among the Willows: The Political Philosophy of Francis Bacon.* The Hague: Martinus Nijhoff, 1968.

Chapter Two

Utopianism and Realism in Shakespeare's *The Tempest*

Paul T. Wilford and Nicholas Anderson

In an uncategorizable drama that nevertheless obeys the principles of classical unity, we see the education of princes, the transformation of spontaneous infatuation into the lasting grounds of affection, the taming of baser instincts, the folly of appetitive rule, the limitations of appealing to low but solid grounds, the reformation of a corrupted soul, forgiveness as benefaction, and we, the audience, learn about the limits of wisdom—even when conjoined with awesome power—to shape political ends. From the opening scene, in which the ship of state metaphor is exploited to great effect, to Prospero's manumission of his "slave" Ariel in the final lines of the play, *The Tempest* abounds in political language, imagery, and metaphor, employing a host of historical, philosophical, and poetic references for exploring questions about the foundations of political order, the nature of the best regime, and the relation between wisdom and politics.

At the intersection of all these questions stands Prospero, who rules like God over the strange isle that is the stage of this drama. Prospero's awesome power to command the elements sets the play's action in motion, and his dominion over nature is the means for effecting his political vision. Nevertheless Prospero's political ambition is astounding, amounting to nothing less than the founding of a new political order for the unification of Italy. The grandeur of the project evinces Prospero's boldness, but this daring is matched by the highest prudence, born of a hard-won understanding of human nature. Prospero's political realism—concealed by the fantastical garb in which it is clothed—is illuminated by a comparison with the other forms of politics operative in the play. In broad terms, what we call "Prospero's noble realism" is juxtaposed on one hand with utopian visions of ideal commonwealths and, on the other, with base Machiavellian scheming and rule by appetitive desire. But Prospero should not be understood as charting a middle course between two extremes—that way of viewing the conceptual landscape obscures not only how different Prospero's political prescriptions are but the distinct view of nature underlying his orientation to the world of convention. As this chapter will show, education is the heart of Prospero's politics: Prospero plays pedagogue to the future princes of Italy. All his political hopes lie in the union of Naples and Milan, in the marriage of his pupils Ferdinand and Miranda.

Shakespeare's *Tempest* exploits the possibilities available in the genre of science fiction for demonstrating the dangers not only of utopian idealism but also cynical realism. The human imagination proves to be both powerful and dangerous. When divorced from reason or morality, it leads either to fanciful speculations or wicked fantasies. Our hopes and dreams quickly become our masters and we become subjects to projects beyond our understanding.

This chapter considers *The Tempest* in the context of (1) the premises of the new natural science; (2) the voyages of discovery; and (3) the tradition of utopian political thought. By reading Shakespeare in light of Francis Bacon, Michel de Montaigne, and Thomas More, we aim to bring into sharper relief Shakespeare's political teaching—a sober realism that tempers ambitions and fosters gratitude.

IMAGINARY REPUBLICS

The play opens in the middle of a tempest with the master of the ship giving orders to the boatswain. Knowledge specific to the mariner's art is needed at this moment to guide the ship. The mariner's art is a technical art and, because of the necessity imposed on the ship by the forces of the storm, those select few on the ship possessing the art that can face the crisis have a claim to guide the ship; that is, knowledge has a legitimate claim to rule over ignorance. King Alonso and Antonio, appearing on deck to learn of the master's whereabouts, are told by the boatswain to keep below. Certain members of the court party—rulers on land—are reluctant to give up their conventional claim to rule. Gonzalo, offended by the boatswain's defiance against conventional hierarchy, appeals to a notion of justice. He declares of the boatswain: "Methinks he hath no drowning mark upon him. His complexion is perfect gallows. Stand fast, good Fate, to his hanging."[1] Gonzalo assumes there is a moral order that supports conventional rule: the boatswain will eventually receive just punishment for his disrespect toward conventional authority; he will perish at the hands of the state, not by the whims of fortune.

Gonzalo's hope belies a faith in a supra-political support for the conventional order, but this reveals his confusion over the relation between conventional and natural hierarchy. Gonzalo's respect for custom aboard ship seems out of character given his anti-hierarchical utopianism, yet this utopianism also relies on a providential order (i.e., nature ordered for the benefit of man).[2] This commitment is the source of Gonzalo's cheerful optimism, which turns misfortune into opportunity. Gonzalo thus exhibits a characteristic resembling that of our protagonist Prospero, whose very name suggests optimism.[3] Among the stranded court party, only Gonzalo remains cheerful and optimistic, telling his fellow Neapolitans to weigh "our sorrow with our comfort" and to rejoice in having survived the wreck. Gonzalo alone notices that their garments "hold notwithstanding their freshness and glosses, being rather new-dyed than stained with salt water."[4] Why does no one else notice this peculiar fact, which contravenes the natural order?[5] Gonzalo's vision is neither clouded by grief nor obscured by ambitious schemes; he exhibits a hopeful, albeit naïve, gratitude for the world. It is in light of Gonzalo's almost childlike wonder that one can best understand his confusion of nature and convention, which is most perspicuous in his imagined commonwealth.

> I' th' commonwealth I would by contraries
> Execute all things; for no kind of traffic
> Would I admit; no name of magistrate;
> Letters should not be known; riches, poverty,
> And use of service, none; contract, succession,
> Bourn, bound of land, tilth, vineyard, none;
> No use of metal, corn, or wine, or oil;
> No occupation; all men idle, all,
> And women too, but innocent and pure;
> No sovereignty [. . .]
> All things in common nature should produce
> Without sweat or endeavor; treason, felony,
> Sword, pike, knife, gun, or need of any engine
> Would I not have; but nature should bring forth
> Of its own kind all foison, all abundance,
> To feed my innocent people.[6]

Gonzalo's vision is representative of one form that utopian dreaming can take: his vision seeks to provide an apolitical solution to the human predicament by imagining humans before the Fall, that is, inhuman humans. Utopian dreaming takes two forms: it either imagines human beings prior to the corruptions of the world as Gonzalo does here, or it envisions a world where the self-inflicted evils of human nature are somehow rectified, whether through extensive education, redistribution of resources, or tremendous artifice. Both approaches, however, tend to overlook that the vice they wish to excise from the commonwealth springs from the same root as the human excellence they so admire. In Gonzalo's polity, there is no strife because there is no hardship, but in a world of ease, there is no self-sacrifice or self-transcendence. Gonzalo's idle men are simple, dumb brutes.

Moreover, the very idea of a commonwealth of such men contains a contradiction; as Antonio points out, its end "forgets the beginning."[7] Although there ought to be no sovereignty in his ideal commonwealth, Gonzalo nevertheless imagines himself king—for all orders require a founder. While Gonzalo's relation to his community is fantastical, it provides a model for Prospero's rule on the island; Gonzalo stands in relation to this imagined commonwealth as Prospero does to his island realm. Their political visions are not subject to the usual constraints imposed by recalcitrant natural necessities.

Gonzalo's respect for custom aboard ship taken in conjunction with his utopian flights of fancy point to his principal oversight. He fails to see how man is naturally political. He cannot see what lies between idyllic, prelapsarian equality and mere convention, which he thinks ought to be respected but which might, he unwittingly suggests, have no more support than the threat of the gallows. Shakespeare's source for Gonzalo's speech is Montaigne's essay *Of Cannibals*. Montaigne compares the supposedly "civilized" customs of Western Europe to the "barbarous" customs of American cannibals. With apolitical, natural man serving as a mirror, the essay is a meditation on human pretension and folly, easily leading one to the conclusion that "custom is king" and that European customs are mere frippery. All the institutions listed in Gonzalo's imagined republic are also absent among the cannibals—a society which, according to Montaigne, surpasses not only the golden age but Plato's imaginary republic. Gonzalo is ironically unaware that the community he describes is composed of cannibals. Some inhuman element underlies his visionary society; it falls short of the fantastic claims made on its behalf by breaking one of the fundamental taboos of humanity. Although political life is not simply natural for the human being, he cannot do without it. Man is a paradoxical being insofar as he is *naturally conventional.* Precisely because cannibalism is not simply unnatural, prohibitions against it are necessary for any commonwealth to exist. As Aristotle reminds us, man, absent the restraint of law, is the worst of animals with regard to food and sex.[8] Just as Gonzalo imagines a society of chaste men and women (as though the eros necessary for the generation of offspring has no base dimension), his vision of a natural human society neglects the parts of human nature that are shaped by convention. The ostensibly natural solution to the perennial political problems fails precisely because it fails to understand that politics is natural for man, absent which his appetites would prove his undoing.

In addition to Montaigne, Shakespeare likely had More's *Utopia* in mind when considering the possibilities for an imaginary republic.[9] In contrast to Montaigne's society of cannibals, More's commonwealth is far more artificial. As recounted by Raphael Hythloday, the commonwealth takes its name from its founder, who acquired sufficient dominion to establish the political order only after victory in war.[10] The founder sees the problem of politics as soluble by means of a virtuous ordering of society—he seeks a conventional solution to the problems of politics. Like Gonzalo's commonwealth, the Utopians have no private property, disdain wealth, and hold all material things in common. More's harmonious vision of society requires a people without a strong distinction between mine and thine. While property is foregrounded in the narrative, such a distinction also undergirds the family.[11] The love Prospero shows for Miranda or the grief of Alonso at having lost Ferdinand are unaccountable in both visions of society. Even though More's *Utopia* upholds a virtuous standard, the political order strips away the motivation that commonly undergirds the pursuit of virtue, namely, the desire for preeminence, for honor, for the recognition of one's own superiority.[12] Nevertheless, there is a measure of realism in More's *Utopia*, and this appears in three features—slaves for menial tasks, mercenaries for foreign wars, and harsh laws against adultery.

Gonzalo's vision thus goes much further than More's *Utopia* in its lack of distinction between mine and thine insofar as it neglects sexual desire, as Sebastian is quick to point out. Marriage, like the prohibition of cannibalism, is a necessary convention for the establishment of a political order.[13] Absent marriage, the distinction between *oikos* and *polis* blurs and the political either disappears or becomes totalizing (like Marx's communist vision in which the state withers away as the distinctions between family, civil-society, and the state are sublated). Common to all these visions (though More exhibits greater sobriety) is a neglect of the particularizing force of erotic love. It is not only that sexual passion is a powerful urge, but that love distinguishes one among many.[14] In loving someone, we elevate an individual, rendering him or her unequal to the rest. One loves *this* person, not as an instance of a class or a member of a species, but as an individual. As Nietzsche reminds us, love is an aristocratic passion: eros upsets all utopian commonwealths.[15]

Eros, however, need not upset all commonwealths, since marriage provides an institutional mechanism to constrain and direct those passions that would otherwise undermine the political order. Marriage is the first, most basic nexus of the conventional and the natural: the human being is, as Aristotle says, a coupling animal, and marriage is the conventional affirmation of this natural propensity.[16] Prospero understands, as we will see, the importance of marriage for political life, and it serves as an essential part of his pedagogic project for Ferdinand and Miranda as well as the key to realizing his political ambitions. It is the primary means by which the passion Gonzalo overlooks is mastered, harnessed, and yoked to the city.

Bacon's utopian vision in *The New Atlantis* provides a third comparison with Gonzalo's imagined commonwealth. Unlike Gonzalo, Bacon does not understand nature as beneficent, nor does nature provide humankind with a standard; rather, nature is so inhospitable that any political solution requires a prior, more fundamental assault upon nature. Man must go to war, nature is his enemy, and politics will not admit of a solution prior to the subjugation of nature. In short, Bacon's political utopianism is the corollary of his scientific project to master nature for the amelioration of our condition. [17] In a world of abundant plenty and the satisfaction of appetites, the tensions and passions behind political strife will be substantially diminished. [18] Although Bacon's political ambition is based on an ostensibly clear-eyed realism about nature, there is a deep idealistic strain in his proposal: if we see nature correctly, we can conquer fortune, and rather than being dependent upon chance for the realization of the best regime, man can provide his own opportunity. In Gonzalo's worldview, the political world with all its injustice is a result of humanity's moral failings and not an accident of an indifferent nature. Bacon, on the other hand, presents nature as not merely indifferent but so cunning that she must be tortured to reveal her secrets. [19] In Bacon's utopia, man, through the conquest of nature, creates his own moral universe. In Gonzalo's vision, a beneficent nature provides the necessary things without the intervention of human art. His vision repudiates the means of Bacon's project, yet the ends are strikingly similar: nature is adequate to human need, and humanity will live in a more comfortable world, a world "T'excel the Golden Age."

POLITICS AMONG BEASTS

In contrast to Gonzalo's utopian vision, there are two base forms of realism presented in the play. Both forms of realism are grounded in an understanding of nature as indifferent—the view of nature underlying Bacon's new science—and both forms are presented through plots of usurpation: the plot of Antonio and Sebastian to overthrow Alonso and the comical plot of Caliban, Stephano, and Trinculo to overthrow Prospero. Both plots show the importance of Prospero's political and poetic education by illustrating the danger of a misguided imagination. Politics guided by utopian visions gives way to flights of the imagination, but so does the politics of the misguided realist. Whereas the former imagines humans cooperating harmoniously on a societal level, the latter shows individuals seeking to satisfy their strongest desires. Whereas the utopian dreamer lets his hopes guide his imagination, the political realist lets his ambitions guide his imagination.

After Gonzalo's imagined republic fails to move anyone else, Ariel puts all the party to sleep, except Antonio and Sebastian. Antonio then persuades Sebastian to murder his brother and take over the kingdom of Naples. Hesitant to act on such a bold plan, Sebastian asks Antonio: "But, for your conscience?" In his response, Antonio displays the understanding of nature that shamelessly allows him to grab power:

> I feel not
> This deity in my bosom. Twenty consciences
> That stand 'twixt me and Milan, candied be they
> And melt ere they molest! Here lies your brother,
> No better than the earth he lies upon,
> If he were that which now he's like—that's dead—
> Whom I with this obedient steel, three inches of it,
> Can lay to bed forever [. . .].[20]

For Antonio, the world is disenchanted and conscience is a false god. Alonso is nothing but clay; no spirit or soul abides in his breast, and so death is no different than sleep. Moreover, Antonio believes neither in an afterlife, where punishment for his deeds would occur, nor in the pangs of guilt in this world. Antonio's view of nature is materialistic; he has no reverence for the dead, no conscience, and no belief in the divine.[21] Antonio lacks wonder, and when one neither believes in gods nor wonders at nature, everything is permitted. The possible is the imaginable. Hence Antonio's persuasion of Sebastian:

> . . . What might,
> Worthy Sebastian, O, what might—? No more.
> And yet methinks I see it in thy face
> What thou shouldst be. Th' occasion speaks thee, and
> My strong imagination sees a crown
> Dropping upon thy head.[22]

Antonio's ambition, if not caused by his "strong imagination," is certainly fueled by it.[23] His imagination drives him to realize his desires, to transform wishes into deeds. But because Prospero's art has contrived the occasion for Sebastian's attempted usurpation, one sees how easily the imagination misleads. Indeed, the past is not prologue to this apparently opportune moment. Not fortune, but Prospero contrives the circumstance in which Antonio's character can reveal itself. Moreover, Antonio's ambition transforms hope, a theological virtue, into a thoroughly political one. In response to Sebastian's lack of hope that Ferdinand has survived the wreck, Antonio says:

> O, out of that no hope
> What great hope have you! No hope that way is
> Another way so high a hope that even
> Ambition cannot pierce a wink beyond,
> But doubt discovery there.[24]

Antonio transforms highest hope into highest ambition—princely rule. Political life may indeed require some form of hope insofar as it is future-directed; thus Prospero in Act V expresses his hope to see "the nuptial / Of these our dear-belovèd solemnized."[25] But whereas Prospero's hope is to yoke young, self-centered love to the broader community through a ceremony of conventional piety—for he wants the city to solemnize Ferdinand and Miranda's wedding—Antonio's hope is nothing beyond his self-interest. Antonio concerns himself not with the political order but merely his place in it; he imagines himself a prince without reflecting on what it means to be one and thus mistakes the trappings of rule for political rule itself. Antonio thinks Sebastian will be king if only the crown drops upon his head, and he thinks of himself as the proper duke of Milan because he can fit into his brother's clothes.[26] If politics is merely convention and solely a realm of appearances, it is hard to see why this view is inadequate.

Antonio's focus on external signs of political rule can be understood as indicative of another instance of the strong separation between nature and convention. His conception of politics rests on a view of nature as wholly indifferent to man (not even providing a standard of conduct). Thus, the given is solely the material upon which to impose the form of one's imagination. Antonio, as we learn, is so lacking in natural filial affection as to remain unrepentant to the end—for which reason Prospero pronounces him "unnatural."[27] Antonio's view of nature and ambition, moreover, leads to a confusion of sleep and wakefulness, of dreams and reality.[28] Thus, although more cynical, he is not so different from the dreamer Gonzalo. Gonzalo imagines as his highest good his hopes for humanity as a whole, while Antonio can imagine no such convergence of individual and common good. His lack of wonder, stemming from his reductive view of nature, forecloses such a possibility. There is no good other than what is clearly one's own good. Antonio's ambitions fall prey to his unrealistic imagination—he sees the world less clearly than he supposes. His realism is idle dreaming.[29]

The other base form of realism, presented through the antics of Stephano, Trinculo, and Caliban, shows us not the cunning of the fox, but a form of politics governed by appetitive desire, which is symbolized in the appetite for wine.[30] For this trio, wine is not only medicinal but takes on a religious status, as Caliban praises the "celestial liquor" and Stephano, priest-like, encourages both Trinculo and Caliban "to swear by the bottle" and "to kiss the book."[31] Having tasted of the "celestial liquor," Caliban quickly kneels to Stephano, first calling him master and then pronouncing him his god.[32] Although Stephano began by forcefully pouring corruption down Caliban's throat, Caliban almost immediately abandons his prudent resistance to imbibing the unknown and quickly develops a strong taste for wine; by cultivating a new appetite in Caliban, Stephano enslaves him. In a matter of minutes, Caliban thinks he has found a replacement for the "tyrant" Prospero.[33] Stephano and his wine win not merely a servant, but quite literally a boot-licking toady.

Caliban's new appetite quickly leads him to abandon his desire for mastery of the island, which he previously claimed by right of inheritance.[34] He is willing to give over all to Stephano to be free of Prospero, but this freedom is understood as absence of labor.[35] Caliban's misunderstanding of freedom is bound up with his lack of understanding of the legitimate grounds for rule. For Caliban, like Antonio, rule appears to be all about power. Thus, if Stephano but burns Prospero's books, then Prospero would be just like himself. That is, Caliban thinks Prospero's power to torment him, to goad him into action, and keep him in servitude is the fundamental difference between them when in truth it is Prospero's self-mastery or virtue that most distinguishes them. If the contrast between Prospero and Caliban is understood as turning on self-mastery, then we glimpse a dangerous possibility inherent in Bacon's project—the possibility that people will submit themselves to those who know how to satisfy their desires. A political order directed by Baconian scientists risks becoming a political order composed of Calibans. The scientist's power to relieve our estate is insufficient grounds for political order; the statesman whose claim to rule rests on efficiently satisfying our appetites debases those whom he ought to ennoble. While appearing to free us from labor and pain, he enslaves us to our pleasures.

Yet Caliban, in contrast to the thoroughly civilized Stephano and Trinculo, nevertheless displays a nature that is open to education—for he is open to wonder.[36] This wonder shows itself in Caliban's initial openness to Prospero's "humane" care. He comes to hate Prospero only after being punished for his attempted rape of Miranda. Nevertheless his capacity for gratitude is not entirely extinguished. He speaks eloquently of the music on the island, showing gratitude for the "sweet airs that give delight."[37] For Caliban, nature is not simply indifferent and subject to manipulation, and his indignation toward Prospero shows a belief in a natural basis for justice: the island is rightfully his and Prospero is the usurper. Thus, Caliban's desire to overthrow Prospero is not simply hedonistic but has prior grounds in a thumotic claim for justice. Stephano, by contrast, although civilized, is *all* appetite.[38]

It is Caliban's propensity to wonder that makes Prospero see his potential for reformation in Act V.[39] The condition for Caliban's education and repentance occurs within the realm of the imagination—for his realization that Stephano is a "dull fool" comes through the contrived circumstances of Prospero's art—yet such an education is not possible without wonder. As opposed to the self-interested ambition of Machiavellian realism or the appetitive fulfillment of Bacon's scientific project, Prospero's pedagogic project offers us another view of politics—one that cultivates wonder and pious gratitude while offering a clear picture of human folly that is absent in utopia.

PROSPERO'S NOBLE REALISM

Before finding himself on his enchanted island, Prospero was an inattentive but beloved Duke of Milan. Consumed by the study of "liberal arts" and "being transported / And rapt in secret studies," Prospero neglected practical affairs, leaving the management of the state to Antonio.[40] Prospero's disdain of "worldly ends" for the sake of "the bettering of [his] mind" is, if nothing else, indicative of the non-political character of his pursuit of knowledge.[41] Prospero turned away from the ephemeral world of politics and became a "stranger" to his state. Having granted his brother de facto rule, Prospero's naive surprise at his deposition by his worldly-minded brother reveals his ignorance of human nature—all the more so since the specimen overlooked was so close at hand (though forgetting the ground one stands on while looking at the heavens is characteristic of the theoretically inclined). Thus, Prospero's declaration: "my library / Was dukedom large enough" encapsulates his youthful orientation to the world.[42] Prospero not only lacked prudence, but knowledge of human affairs, insight into human depravity, and, above all, self-knowledge. Overcoming these deficiencies is the core of Prospero's education.

Nevertheless, speaking of the provisions given by Gonzalo, Prospero describes his prized possessions in the present tense: "Knowing I loved my books, he furnished me / From mine own library with volumes that / I prize above my dukedom."[43] Despite his sufferings, Prospero still values knowledge above principalities. If he has learned from past political failures, then the play raises the question: Is it possible for one to engage in worldly affairs while still prizing the pursuit of truth over political ends? Prospero's answer is a qualified "yes": the philosopher might satisfy his desire for contemplation while providing for the political realm through the judicious education of princes. Prospero has learned to temper his pursuit of knowledge for the sake of the political. But is this a moderation required by necessity or a second sailing truer to the original impulse? Is this the mature means to pursue the same youthful end or has another interest become just as important to Prospero as his books?[44]

The new orientation to practical affairs stems from two interrelated concerns and is aimed at realizing two interdependent goods: (1) Prospero's love for Miranda and (2) Prospero's project for Italian politics. Prospero claims, "I have done nothing but in care of thee," suggesting that his love for Miranda precipitates the tempest with which the drama begins.[45] In addition, when recounting their travails upon being banished and Miranda worries that she had been a nuisance, Prospero assures her that in the depths of his despair "O, a cherubin / Thou wast that did preserve me."[46] At sea with few hopes, weeping and groaning under the weight of his fate, Prospero took courage from his paternal duty—Miranda gave him reason for enduring "what should ensue."[47] *In extremis*, therefore, Prospero's daughter rather than the satisfactions of contemplation constitutes his reason for living. This loving attachment to what is simultaneously his own but also other than himself brings Prospero out of his former "closeness" into the realm of worldly responsibility.[48] Prospero's second education begins with his banishment. He learns not only about human wickedness, the lengths to which ambition will go, and how easily it is to be deceived, but also about the force of familial love—something he neglected when engrossed with his books, but which provides meaning and purpose in dire circumstances. Yet Prospero's education remains substantially incomplete until Caliban's attempted rape of Miranda. That Prospero had not foreseen this possibility and failed to guard against it indicates how little awareness he had hitherto of the force of natural desires. The incident may have also proved to Prospero that the island is not a fit place for Miranda—her good requires participation in a society composed of more than her father and Caliban.[49]

By the end of the first act, we see Prospero's fatherly care complemented by a distinctly political and profoundly ambitious project: the unification of Italy through the marriage alliance of Naples and Milan. Is this for the sake of Miranda or to satisfy Prospero's ambition? Fortune provides Prospero with the opportunity both to secure Miranda's future and to found a new political order, but which end serves which remains unclear.

Regardless, Prospero's primary concern on the island hitherto has been Miranda's education:

> Here in this island we arrived, and here
> Have I, thy schoolmaster, made thee more profit
> Than other princes can, that have more time
> For vainer hours and tutors not so careful.[50]

Like Machiavelli, Prospero is a schoolmaster of princes. For Miranda, this has meant primarily an education of the passions, i.e., primarily a moral education. Though Prospero describes taking great pains, we never hear of Miranda studying "the liberal arts." There is no explicit mention of her learning to read—not to mention being initiated into "secret studies." At the very least, we can be certain that Prospero has decided to forego teaching her any of his awesome magical powers. She never complains of this fact, and seems somehow perfectly content with not knowing the causes of her father's power.[51] Miranda, for all her virtues, is not philosophically inclined: she is not, like her father, consumed with "bettering her mind" and she seems relatively unperturbed by her lack of self-knowledge. Though she speaks of "bootless inquisitions," she seems to have been content not to press her father beyond his wont and gives little indication of having chafed at remaining, as Prospero says, "ignorant of what thou art, naught knowing / Of whence I am."[52]

The stage is now set for the final piece of Miranda's education: in the span of three hours Miranda will run through a host of erotic experiences from physical attraction to transgressive desire, from reciprocal declarations of love to a playful, teasing friendship—all in preparation for the solemnized nuptials that await her return to Naples. Her rapid maturation occurs in tandem with the maturation of Prospero's second, more experienced pupil, Ferdinand.[53] Through their courtship, guided by Prospero, Miranda's gentle nature, compassionate temperament, and inclination to wonder will be shaped into the appropriate counterpart to Ferdinand's chastened pride, moderated ambition, and strategic cunning.

Prospero's political project, then, takes the form of making others fit for rule. But why does Prospero not rule directly? Why does he plan to set his two pupils on the throne rather than rule himself? It is tempting to jump to the conclusion that Prospero learned from his past failures that the philosopher cannot rule directly. The vision of a community ruled by the wise is, like Gonzalo's imagined commonwealth or More's *Utopia*, the vision of a dreamer. But Prospero does rule on the island, so why not continue his rule in Italy? Is it merely that the conjunction of wisdom and power that makes Prospero's rule so effective on the island unavailable on the mainland? If so, Shakespeare would then be teaching us something about the limits of wisdom's efficacy: Prospero's power is commensurate to his wisdom *only* on the island.[54] This is certainly part of Shakespeare's teaching, but it must be understood in relation to two further considerations, both of which evince Prospero's wisdom: Prospero's knowledge of his own mortality and the problem of omniscient and omnipotent—even if benevolent—rule.[55]

Despite Prospero's magnificent powers, his mastery over the elements of nature, and his ability to manipulate the imaginations of those around him, his plan can only come to fruition on account of a chance occurrence outside of his agency.

> By accident most strange, bountiful Fortune,
> Now my dear lady, hath mine enemies
> Brought to this shore; and by my prescience
> I find my zenith doth depend upon
> A most auspicious star, whose influence
> If now I court not, but omit, my fortunes
> Will ever after droop.[56]

Thus, even the indirect rule of the wise through education depends on forces beyond the control of the wise. Prospero's admitted reliance on Fortune reveals his view of nature, which echoes Antonio's more than Gonzalo's.[57] It is not providence that brought his enemies to the island but a chance occurrence in an indifferent cosmos.

Yet Prospero, unlike Antonio, retains a sense of gratitude and a reasoned commitment to moral rule despite his recognition that conditions favorable to political order are subject to fortune. His moral integrity, rather than being undermined by an awareness of nature's indifference, in fact seems to stem in part from his belief that everything human is fleeting—merely an "insubstantial pageant." Prospero's awareness of the contingency of human affairs is an aspect of his philosophic confrontation with death. Prospero remarks that upon returning to Milan, "every third thought shall be my grave."[58] He does not avoid the terrible fact of mortality, and yet it is not everything.

Prospero knows that confronting death with equanimity ("our little life is rounded with a sleep") is not a reasonable task to ask of most people—Antonio demonstrates the perils of thinking too lightly of death. Thus Prospero instills in others, through his stagecraft of carefully managed spectacle and contrived circumstance, a belief in "immortal providence." Prospero's noble lie that the cosmos supports moral action supports a generous hope. He attempts to inculcate a faith that fosters a brave orientation to the unknown. Its political function is apparent when contrasted with the hopes of Antonio's fevered imagination. For Antonio political life is necessarily a zero-sum game; there is no such thing as a salutary political order because there is no such thing as a salutary moral order, but only "Who, Whom?" power politics. Understanding why Prospero, who like his brother does not believe in a providential moral order, nevertheless pursues a noble realism aimed at establishing an enduring political order is at the heart of the play's teaching.

Prospero's understanding of the contingent, ephemeral nature of politics informs not only his judgment of what is possible, but also the necessary means to that end. Thus, although ambitious, Prospero's project does not verge into the dreamlike territory of utopianism. His grand political aim of unifying Italy is realizable through concrete, specific educational goals: Miranda must learn to moderate her pity, Ferdinand temper his ambition lest he become a cruel ruler, Alonso taught to be remorseful through the guilt of his past deeds, and Antonio and Sebastian—if not educated—unmasked so that their imaginative ambitions will not pose a threat on the return to Italy. But how does Prospero achieve these ends? What does his pedagogic project show us about his noble realism?

Gonzalo unknowingly provides insight into Prospero's method while recounting the events of the play: Ferdinand "found a wife / Where he himself was lost; Prospero his dukedom / In a poor isle; and all of us ourselves / When no man was his own."[59] No man was his own because, through the conjurations of Prospero's art, each one acted out a role—a role revelatory of their nature. Antonio and Sebastian play the role of usurpers, Stephano plays the role of a tyrant, Alonso plays the role of a grieving father, and Miranda and Ferdinand play the role of star-crossed lovers, who love against the will of a paternal power.[60] Each situation reveals the nature of the individuals in ways that are rare in actual political life; each character is presented with an opportunity to find himself. (This is true also of Stephano, Trinculo, and Caliban, but of the comic trio only Caliban learns anything.) Yet none of the characters is cognizant of Prospero's machinations; they move about the island as though following a script, reacting to contrived circumstances precisely as Prospero intends. Though beneficent, Prospero's rule is paternalistic to the point of puppetry; he precludes genuine agency, while granting the illusion of freedom. This should give us pause.[61]

However, it is easy to overlook this darker theme of the play, especially when we are captivated by the wholesome and gratifying drama of young lovers, who "at first sight . . . have changed eyes."[62] Miranda and Ferdinand's education and marriage not only serves as the cornerstone for Prospero's political project, but it saliently demonstrates Prospero's hard-won knowledge of human nature. Ferdinand shows himself to be an ambitious young man. Having weathered the tempest, he takes himself, with little evidence, to be the sole survivor of his party and declares himself the king of Naples. Within thirty lines, he offers to make Miranda the queen of Naples and rashly draws his sword against her father.[63] Such bold action, perhaps characteristic of all young men, must be reined in. In making "uneasy" the "swift business" of love, Prospero will discipline Ferdinand's hot temper and strong passions.[64]

Prospero begins by setting Ferdinand the task of gathering firewood, Caliban's principal labor.[65] Ferdinand performs the menial task willingly and the banausic work quickly shapes his soul. From thumotically resisting being manacled, Ferdinand has learned that "Some kinds of baseness / Are nobly undergone; and most poor matters / Point to rich ends."[66] We can hardly imagine any of the conspirators making such a claim—their desires and ambitions seek immediate gratification. Ferdinand, forced into becoming a "patient log-man," learns to endure hardship for a higher end.[67] Miranda pities Ferdinand and pleads to perform the work for him. Ferdinand, of course, cannot let Miranda so dishonor herself. Ferdinand learns to humble himself, for love makes us willing to endure what would otherwise be the indignity of servitude. Through patient submission, and through the reward of Miranda's affection, Ferdinand's initial wonder at Miranda becomes admiration—the only foundation for enduring love. Thus he exclaims at learning her name: "Admired Miranda! / Indeed the top of admiration, worth / What's dearest to the world."[68] This exclamation describes the gift that has been granted to Ferdinand through his encounter with Prospero. It is, as Prospero says of Miranda, "a gift and thine own acquisition / Worthily purchased."[69] Ferdinand's labor for the sake of Miranda has allowed him to see the world as marvelous, and thus to see it with gratitude. The world is more than an arena for his ambition.

Like all young lovers who are to avoid a tragic end, Miranda and Ferdinand must learn to rule themselves—an education that begins by each wishing to serve the other.[70] Love makes them willing to submit, but this passion must be further tempered. Hence, Prospero emphasizes chastity; having privately called upon the "heavens [to] rain grace / On that which breeds between 'em,"[71] he warns the young lovers that should their passion get the best of them "No sweet aspersion shall the heavens let fall / To make this contract grow; but barren hate, Sour-eyed disdain, and discord."[72] Only by mastering and directing this most intense natural passion to the form of a conventional institution will they become fit to rule. Hymen must lead these two toward the marriage bed, lest weeds choke rather than flowers spring from their union.[73]

Warning, threats, and oaths, however, are not sufficient for a flourishing union.[74] Although Ferdinand and Miranda possess "two rare affections," they are not wise enough, as Prospero seems to be, for their reason to rule unaided. Prospero calls upon his art and offers the couple a moral vision to balance his admonitions: a positive ideal to complement the previous bulwarks against physical temptation. In Prospero's pageant, pagan gods dance and sing and celebrate the beauty of self-governance. The gods sanctify their union and through poetic spectacle endow chastity with splendor. Self-mastery is not delayed gratification but beautiful fecundity.

Juno, the goddess of marriage, calls on Ceres, the goddess of agriculture, to celebrate the marriage of the two young lovers, but Ceres, having forsworn the company of Venus and Cupid, will only come if such erotic temptation is in abeyance. (Ceres, after all, lost her daughter Persephone to the god of the underworld on account of erotic passion.) Juno and Ceres then sing about the harvest and an abundance of goods. If the couple remains chaste, then the fertile richness that Juno and Ceres describe will be theirs.[75]

Moreover, the spectacle is also political. Juno, the goddess of marriage, is the "highest queen of state" because marriage serves as the foundation of the state by yoking together the natural to the conventional.[76] The institution of marriage, supporting reason's rule over the passions, exemplifies how convention can be a bulwark for morality. A marriage of two noble, self-ruling souls will serve as the foundation of a nobly ruled state. This initial marriage ceremony fulfills its intended purpose, for in response to Prospero's monologue, in which he reveals the "vanity" of his art, the couple answers together as one: "We wish your peace."[77] Together Ferdinand and Miranda can rule one another—and it is this pious and chaste "we" that will serve as the foundation of the new Italian regime.

Prospero's art orients Ferdinand and Miranda in an imaginative view of the whole that allows them to believe in the world's goodness. Prospero's theatrical manipulation of their imagination supports the couple's belief that the gods reward virtue. Ferdinand states: "Let me live here forever. / So rare a wondered father and a wise / Makes this place paradise."[78] Far from cursing the world, Ferdinand ends the play believing in a moral order and a merciful world: "Though the seas threaten, they are merciful. / I have cursed them without cause."[79] Further, in reply to his father's question about whether Miranda is a goddess, Ferdinand states: "Sir, she is mortal, / But by immortal providence she's mine."[80] The belief in immortal providence—which supports a grateful orientation toward the world—will guide Ferdinand's future actions as a ruler.

Miranda, for her part, must learn to temper her pity. When we first encounter her pitying those in the tempest, we see what damage her pity would do to the world if only she had the power.[81] Although Miranda once pitied Caliban, taking pains to "make him speak," she came to see him as a "villain" deserving of his confinement and subordinate condition.[82] Miranda nevertheless quickly assumes that the object of her pity possesses a good nature. Thus, the hardest lesson for Miranda is that some natures are evil. In addition, she must learn that suffering should not always be immediately relieved. Ferdinand's labor teaches Miranda the important lesson that some suffering, even in those possessing good natures, is inevitable and necessary, and sometimes even beneficial. Miranda's development is in evidence when she plays chess with Ferdinand. Ferdinand attempts to cheat Miranda ("Sweet lord you play me false"), yet she accepts this cheating and understands that a certain amount of ambition may be necessary for sustaining a regime: "Yes, for a score of kingdoms you should wrangle, / And I would call it fair play."[83] Miranda is ready to play her part in the political rule of Italy. She no longer has an overly "piteous heart." She is now self-possessed and collected.

With the marriage of Miranda and Ferdinand, Milan (redeemed from its "ignoble stooping") and Naples will be unified and supported by Tunis; thus there will be no need for an alliance with Rome, which is never mentioned in the play.[84] The marriage of the young lovers unites ambition with pity and gratitude, providing the necessary support for the compassionate rule of a unified Italy. Prospero's political project is not complete, however, until his final hope is fulfilled, that is, "to see the nuptial / Of these our dear-beloved solemnized."[85] The ceremony produced by Prospero's art readies Miranda and Ferdinand for political rule, but the political community must also sanctify their union. The first ceremony supports the couple's natural basis for rule—that is, Ferdinand and Miranda have a claim to rule others because they can rule themselves. But if the two lovers are to rule not only themselves but also others, their bond of affection requires confirmation under the auspices of established custom. The best marriages are founded on two blessings: the first from nature and the second from convention. The best regimes likewise require these two blessings, resolving, however briefly, the tension between nature and convention.

Prospero's understanding of politics as education is predicated on a sober view of human nature. Yet, in contrast to Machiavellian politics, it does not understand man's highest hopes in terms of his capacity for acquisition; nor does it understand the human race—as Bacon's scientific utopia might—as a race of unreformed Calibans. The rule of Prospero, through the indirect means of education, is a form of rule that preserves and encourages wonder. It allows the best and most noble parts of the human being to flourish while keeping in check—but certainly not eliminating—the base aspects of human nature. The new science, on the other hand, cannot educate souls, and might even hinder it, for it harms wonder and eases labor. A Ferdinand educated by modern science risks becoming at best like Antonio and at worst like Stephano—a ruthless Machiavellian operator or a pleasure-seeking tyrant. Despite the immense power of the new science in discovering and manipulating the secrets of nature, its knowledge is inadequate to the demands of ruling—for it is purely instrumental. It knows *how* to master nature, but it does not know *why* or *wherefore*.[86] In contrast, Prospero's rule by education, through its formation of wonder, situates us in a greater cosmic context in which our ambition is tempered and our imagination does not delude us into seeking permanent solutions to perennial problems. Through the indirect means of education, the poet-philosopher can become, in Shelley's words, "the unacknowledged legislator of the world."[87] Realistic reflections on the political life of man must eventually confront Prospero's harsh truth: human institutions are ephemeral, and all things pass away. But true wisdom entails seeing this without giving into despair; one must not become deaf to the pleasant notes of life, the moments of grace that give delight and hurt not. Prospero provides the model for this orientation, exhibiting in his most vulnerable and self-revelatory moment a reconciled recognition of the fleeting pageantry of life:

> Be cheerful, sir.
> Our revels now are ended. These our actors,
> As I foretold you, were all spirits and
> Are melted into air, into thin air;
> And like the baseless fabric of this vision,
> The cloud-capped towers, the gorgeous palaces,
> The solemn temples, the great globe itself,
> Yea, all which it inherit, shall dissolve,
> And, like this insubstantial pageant faded,
> Leave not a rack behind. We are such stuff
> As dreams are made on, and our little life
> Is rounded with a sleep.[88]

Yet Prospero is not without hope.[89] He has retained sufficient wonder such that he so delights in the spectacular dance of the gods that he briefly forgets the baser parts of life (represented by the comic trio). Prospero demonstrates how philosophy is not only a private, cloistered pursuit of knowledge, but can be genuinely philanthropic, inspiring in others a wonder similar to that which animates its own search for wisdom.

CONCLUSION: PLAYWRIGHT AS PEDAGOGUE

Having forsworn his "rough magic" at the beginning of act V, breaking his staff and drowning his book,[90] Prospero closes the drama with an epilogue addressed to the audience, a brief soliloquy composed of octosyllabic rhyming couplets.

> Now my charms are all o'erthrown,
> And what strength I have 's mine own,
> Which is most faint. Now 'tis true
> I must be here confined by you,
> Or sent to Naples. Let me not,
> Since I have my dukedom got
> And pardoned the deceiver; dwell
> In this bare island by your spell,
> But release me from my bands
> With the help of your good hands.
> Gentle breath of yours my sails
> Must fill, or else my project fails,
> Which was to please. Now I want
> Spirits to enforce, art to enchant,
> And my ending is despair,
> Unless I be relieved by prayer,
> Which pierces so that it assaults
> Mercy itself, and frees all faults.
>   As you from crimes would pardoned be,
>   Let your indulgence set me free.[91]

This speech, traditionally understood as Shakespeare's farewell to the stage, echoes in both substance and style the closing lines of *Midsummer Night's Dream*. This resonance points the reader to *Midsummer,* where, as in *The Tempest,* the similarity of drama and dreaming is a theme of the play, a theme stated explicitly in *Midsummer*'s epilogue as spoken by Robin Good-fellow:

> If we shadows have offended,
> Think but this, and all is mended,
> That you have but slumber'd here
> While these visions did appear.
> And this weak and idle theme,
> No more yielding but a dream.[92]

The connection between dreaming and poetry is not restricted to the playful Puck, but is, in fact, stated more explicitly and forcefully by the serious and grave Theseus, who appears to condemn the falsehoods generated by the overheated imaginations that consume the minds of lovers, madmen, and poets:

> The poet's eye, in fine frenzy rolling,
> Doth glance from heaven to earth, from earth to heaven;
> And as imagination bodies forth
> The forms of things unknown, the poet's pen
> Turns them to shapes and gives to airy nothing
> A local habitation and a name. [93]

The poet's art *seems* to fool us into believing the potential actual, the unreal real, the dream a reality. It is possible, thus, to read the epilogue of *The Tempest* as Shakespeare's reflection on the dreamlike unreality, nay the impossibility of all that has preceded. Poetry lacking "spirits to enforce" and "art to enchant" seems to end in "despair."[94]

But there is a second possible reading of Theseus's speech; for *Midsummer Night's Dream* is, after all, about the founding of Athens, and how else are new modes and orders brought into being other than through the truly poetic art of legislation?[95] Thus, there is a similarity between the poet and the great legislator—both bring something into being, both give form to things unknown. In Prospero's words, which echo both a famous speech of Medea's in Ovid's *Metamorphoses* and *The Bible*, this capacity is extraordinary, rivaling the power of God: Prospero's (and Shakespeare's) magic distinguishes sea from sky, tames lesser gods, controls thunder and lightning, precipitates earthquakes, and even resurrects the dead.[96]

The connection between poetry and politics implicit in Theseus's character opens a perspective on Prospero as poet-legislator. As we have seen, Prospero's love for Miranda draws him into worldly affairs and makes him a benefactor of humanity. He not only forgives those who wronged him—and this forgiveness is a mark of his magnanimity—but he lays the foundations for a political order that will benefit future generations entirely unknown to him. He brings into being a fancy of his imagination. In light of the *Epilogue,* however, how should we understand Prospero's grand political project? And, why is Shakespeare's farewell to the stage a plea for forgiveness and freedom?

Prospero's—and by extension Shakespeare's—realism is easy to miss, while we are distracted by magic, amused by carousing drunkards, and charmed by youthful love, yet it is the central nerve of the play, evident from beginning to end, from the Boatswain's frank confession to having greater regard for his own self-preservation than the safe transportation of King Alonso to the pain of Caliban's realization that he worshiped a false god. While the play abounds in fantastical magic, the depiction of human nature, its highs and its lows, its possibilities and its shortcomings, is unerringly clear-eyed. Above all, Shakespeare is realistic about what wisdom can hope to achieve. The Baconian project is either a fanciful dream or a nightmare—political life cannot be based on the satisfactions of the body—and the idealized harmony of *Utopia* presupposes a people without mine and thine. What might actually be possible is a good marriage and rule by a virtuous pair, who know nothing of Prospero's art and so can wield none of his power, but whose union unites Northern Milan with Southern Naples, and thereby forges a kingdom sufficiently powerful to counter that unnamed city, and which can, moreover, reliably count on an alliance with Tunis—the descendent of that unnamed city's old rival. But even this is profoundly unlikely, depending on a contingency that is beyond mastery, and subject to woe, destruction, ruin and decay—like all human institutions. Shakespeare asks for forgiveness because even Prospero's noble realism is most unlikely to be actualized.

Yet Shakespeare's teaching is not exhausted by this somber political reflection. Whereas Prospero's education is manipulative, Shakespeare's education requires liberal participation on the part of the audience. Like Prospero, Shakespeare directs the dramatis personae as he desires, but the action is for the sake of another's education: the spectator (or reader) whose reflection on the drama is itself a feature of the deepest education Shakespeare can offer. We are simultaneously outside the play—distant, omniscient lookers-on—and sympathetic witnesses. Our own passions are manipulated like those of Ferdinand and Miranda, but this occurs only indirectly, and through our own willingness to be so moved—through our own active receptivity. To provoke his audience to suffer with the dramatis personae is part of the pedagogic means available to the playwright, but only certain souls will reflect on the passions provoked by the drama. In *The Tempest*, this meta-level reflection made explicit in the *Epilogue* governs the whole. This play opens up for the spectator a reflection on the mimetic power of man more comprehensively than all of Shakespeare's previous dramas. Perhaps man's poetic power underlies his capacity for speech and the possibility of political life. By stepping forth and calling out to the audience, Shakespeare provokes us to recognize how we are participants in the spectacle; we too become active and thereby open to passion, which is the stuff of our deepest education, the substance of our most serious reflections. Prospero's political project may be an idle dream, but Shakespeare's pedagogic project is a real possibility. If we are open to Shakespeare's music, we too might learn to be grateful, like Caliban, for the "Sounds and sweet airs that give delight and hurt not."[97]

NOTES

The authors would like to thank Prof. Robert Faulkner for exemplifying that generosity of spirit that enables one to remain open to hearing those "sounds and sweet airs that give delight and hurt not." His magnanimity is an inspiration to us both.

1. William Shakespeare, *The Tempest*, ed. Barbara A. Mowat and Paul Werstine (New York: Simon & Schuster Paperbacks, 2009), 1.1.29–32.

2. This is a reflection of his character, "whose honor cannot be measured or confined" (Shakespeare, *Tempest*, 5.1.135–6). But what is the nature of this honor? Is honor something natural or conventional? In Gonzalo's case it appears to be both. As for the providential order Gonzalo wishes existed, it does exist on the island, insofar as evil is turned to good, the just are rewarded, and no one suffers the consequences of their own stupidity or wickedness—not even Caliban, Trinculo, or Stephano.

3. David Lowenthal, "The Tempest" in *Shakespeare's Thought: Unobserved Details and Unsuspected Depths in Thirteen Plays* (Lanham, MD: Lexington Books, 2017), 25.

4. Shakespeare, *Tempest*, 2.1.64–67; cf. 1.2.258–260.

5. As Tanner observes, the island brings out character's predisposition to view the world positively or cynically (*Prefaces to Shakespeare*, 816). On the island Milton's adage is true: "The mind is its own place, and in itself / Can make a heav'n of hell, a hell of heav'n" (*Paradise Lost*, I.254–255).

6. Shakespeare, *Tempest*, 2.1.162–180. Note the absence of religion, which is apparently unnecessary because the people are without sin (as Gonzalo underscores twice). Might this innocence have something to do with the absence of sexual desire? Gonzalo's vision is of Prelapsarian man—no shame, no knowledge of good and evil, and so no custom, law, or politics.

7. Shakespeare, *Tempest*, 2.1.173–4.

8. Cf. Aristotle, *Politics*, trans. Carnes Lord (Chicago, IL: The University of Chicago Press, 2013), 1253a 30–40. Aristotle's reference to the Odyssey and the Cyclopes is illuminating here as well. For more on this reference and the importance of the prohibition of cannibalism in the development of political life, see Michael Davis, *The Politics of Philosophy: A Commentary on Aristotle's* Politics (Lanham, MD: Rowman & Littlefield Publishers, 1996), 13–32.

9. In addition, the travel literature of the era provided rich material for Shakespeare's creative imagination. In particular, Shakespeare would have read the reports of the shipwreck of Sir Thomas Gates and his subsequent safe return to the colony of Virginia in 1609–1610. For a helpful account of this material see Tanner, *Prefaces to Shakespeare*, 794–800.

10. Thomas More, *Utopia*, ed. George M. Logan and Robert M. Adams (Cambridge, Cambridge University Press, 2002), 42. "Utopus, who conquered the country and gave it his name . . . and who brought its rude, uncouth inhabitants to such a high level of culture and humanity that they now surpass almost every other people, also changed its geography." While the story of utopia is recounted by Raphael Hythloday, for present purposes we will not try to distinguish between More and his literary character, who often seems his mouthpiece, especially when describing the challenges of advising princes in Bk. I. On the complexity and subtly of More's argument see Richard G. Stevens, "On the Practicality of More's Utopia," *Social Research* 33, no. 1 (Spring, 1966).

11. While there remain discrete families in Utopia their integrity as a distinct source of identity is subordinated to the needs of the commonwealth. To the extent that "the whole island is like a single family," individual families are less inviolable (More, *Utopia*, 59).

12. This source of social discontent is supposedly absent from Utopia, but whereas the account of the arrangements by which material needs are satisfied is lengthy and developed, it is simply asserted that although man alone out of "sheer pride" glories "in getting ahead of others by a superfluous display of possessions, . . . this sort of vice has no place whatever in the Utopian scheme of things" (More, *Utopia*, 55). How Utopia checks the sin of pride, the foremost sin in Christianity, is never fully elaborated.

13. See Ronna Burger, "Definitional Law in the Bible" in *The Eccentric Core: The Thought of Seth Benardete,* ed. Ronna Burger and Patrick Goodin (South Bend, IN: St. Augustine's Press, 2018).

14. For a helpful account of the particularizing force of love and the difficulty this presented to Medievals attempting to foreground the Christian teaching on *agape* or *charitas* see Roger Scruton, "Philosophy of Love" in *Death-Devoted Heart: Sex and the Sacred in Wagner's Tristan and Isolde* (Oxford University Press, 2003).

15. Friedrich Nietzsche, *Beyond Good and Evil*, trans. Walter Kaufmann (New York: Vintage Books, 1989), §260.

16. Aristotle, *Nicomachean Ethics*, trans. Robert C. Bartlett & Susan Collins (Chicago, IL: The University of Chicago Press, 2012), 1162a16–20.

17. On the grounds of Bacon's Utopianism, see Richard Kennington "Bacon's Ontology" in *On Modern Origins,* 33–48; note Kennington's remark "this is utopia, the perfect marriage of theory and practice" (38).

18. This project also addresses the psychological and spiritual needs that undergird our religious passions and thereby affect political life. To make man master and possessor of nature is to supplant God. Man is no longer subordinate to a higher being, but appears to become his own master. The question whether man is actually liberated or in fact subordinated to powers that he ultimately cannot control is central to evaluating the Baconian project.

19. In *The Great Instauration*, for example, Bacon writes: "the nature of things betrays itself more readily under the vexations of art than in its natural freedom" (Francis Bacon, *Selected Philosophical Works*. [Indianapolis, IN: Hackett Publishing Company, 1999], 82). Further, Bacon transforms Machiavelli's teaching in chapter 25 of *The Prince*, expanding the mastery over *fortuna* to "the empire of man over things," which depends "wholly on the arts and sciences" (147).

20. Shakespeare, *Tempest,* 2.1.318–325.

21. Antonio further displays his materialism and lack of wonder when he attributes the drowsiness felt by the other members of the court party not to anything "wondrous" but to the "quality of the climate" (Shakespeare, *Tempest,* 2.1.218–220). Given how "strange" the island is, perhaps Alonso's judgment that "there is in this business more than nature / was ever conduct of" is, in fact, more reasonable than Antonio's skepticism (5.1.294–295). Antonio's realism accords with a stubborn insistence on the denial of the miraculous, preventing him not only from seeing the wonders of the isle but recognizing the great gift of grace that is his brother's forgiveness, which unlike that bestowed on the repenting King of Naples, is wholly unmerited. On the island's strangeness, note that "strange" or its cognates appears 29 times in the play.

22. Shakespeare, *Tempest,* 2.1.226–231.

23. As Paul Cantor observes, comparing Antonio and Lady Macbeth: "A strong imagination seems characteristic of Shakespeare's usurpers—they readily leap ahead in their minds to picture themselves already possessed of what they most desire" ("Shakespeare's *The Tempest*: Tragicomedy and the Philosophic Hero" in *Shakespeare's Last Plays: Essays in Literature and Politics,* ed. Stephen W. Smith and Travis Curtright [Lanham, MD: Lexington Books, 2002], 7).

24. Shakespeare, *Tempest,* 2.1.272–276.

25. Shakespeare, *Tempest,* 5.1.366–367.

26. Shakespeare, *Tempest,* 2.1.313–314.

27. Shakespeare, *Tempest,* 5.1.89.

28. Shakespeare, *Tempest,* 2.1.232–239.

29. No one else in the play is described as evil, not even Caliban. Only Antonio is said to have an "evil nature" which was awakened by Prospero's unbounded generosity and confidence (Shakespeare, *Tempest,* 1.2.113–117). Prospero's remark indicates what he has learned about the conditions under which particular natural potencies are actualized.

30. Wine is explicitly excluded from Gonzalo's commonwealth, as viticulture constitutes a marker of civilization. For the possibility that wine is particularly important consider the view implied in the story of Noah as the first viticulturist (*Genesis,* 9:20–25). Here the motifs of the Fall (*Genesis,* 3:7–19) are repeated, namely, the movement from nakedness and shame to

banishment. Cf. Homer's description of the Cyclopes first encounter with wine at the hands of Odysseus (Homer, *The Odyssey*, trans. Richmond Lattimore [New York, NY: Harper & Row Publishers, Inc, 1967], Book 9.105–115, 345–374). Consider also Sebastian's preemptive concern with wine, even before Gonzalo states there would be no vineyards; Sebastian indicates what he thinks is the most decisive product of artifice, which, ironically, is the means civilized man employs for self-forgetting, i.e., returning to the unreflective existence of Gonzalo's natural man (Shakespeare, *Tempest*, 2.1.161).

31. Shakespeare, *Tempest*, 2.2.75–150.

32. Shakespeare, *Tempest*, 2.2.120–122.

33. Shakespeare, *Tempest*, 2.2.190–192.

34. Shakespeare, *Tempest*, 1.2.396.

35. Shakespeare, *Tempest*, 2.2.164–193. Note how quickly Caliban has moved from announcing that he will serve Stephano, especially in the office of fetching wood, to believing he won't work at all (cf. 2.2.166–7). Contrast this view of freedom with freedom as self-mastery exemplified by Prospero in his decision to abjure his power, in his promise-making and keeping, and in his forgiveness of his enemies. Promise-keeping is an exemplary instance of human agency, since one commits oneself to a specific action in an indeterminate future, thus evincing our belief in the efficacy of practical reasoning and our capacity for self-determination. Like forgiveness, promise-making is uniquely human, but requires an astonishing degree of *rational* self-mastery (5.1.33–36; 5.1.377).

36. Caliban is also less taken in by the superficial frippery of civilization. When approaching Prospero's cave with murderous intent, Stephano and Trinculo are easily distracted by "glistening apparel"—mere signs of custom—whereas Caliban remains focused on murder. Shakespeare, *Tempest*, 4.1.246–276.

37. Shakespeare, *Tempest*, 3.2.148–156. Whereas Stephano and Trinculo chatter in drunken prose, Caliban speaks mostly in verse throughout the play. He exhibits a mastery over language that his co-conspirators lack, suggesting he has learned more from Prospero than just how to curse, something which prepares him for repentance in the final scene (5.1.351–53).

38. Stephano's willingness not only to kill Prospero but also to forcibly take Miranda for his queen is indicative of "civilized baseness" as opposed to the "natural baseness" of Caliban. That is, Stephano wishes to rape Miranda just as Caliban did, but he will call it "making her my queen" (Shakespeare, *Tempest*, 3.2.116). Whereas Caliban's action can be understood as springing from an unmediated natural passion, Stephano's stems from imagination. Note the pun in that same speech, after Stephano's affirmation of himself and Miranda as King and Queen of the island, he calls Trinculo and Caliban his "viceroys" or his kings of vice. All those vices Gonzalo wished to avoid are present in Stephano's kingdom. This juxtaposition shows how Gonzalo's vision is negatively determined: his utopian vision is not man at his highest, but man absent all the potential for vice that attends upon civilization. Furthermore, consider how Stephano is introduced to the audience: drinking while singing a bawdy tune comparing sex to scratching an itch (2.2.43–56).

39. Throughout the play Prospero treats Caliban as an agent with moral choice, whereas Stephano, Trinculo, and Antonio only see Caliban as a commodity (Shakespeare, *Tempest*, 5.1.319–321). This is how the English view Caliban as well, who in the allure of spectacle and coin forget their own humanity (2.2.29–30, 69–72), but perhaps this is because "any strange beast there makes a man" (2.2.31–2).

40. Shakespeare, *Tempest*, 1.2.91–95.

41. Shakespeare, *Tempest*, 1.2.109–10.

42. Shakespeare, *Tempest*, 1.2.130–131.

43. Shakespeare, *Tempest*, 1.2.198–200.

44. In addition to works already cited, our interpretation is indebted to Paul A. Cantor, "Prospero's Republic: The Politics of Shakespeare's *The Tempest*" in *Shakespeare as a Political Thinker*, ed. John E. Alvis and Thomas G. West. (Wilmington, DE: ISI, 2000); Janet Dougherty, "The Poetic Art of the Possible: Shakespeare's *Tempest*," St. John's College Digital Archives, http://digitalarchives.sjc.edu/items/show/3459; Nathan Schlueter, "Prospero's Second Sailing: Machiavelli, Shakespeare, and the Politics of the Tempest," in *Shakespeare's Last Plays: Essays in Literature and Politics*, ed. Stephen W. Smith and Travis Curtright (Lanham,

MD: Lexington Books, 2002); Peter Augustine Lawler, "Shakespeare's Realism in *The Tempest*" in *Shakespeare's Last Plays*; and Timothy Burns, *Shakespeare's Political Wisdom* (New York: Palgrave Macmillan, 2013), 183–217.

45. Shakespeare, *Tempest*, 1.2.19.

46. Shakespeare, *Tempest*, 1.2.182–83.

47. Shakespeare, *Tempest*, 1.2.188.

48. Shakespeare, *Tempest*, 1.2.110.

49. It is possible to interpret this sequence of events as Prospero's deliberate manipulation of Caliban for the sake of Miranda's education, but this seems unlikely given Caliban's account of the fatherly affection Prospero once lavished on him.

50. Shakespeare, *Tempest*, 1.2.205–208.

51. Miranda is kept in the dark about the extent and mechanism of Prospero's power, which is most evident in her complete ignorance of Ariel's existence.

52. Shakespeare, *Tempest*, 1.2.21–22.

53. Shakespeare, *Tempest*, 3.1.49–56.

54. Cf. David Lowenthal, "The Tempest," 25; 50–51.

55. As Burns spells out so clearly, Prospero's rule on the island is by means of deception and manipulation (*Shakespeare's Political Wisdom*, 209, 216–17). Not only Miranda and Ferdinand but all the island's inhabitants are like children in relation to Prospero.

56. Shakespeare, *Tempest*, 1.2.213–219.

57. Shakespeare, *Tempest*, 2.1.241.

58. Shakespeare, *Tempest*, 5.1.369.

59. Shakespeare, *Tempest*, 5.1.251–254.

60. On Ferdinand and Miranda's similarities to Romeo and Juliet see Allan Bloom, *Love and Friendship* (New York: Simon & Schuster, 1993), 283–285.

61. The manipulation of characters' actions and emotions by Ariel almost always occurs by means of music (e.g., see stage direction *The Tempest* at 1.2.451; 2.1.201–2; 3.2.135–6; 3.3.23, 3.3.102), but music is more than the means of manipulation; for example, Ariel sings when helping Prospero change once he has divested himself of his "rough magic" at 5.1.98–104. A full account of the meaning of music in the play is beyond the scope of this chapter, but music as a tool for governing the actions of others might be an analogue for rule by persuasion rather than threats of punishments. If this is correct, then it suggests that if rational speech were as effective in political life as music is on the island, the philosopher could rule. But as we know from the play, not everyone is equally responsive to music; Antonio seems almost deaf to its charms and Caliban, though receptive, nevertheless requires physical goading. Even on the island, music is insufficient to bring harmony to the affairs of men.

62. Shakespeare, *Tempest*, 1.2.529–530.

63. Shakespeare, *Tempest*, 1.2.538–565.

64. Shakespeare, *Tempest*, 1.2.542–545.

65. In addition to gathering firewood, there are a number of similarities between Ferdinand and Caliban: both are young, thumotic men, both are described as imprisoned (Shakespeare, *Tempest*, 1.2.434–436, 1.2.595–600), both describe the music on the island in similar, "sweet" terms (1.2.465–473, 3.2.148–156), both seek some sort of sovereignty, and both confuse a mortal for a divinity (1.2.505–11, 2.2.120–122).

66. Shakespeare, *Tempest*, 3.1.2–4.

67. Shakespeare, *Tempest*, 3.1.79.

68. Shakespeare, *Tempest*, 3.1.47–49.

69. Shakespeare, *Tempest*, 4.1.14–15.

70. Shakespeare, *Tempest*, 3.1.24–36, 74–79, 101.

71. Shakespeare, *Tempest*, 3.1.90–91.

72. Shakespeare, *Tempest*, 4.1.16–24.

73. Among the many significant parallels between *As You Like It* and *The Tempest*, the most important is the role of marriage in redressing the political situation; in both cases, Hymen must have a place at the nuptials. Cf. Mera J. Flaumenhaft, "Is All the World a Stage? Marriage and a Metaphor in As You Like It," in *Perspectives on Politics in Shakespeare*, ed. John Albert Murley and Sean D. Sutton (Lanham, MD: Lexington Books, 2006).

74. Shakespeare, *Tempest*, 4.1.56–58.
75. Shakespeare, *Tempest*, 4.1.119–130.
76. Shakespeare, *Tempest*, 4.1.114.
77. Shakespeare, *Tempest*, 4.1.181.
78. Shakespeare, *Tempest*, 4.1.137–139.
79. Shakespeare, *Tempest*, 5.1.209–210.
80. Shakespeare, *Tempest*, 5.1.224–225.
81. Shakespeare, *Tempest*, 1.2.10–14.
82. Shakespeare, *Tempest*, 1.2.424–436.
83. Shakespeare, *Tempest*, 5.1.203–204.
84. The challenge of holding on to both Naples and Milan simultaneously was central to the turmoil of Italian politics throughout the Renaissance (Cf. More, *Utopia*, 28–29). With Naples and Milan united, and the support arising from the political marriage with Tunis, Shakespeare responds to Machiavelli's call for the unification of Italy. Such unification constitutes a new founding, and thereby requires a reworking of the founding myth of Rome. Shakespeare first points to the reworking of the Aeneas myth during Gonzalo, Adrian, Antonio, and Sebastian's discussion of "Widow Dido" in *The Tempest* at 2.1.75–110. Ferdinand, resembling Aeneas, finds himself on the shores of a foreign land after a fierce storm has thrown him off course while sailing to Italy. Instead of abandoning the love he meets in this foreign land, however, Ferdinand will return to Italy with a wife and an alliance with Tunis (the descendant of Carthage). Miranda will serve as co-regent of a unified Italy; she is Dido redeemed. Compare also *The Aeneid* lines 4.131–177 and the marriage ceremony of Ferdinand and Miranda (4.1.95–102). In the former, Venus (the mother of Aeneas) and Juno act together to secure the love of Dido and Aeneas, whereas, by Prospero's art, Venus is absent in the confirmation of the latter couple's love. This fact, as well as Prospero's education of the young couple, seems to account for the differences of fate between the two young couples (Virgil, *The Aeneid*, trans. Robert Fitzgerald [New York, NY: Vintage Classics, 1983], 99–100).
85. Shakespeare, *Tempest*, 5.1.366–367.
86. Moreover, the mastery of nature tends to infantilize individuals. Since it requires less and less of us, protecting and providing for us, we remain perpetually, if not children, then adolescents. We never *need* to become responsible adults and so we never do. See Harvey Mansfield, "Rational Control: Or, Life Without Virtue," *The New Criterion* (September 2006).
87. Percy B. Shelley, *Shelley's Poetry and Prose*, ed. Neil Fraistat and Donald H. Reiman (New York, NY: W.W. Norton and Company, 2002), 535.
88. Shakespeare, *Tempest*, 4.1.164–175.
89. Shakespeare, *Tempest*, 5.1.366.
90. Shakespeare, *Tempest*, 5.1.42–66.
91. Shakespeare, *Tempest*, Epilogue.1–20.
92. Shakespeare, *A Midsummer Night's Dream*, Epilogue.1–6.
93. Shakespeare, *A Midsummer Night's Dream*, 5.1.13–18.
94. Shakespeare, *Tempest*, *Epilogue*.14–15.
95. For a book-length commentary on *Midsummer* as a reflection on Athens's founding see Jan Blits, *The Soul of Athens: Shakespeare's Midsummer Night's Dream* (Lanham, MD: Lexington Books, 2003).
96. Shakespeare, *Tempest*, 5.1.42–66.
97. Shakespeare, *Tempest*, 3.2.149.

BIBLIOGRAPHY

Aristotle. *Nicomachean Ethics*. Translated by Robert C. Bartlett and Susan Collins. Chicago, IL: The University of Chicago Press, 2012.
———. *Politics*. Translated by Carnes Lord. Chicago, IL: The University of Chicago Press, 2013.
Bacon, Francis. *Selected Philosophical Works*. Indianapolis, IN: Hackett Publishing Company, 1999.

Blits, Jan. *The Soul of Athens: Shakespeare's Midsummer Night's Dream.* Lanham, MD: Lexington Books, 2003.

Bloom, Allan. *Love and Friendship.* New York: Simon & Schuster, 1993.

Burger, Ronna. "Definitional Law in the Bible." In *The Eccentric Core: The Thought of Seth Benardete,* edited by Ronna Burger and Patrick Goodin, 3–17. South Bend, IN: St. Augustine's Press, 2018.

Burns, Timothy. *Shakespeare's Political Wisdom.* New York: Palgrave Macmillan, 2013.

Cantor, Paul A. "Shakespeare's *The Tempest*: Tragicomedy and the Philosophic Hero." In *Shakespeare's Last Plays: Essays in Literature and Politics,* edited by Stephen W. Smith and Travis Curtright, 1–15. Lanham, MD: Lexington Books, 2002.

Cantor, Paul A. "Prospero's Republic: The Politics of Shakespeare's *The Tempest*" in *Shakespeare as a Political Thinker,* ed. John E. Alvis and Thomas G. West, 241–259. Wilmington, Delaware: ISI, 2000.

Davis, Michael. *The Politics of Philosophy: A Commentary on Aristotle's Politics.* Lanham, MD: Rowman & Littlefield Publishers, 1996.

Dougherty, Janet. "The Poetic Art of the Possible: Shakespeare's *Tempest*," St. John's College Digital Archives, http://digitalarchives.sjc.edu/items/show/3459.

Flaumenhaft, Mera J. "Is All the World a Stage? Marriage and a Metaphor in *As You Like It.*" In *Perspectives on Politics in Shakespeare,* edited by John Albert Murley and Sean D. Sutton, 71–104. Lanham, MD: Lexington Books, 2006.

Homer. *The Odyssey.* Translated by Richmond Lattimore. New York, NY: Harper & Row Publishers, 1967.

Kennington, Richard. "Bacon's Ontology." In *On Modern Origins,* edited by Pamela Kraus and Frank Hunt, 33–48. Lanham, MD: Lexington Books, 2004.

Lawler, Peter Augustine. "Shakespeare's Realism in *The Tempest.*" In *Shakespeare's Last Plays: Essays in Literature and Politics,* edited by Stephen W. Smith and Travis Curtright, 91–110. Lanham, MD: Lexington Books, 2002.

Lowenthal, David. *Shakespeare's Thought: Unobserved Details and Unsuspected Depths in Thirteen Plays.* Lanham, MD: Lexington Books, 2017.

Mansfield, Harvey. "Rational Control: Or, Life Without Virtue," *The New Criterion* (September 2006).

More, Thomas. *Utopia,* edited by George M. Logan and Robert M. Adams. Cambridge, Cambridge University Press, 2002.

Nietzsche, Friedrich. *Beyond Good and Evil,* translated by Walter Kaufmann (New York, NY: Vintage Books, 1989), §260.

Schlueter, Nathan. "Prospero's Second Sailing: Machiavelli, Shakespeare, and the Politics of *The Tempest.*" In *Shakespeare's Last Plays: Essays in Literature and Politics,* edited by Stephen W. Smith and Travis Curtright, 179–195. Lanham, MD: Lexington Books, 2002.

Scruton, Roger. "Philosophy of Love." In *Death-Devoted Heart: Sex and the Sacred in Wagner's Tristan and Isolde,* 119–160. Oxford: Oxford University Press, 2003.

Shakespeare, William. *The Tempest,* edited by Barbara A. Mowat and Paul Werstine. New York: Simon & Schuster Paperbacks, 2009.

———. *A Midsummer Night's Dream,* edited by Barbara A. Mowat and Paul Werstine. New York: Simon & Schuster Paperbacks, 2004.

Shelley, Percy B. *Shelley's Poetry and Prose,* edited by Neil Fraistat and Donald H. Reiman. New York, NY: W.W. Norton and Company, 2002.

Stevens, Richard G. "On the Practicality of More's *Utopia.*" *Social Research* 33, no. 1 (Spring 1966): 30–46.

Tanner, Tony. *Prefaces to Shakespeare.* Cambridge, Massachusetts: Belknap Press, 2010.

Virgil. *The Aeneid.* Translated by Robert Fitzgerald. New York, NY: Vintage Classics, 1983.

Chapter Three

Frankenstein and the Ugliness of Enlightenment

Jeff J. S. Black

All writings escape the control of their authors, and Mary Shelley's *Franken-stein* is no exception. In transformations from page to stage to screen, our crude imaginations have reshaped her articulate, agile, tormented monster into something inarticulate, lumbering, and single-minded; likewise, our crude understandings have reduced her "hideous progeny,"[1] *Frankenstein* itself, to a cautionary tale about the dangers of modern technology[2]—to what one scholar calls "the governing myth of modern biology."[3] But in its original form, *Frankenstein*, like its monster, was also articulate, agile, and tor-mented. The novel's original concerns cut deeper than the dangers of tech-nology. Its concerns cut all the way to the dangers of enlightenment itself.

Anatomizing the original, 1818 text of Shelley's novel, we find that it consists of five nested stories of enlightenment, understood as Jean-Jacques Rousseau describes it in his *Discourse on the Sciences and the Arts*, or *First Discourse*. "It is a grand and beautiful sight," Rousseau writes near the beginning of that work,

> to see man emerge from obscurity somehow by his own efforts; dissipate, by the light of his reason, the darkness in which nature had enveloped him; rise above himself; soar intellectually into celestial regions; traverse with Giant steps, like the Sun, the vastness of the Universe; and—what is even grander and more difficult—come back to himself to study man and know his nature, his duties, and his end.[4]

In *Frankenstein* we find five stories in which one or two beings emerge from obscurity somehow by their own efforts, achieve a degree of illumination, but *fail* to return to themselves, to learn their nature, their duties, and their

end. Enlightenment, in each of these stories, turns out to be fragile, dangerous, and ugly.

This five-part structure is not evident in the familiar skeleton of the novel,
which can be laid out as follows. Victor Frankenstein, a young student,
makes and animates a monster. Horrified by his work, he abandons the
monster, who disappears. A few months later, Frankenstein learns of the
murder of his youngest brother. A family servant is executed for the crime,
but Frankenstein fears the true murderer is his monster. This suspicion is
confirmed during a solitary hike in the Alps, where the monster confronts
Frankenstein, tells his story, and demands Frankenstein build him a companion.

Despite the monster's crimes, to Frankenstein his demand at first seems
just. Frankenstein travels for research, and to gather materials. After laboring
for several months, he nearly completes an artificial woman; but at the last
moment, fearing she will birth a species of monsters to terrorize humanity, he
destroys his work. The monster witnesses Frankenstein's betrayal, and vows
revenge. Soon, he has also murdered Frankenstein's friend, Henry Clerval.
Frankenstein himself is tried for this crime, but acquitted; he then prepares to
marry his cousin Elizabeth Lavenza, telling her he has a dreadful secret to
share, once they are wed. He sends Elizabeth to bed on their wedding night,
expecting again to confront the monster. But he misunderstands the monster's vow of revenge. Two terrible screams ring out, and Frankenstein finds
Elizabeth dead by the monster's hand. It is Frankenstein's turn to vow revenge, and he pursues his monster north.

In the frozen north Frankenstein meets Robert Walton, an arctic explorer,
to whom he tells his story. Walton writes it down, and reports certain episodes in letters to his sister, Mary Seville[5]—who happens to share both the
first name and the initials of *Frankenstein*'s author, Mary Shelley. When
Walton meets him, Frankenstein has almost caught up with his monster. But
he is also near death, and too weak to continue his pursuit. Soon after concluding his story, Frankenstein dies aboard Walton's ship. That night, Walton finds the monster crouched over Frankenstein's corpse. Walton speaks
with the monster; then the monster leaps from Walton's ship and disappears
on the ice. The novel ends with Walton sailing home, bringing the story of
Frankenstein and his monster back to his sister, and to humanity.

Frankenstein's familiar skeleton is nevertheless arranged in a peculiar,
nested way. The novel begins and ends with Walton's letters to his sister
Mary. These letters enclose Walton's transcript, corrected by Frankenstein,
of Frankenstein's story, told to Walton on the arctic ice. This story contains
Frankenstein's report of the monster's own story, told to Frankenstein on the
alpine ice. The monster's story contains in turn a story about some cottagers
living in Germany. And all four of these stories, each one nested in the one
before it, like generations of children in their mothers, are contained in the

story that is *Frankenstein* itself. Joining all five of these stories together are letters written by one of the cottagers to another, letters copied by the monster, given by him to Frankenstein, left by Frankenstein to Walton,[6] and published by Mary Shelley. Each of these five stories, moreover, is a story of enlightenment. The innermost story, about the German cottagers, lays down the paradigm of enlightenment, which promises that if human beings become wise, they will also become happy and good. The monster's story shows the fragility of this happiness and goodness, while Frankenstein's story explains the reasons for this dangerous fragility. Walton's story asks whether, given the danger, enlightenment is worth the pursuit; and Shelley's story—*Frankenstein* itself—adumbrates an answer.[7]

By anatomizing *Frankenstein*'s five component stories of enlightenment, laying each one out in turn in their functional order, we will see that the novel's concerns with the dangerous fragility of enlightenment, with its vulnerability to chance, and with the resultant paradoxical need for the one seeking enlightenment both to be taught and to learn "somehow by his own efforts,"[8] parallel the concerns of Rousseau's major writings: the *First Discourse*, the *Discourse on the Origins of Inequality* or *Second Discourse*, and *Emile, or On Education*. There are signs throughout the novel of Shelley's deep engagement with Rousseau, though there is also reason to wonder how well she understood Rousseau's thought, and whether her own enlightenment was also a failure. To reach this point, we will begin with the heart—not to say the brain—of *Frankenstein*: the story at the novel's center. We will anatomize Shelley's "hideous progeny" from the inside out.

THE HISTORY OF THE MONSTER'S BELOVED COTTAGERS

The brief story at the heart of *Frankenstein* sets down the paradigm of enlightenment, but in a disguised way. On its face, it is a tale of intrigue and betrayal that ends with the happy victory of love, and that seems to have nothing to do with the monster at all. A wealthy Turkish merchant, long a resident of Paris, is condemned to death. The public judges him the innocent victim of the government's hatred of his religion and envy of his wealth. Felix De Lacey, a patriotic, virtuous, and intelligent nobleman of moderate means, is among those outraged by this injustice.[9] He vows to liberate the Turk from prison.

Felix seeks to right a wrong, but a stronger motive soon supervenes. When he visits the Turk in secret to communicate his plan, Felix falls for Safie, the Turk's beautiful daughter. The Turk offers Felix money in return for his freedom, which Felix refuses. So, seeing Felix's interest in his daughter, the Turk instead proposes that they marry, promising this will happen once the Turk is safely home. Felix cannot bring himself to agree to this mercenary exchange, but he sees in Safie a just reward for the risks he runs, and the promise of happiness.[10] Safie seems to reciprocate his affection; she writes him ardent letters, translated by an intermediary, thanking him for his help, and deploring her own fate. These are the letters the monster copies and passes to Frankenstein to prove the truth of his story.[11]

Safie's letters speak of her longing for freedom. She tells Felix how her mother was a Christian Arab who was enslaved for her religion, and wedded to the Turk for her beauty. But her mother was born free, and refused to succumb to her slavery. She rebelled by secretly instructing Safie in Christianity, and by encouraging her spiritual independence and intellectual development to a degree forbidden to Muslim women. These qualities lead Safie to seize the chance to marry Felix, a Christian, to escape the fate of harem life.[12]

Felix acts on the eve of the Turk's execution. After sharing his plan with his father and his sister Agatha, and arranging for them to flee Paris, Felix breaks the Turk from prison, and conveys the Turk and Safie from Paris to the port of Livorno in Italy, there to await passage to Turkish lands. Safie will stay with her father until he sails; then she will return to France with Felix. But the Turk, loathing the thought that Safie will marry a Christian, plans to betray Felix and flee Europe with Safie, as soon as he can.

Then news arrives that Felix's father and sister have been jailed in Paris for their role in the Turk's escape. Rather than fleeing Paris, they had remained while Felix acted, and were discovered in hiding.[13] Moved by the image of his family in chains, Felix surrenders to the authorities, who deprive him and his family of their rank and fortune, and exile them from France. Felix's ruin gives the Turk the chance to return home with Safie, over her protests at his faithlessness and ingratitude. But then the Turk somehow learns, or claims to learn, that the French have found him in Italy. He immediately flees alone to Constantinople, leaving Safie in Italy in charge of his property. Safie takes this chance, having read in her father's papers of Felix's exile, to abandon her father, steal his property, and rejoin Felix at his cottage in Germany.

On its face, this story at the heart of *Frankenstein* only hints that it is a story of enlightenment. Somehow, by their own efforts, Felix and Safie escape the obscurity of their circumstances to live free together in their German cottage. Felix's upbringing and education lead him to rebel against the intolerance and injustice of the Parisian authorities, and to seek his happiness with the beautiful Safie. Safie's upbringing and education lead her to rebel against the intolerance and injustice of Turkish harem life, and to seek a marriage with Felix in which she can cultivate her virtue and intellect. But these hints become more emphatic if we consider the meaning of our protagonists' names. "Safie" is a variant of "Sophie": which comes from *sophia*, the Greek word meaning "wisdom," and is the name Rousseau gives to Emile's beloved in *Emile*.[14] "Felix," which in Latin usually means "happy" or "fortunate," comes from the Greek word *phuō*, the root of *phusis*, which means "nature." Felix is thus Shelley's version of Emile, Rousseau's child raised according to nature.[15] Even "Agatha," the name Shelley assigns to Felix's sister, means "good" in Greek. So the story at the heart of *Frankenstein* is a brief version of Rousseau's *Emile*, in which wisdom is married to happiness, or to happy chance—or even to nature—at home with the good. It is *the* story of enlightenment, of the kept promise that if human beings become wise, they will also become happy and good. It was doubt about the complete truth of this story that birthed Rousseau's philosophic system, prompting him to publish the *First Discourse*, the *Second Discourse*, and *Emile*.

The history of the monster's beloved cottagers also follows Rousseau's *Second Discourse* in particular by indicating the importance of accidents. We never learn why Felix's family fails to flee Paris, nor how the French authorities learn of the Turk in Italy. But the former chance nearly destroys Felix and Safie's happiness, and only the latter chance makes their happiness possible. Enlightenment depends not just on our own efforts, but on the cooperation of circumstances. Worse, the enlightenment of the monster's beloved cottagers turns out to be dangerously fragile—as the monster himself is about to relate.

THE MONSTER'S STORY

Guided by the story of enlightenment at the heart of *Frankenstein*, we expect to hear more from the monster than a story about the dangers of forbidden technology run amok. And we are not disappointed. When the monster confronts Frankenstein on the alpine sea of ice, he tells Frankenstein a second story of enlightenment: one that depicts both the monster's own enlightenment, and that of his beloved cottagers, as failures.

Waking to life in Frankenstein's apartment, the monster is at first moved only by his sensations. He sees light, and closes his eyes; but then he sees darkness, feels pain, and opens his eyes again. He feels cold, and takes some nearby clothing to warm himself; but once in the sun he feels hot, and shelters in a nearby forest. Soon he feels hunger, leading him to eat berries; thirst, leading him to drink at a stream; and fatigue, leading him to sleep. At night, the cold and dark return, and the monster weeps in pain—until he sees moonlight, feels pleasure, and wonders. All these motions happen mechanically, since his mind is empty of distinct ideas.[16] But their tendency is clear: away from painful darkness, and toward pleasant, wonderful, sometimes overpowering, light. The monster's first days recall the development of the savage of Rousseau's *Second Discourse*, whose needs generate passions, which generate reason.[17] From the first the monster is headed for enlighten-ment.

As the monster's sensations become distinct, they form distinct ideas. Wandering in the woods, he finds an abandoned campfire. Playing the satyr's role in the allegory of the frontispiece of Rousseau's *First Discourse*, the monster finds the fire's warmth pleasant, but it burns him when he touches it.[18] By experiment he learns to feed the fire, to fan it to life, and to use it to cook nuts and roots.[19] But food is scarce, so he abandons his fire to forage. When he happens on a shepherd's hut, he scares its occupant away, and finds more food and another fire inside. Though this hut is a kind of paradise for him, soon hunger forces him to leave it too. He happens on a village, where the sight of food draws him into a cottage. The terrified villagers assemble to repel him with a hail of missiles.[20]

The scarcity of food forces the monster into his first encounters with society. But these encounters aggravate his susceptibility to circumstances, making him vulnerable to accidents. He mentions three as decisive for his development. First, while fleeing the villagers he hides in a hovel, which he improves so that it shelters and conceals him, like his paradisiacal shepherd's hut. But this hovel happens to adjoin a cottage. It has food and water for the taking, and a crack in a covered window allows the monster to observe its three occupants unseen. The blind old man, the young man, and the young girl seem kind, sad, and poor. Perhaps by contrasting their behavior with that of the terrified shepherd and villagers, the monster has his first experience of beauty—a peculiar and overpowering sensation that mixes pleasure and pain, unlike those due to cold or warmth, hunger or food.[21] The monster becomes unwilling to continue stealing the cottagers' supplies; instead, he forages and gathers wood for their fire while they sleep. He becomes an invisible family member, and when they notice his benefactions, they call him "*wonderful*," and "*a good spirit*."[22] The monster also hears his cottagers communicating pleasure and pain through speech. He begins to acquire this divine power by learning their names: the old man is "father," the young girl "Agatha" or "sister," and the young man "son," "brother," or "Felix."[23] But he also contrasts the cottagers' beauty with his own ugliness, which he first sees in a pool of water.[24] These comparisons lead the monster, like the savage of Rousseau's *Second Discourse*, to begin to reflect; but the first glance he directs on himself does not produce his first stirring of pride.[25] Instead he finds his own looks terrifying, and begins to call himself "monster."[26]

This is the less moving part of his story, the monster tells Frankenstein: the part explaining how he became what he once was.[27] Despite his concern with how others see him, a concern Rousseau would call a sign of *amour-propre*,[28] the monster insists that at this point he is good. He does not need to harm others to survive or flourish: he is a vegetarian who will not steal from those worse off.[29] He admires beauty and benevolence, and wants to imitate them and be admired in return. But the more moving part of the monster's story, explaining how he becomes what he now is,[30] begins with a second accident, which teaches him to speak, write, and read.

One day a beautiful woman arrives at the cottage. The monster overhears her name: Safie. Safie cannot speak, write, or read the cottagers' language, so Felix teaches it to her, while the monster listens in. The monster boasts to Frankenstein that he improved more rapidly than she did—he is a quicker study than wisdom herself.[31] For his lessons, Felix reads from and explains a book of history. The monster wonders at the many stories of murder, and at humankind's consequent need for government and law. Stories of vice and bloodshed disgust him, and he sorrows at the fate of the Native Americans.[32] He learns that human society is based on property and inequality.[33] And he learns about male and female, the birth and growth of children, and family. It takes Safie's arrival to teach the monster about sex, since Felix and Agatha are brother and sister, and the old man is their father. The monster feels no sexual desire for Agatha or Safie, suggesting that he already sees them as members of a different species,[34] and that, like Rousseau's primitive man, he feels no natural need for sex.[35]

Reflecting on Felix's lessons, the monster recognizes that he lacks both rank and riches, the only possessions human beings esteem. He admires beauty, but he is horribly ugly. He may not even be human: he has yet to see anyone like him, he has no family, and he has no memory of his birth or growth. These reflections are agonizing. "I tried to dispel them," he tells Frankenstein, "but sorrow only increased with knowledge," which "clings to the mind . . . like lichen on a rock."[36] The monster longs to escape all thought and feeling, to return to his life in the woods. But he knows that death alone—a fate he learned of through Felix's lessons, a fate he fears and does not understand[37]—can release him. Safie's arrival reunites her with Felix, joining wisdom with happiness, but it makes the monster miserable.

The last part of this second accident gives the monster's misery more meaning. He finds several books while gathering wood in the forest: Milton's *Paradise Lost*, the first volume of Plutarch's *Lives*, and Goethe's *Sorrows of Werther*, all written in a language he can read. He studies these books, taking each for a "true history."[38] Unlike Rousseau's Emile, whose first reading, *Robinson Crusoe*, is carefully chosen and edited to depict only his true needs,[39] these chance readings give the monster imaginary ones. Goethe's Werther puzzles him: why should a being with a deep and honest character, whose opinions the monster shares, kill himself for love? This book renews the monster's despair.[40] He admires and loves Plutarch's founders of Greece and Rome, but prefers the peaceful lawgivers, Numa, Solon, and Lycurgus, to the violent heroes Romulus and Theseus. He understands this to be a chance preference, though: had he first observed a young soldier, the monster tells Frankenstein, rather than his cottagers, he would have judged differently.[41] But *Paradise Lost* moves the monster the most, by showing him situations resembling his own. Like Satan, who envies the happiness of God, the monster finds he envies the happiness of his cottagers.[42] Like Adam, he sees no link between himself and any other being; but unlike Adam, his creator has not fashioned him an Eve.[43] To this chance reading, the monster owes his first feeling of envy, and his first desire for a companion. Despite suffering from his taste from the tree of knowledge, the monster overlooks his resemblance to Eve.

In a pocket of the clothing taken from Frankenstein's apartment, the monster finds pages from a journal, which he deciphers.[44] They describe his origin in horrible detail.[45] The monster immediately likens his maker to Milton's God, and himself to Satan. But Milton's God made man beautiful, after his own image, out of pity; whereas the monster's form is an ugly imitation of Frankenstein's, "more horrid from its very resemblance."[46] And Satan had the admiration and encouragement of the other devils in his rebellion against God; whereas the monster has no fellows, and is admired and encouraged by no one.[47] Frankenstein's journal pages, interpreted through *Paradise Lost*, give the monster someone to blame for his ugliness, and hence for his solitude.

The monster resolves to end his solitude by revealing himself to his cottagers.[48] He knows his ugliness causes horror, but his voice, though harsh, does not,[49] so he plans to address himself to the blind old man. He hopes the old man will defend him before the other cottagers, convey his admiration for them, and elicit their compassion. Once the old man is alone, the monster knocks, enters, and speaks with him. He pleads that he is a victim of injustice, and throws himself on the old man's mercy, just as the other cottagers return. But when these self-liberated opponents of injustice and intolerance see the monster—without hearing his pleas—their enlightenment fails them. Agatha faints, Safie flees, and Felix attacks, driving the monster back to his hovel.[50] There, in rage and despair, he declares war on humanity, and on his maker in particular.[51] He opens hostilities by burning the cottagers' home. Then he goes in search of Frankenstein, to demand pity and justice.[52]

The third accident befalls the monster when he reaches Frankenstein's home town. Pondering how to address his maker, he happens on a small child. This child, he thinks, will not feel horror at his ugliness, because this horror is learned and conventional, rather than natural.[53] Perhaps the monster doubts the naturalness of the contrast with his cottagers that first made him judge himself ugly.[54] If he could raise this child to be his friend, the monster thinks, he would not be alone.[55] He seizes the child, who screams, calls him "monster," and threatens punishment by his father—"Monsieur Frankenstein."[56] Hearing his maker's name, the monster commits his first murder. He grasps the child's throat, and William Frankenstein is dead. On his body the monster finds a locket, which he slips unseen into the pocket of a nearby girl.

When this locket is discovered on her person, Justine Moritz is executed for the murder of Frankenstein's brother.

Thus ends the more moving part of the monster's story, tracing his fall from original goodness to "malignity."[57] Yet the monster still hopes for Frankenstein's pity and justice, despite the murder he has just committed. His hatred for Frankenstein is not total; nor does it fully explain William's murder. The monster kills the child also for the child's revulsion at the monster's ugliness. If William was truly unprejudiced, then his revulsion was not learned, but natural—and neither ignorance nor enlightenment is sufficient protection from the monster's appearance. As for poor Justine Moritz, the monster claims it was his enlightenment—through Felix's history lessons—that taught him to frame her.[58] But he uses a locket containing a portrait of Frankenstein's beautiful mother, which he briefly contemplates. This too reminds him that he is ugly. The smiles of beautiful women will never be for him.

After telling his story, the monster demands that Frankenstein build him a female companion.[59] He insists this is Frankenstein's duty, because a creator must make his creation capable of happiness. If Frankenstein does not comply, the monster will murder the rest of his family, and many others. Frankenstein's choice, the monster alleges, will determine whether the monster remains wicked, or recovers his original goodness—whether he becomes Frankenstein's Satan, or his Adam.[60]

Frankenstein agrees about his duty,[61] but fears that if he makes the monster a companion, "their joint wickedness might desolate the world."[62] He doubts, in other words, the monster's claim that he is wicked because he is alone. To reassure him, the monster promises that he and his mate will quit human society. "It is true, we shall be monsters, cut off from all the world," he concedes, but he predicts their joint solitude will bind them more closely together.[63] The monster's promise allays Frankenstein's fears, and makes him compassionate: on reflection he attributes the monster's wickedness wholly to his solitude.[64] He consents to make a female companion. And the monster keeps his word. Not until Frankenstein repents of his promise, and destroys his second creation, does the monster destroy what remains of Frankenstein's family.

Once again, the monster is misled, and misleads Frankenstein, by his chance reading of *Paradise Lost*. The monster kills out of wickedness, and is wicked out of solitude. But he is solitary because he is ugly. *Can* Frankenstein make him a companion? If every human being, enlightened or ignorant, finds the monster ugly,[65] and he finds himself ugly,[66] it is reasonable to infer—as Frankenstein later realizes—that the monster's companion will also find him ugly.[67] Worse, it is reasonable to expect—as we will soon see—that the companion will also *be* ugly. *Paradise Lost* offers the monster only the alternative of Adam or Satan: it does not offer an image of independent solitude, like Rousseau's edited *Robinson Crusoe*. The monster is alone, not by Frankenstein's improvidence, but because he is ugly. So why is he ugly?

VICTOR FRANKENSTEIN'S STORY

The third component story of *Frankenstein* explains the monster's ugliness. Told by Frankenstein to Walton aboard ship on the arctic sea of ice, it explains how enlightenment made Frankenstein a monster. Victor's life begins as happily as possible. His parents are kind, his father indulgent and rarely dictatorial.[68] But his family is strangely constituted. Victor's parents differ widely in age, as do his siblings.[69] His parents' marriage happens because of the death of a friend, while the death of an aunt brings Victor's cousin, Elizabeth Lavenza, into their household, first as Victor's sisterly playmate, but later as his intended bride.[70] Victor's habit of calling his family his "friends"[71] could be due to the ranges of age and filiation, and the hints of incest and death, that his accidental family embraces.

Alphonse Frankenstein, Victor's father, is old, and has retired from a political life to educate his children.[72] He is the cause of Victor's first accident. One day, the teenage Victor finds a book by Cornelius Agrippa, a sixteenth-century alchemist. He is dazzled by the theory of chemistry and the other wonders in its pages. But when he shares his wonder with his father, Alphonse replies, "Ah! Cornelius Agrippa! My dear Victor, do not waste your time upon this; it is sad trash."[73] Looking back, Victor thinks he would have abandoned the book, had his father explained that Agrippa's system had been replaced by a more rational and powerful modern chemistry. Instead, he judges his father's remark ignorant, and acquires and reads Agrippa's complete works, followed by those of Paracelsus and Albertus Magnus.[74]

According to Victor, this chance remark fixed his thoughts on natural philosophy, and first propelled him toward his ruin.[75] The alchemists' projects—raising ghosts and devils, and finding the elixir of life—became Victor's. As suggested by his reaction to his father's remark, Victor's motive in these studies was pride, or emulation. Alchemy appealed to him not only because it reveals the occult properties of materials, but also because it teaches esoteric matters known to few. Like the wise man in Rousseau's *First Discourse*, Victor dreams that his private knowledge will bring public acclaim: "what glory would attend the discovery, if I could banish disease from the human frame, and render man invulnerable to any but a violent death!"[76]

Victor's subsequent studies distance him somewhat from his alchemists. To their discredit, they are ignorant of distillation, steam power, the air-pump, and electricity.[77] His father sends him to lectures on natural philosophy, but a second accident makes Victor miss all but the last few, which he therefore cannot understand. He becomes disgusted with natural philosophy, preferring mathematics, German, and Greek.[78] But his haphazard home schooling never introduces a modern chemical system to replace alchemy. Then, just as Victor is about to leave for college, another accident happens: his mother Caroline contracts scarlet fever from Elizabeth, and dies.[79] Losing his mother to death, "that most irreparable evil,"[80] must have reanimated in Victor his alchemical dreams of immortality.

A final decisive accident happens on Victor's arrival at the University of Ingolstadt. Living alone, far from his family, unable to make new friends, pursuing his desire for knowledge in solitude, he happens to meet two professors: Krempe and Waldman. When Victor confesses to Krempe his interest in alchemy, Krempe responds like Victor's father: he calls the subject antiquated, and insists Victor begin his studies anew.[81] But Krempe fails to interest Victor in modern natural philosophy, because he insists it means to annihilate the alchemists' visions of immortality and power[82]—the very visions that animate Victor. When Victor makes the same confession to Waldman, though, Waldman shows no contempt for Agrippa, and calls the alchemists the founders of modern philosophy. Charmed by this "man of the woods," Victor learns from him that modern science improves on the alchemists' miraculous visions with the "new and almost unlimited powers" promised by scientists like Harvey and Boyle.[83] Waldman overcomes Victor's prejudice against modern chemistry, where the cramped Krempe could not, and Victor becomes the student of both professors.[84] The day he met Krempe and Waldman decided his fate, Victor tells Walton, since it set him to study almost nothing but chemistry.[85] It did not hurt, he adds, that Waldman had a benevolent aspect and a sweet voice, whereas Krempe's ugliness kept Victor from taking his advice.[86] Victor's sensitivity to beauty, which takes ugliness for an argument, will have terrible consequences when he completes his monster.

Seeking to end disease, Victor studies the principle of life. He studies physiology, anatomy, and the causes of decay. An "almost supernatural enthusiasm" drives his work, which requires dissections and vivisections.[87] But he does not fear divine punishment for these labors; his father kept all supernatural horrors from his mind,[88] presumably including the fear of hell. Instead, he needs an *almost* supernatural enthusiasm because he has a natural aversion to the ugliness of dead things. At last, after analyzing the causes of death and birth, he is suddenly enlightened.[89] He discovers the cause of generation and life—a secret reserved for him alone—and gains the power to animate dead matter.[90]

Victor's newfound power is general. He can animate anything from a worm to a human being, but he chooses to animate a being like himself. Even if the results of his first attempt are not perfect, he reasons, like any other experiment they will inform future improvements. But he faces a practical constraint: making minute parts will take time. So he decides to make an eight-foot tall, proportionate humanoid.[91] Victor does not explain why he rejects a slow procedure. Perhaps he fears another will animate a dead being before he does, though there is no sign that he has competitors; perhaps his family history has impressed him with his own mortality. He visits dissecting theaters and charnel- and slaughterhouses to gather his materials. If he succeeds in animating an artificial being, he hopes to learn how to reanimate the dead—something he cannot yet do.[92]

We should not imagine Victor sewing together corpse limbs, then animating them with electricity—later depictions of the monster notwithstanding. No human corpse could furnish proper parts—like hands, feet, or heart—proportioned to an eight-foot-tall humanoid. Also, if Victor cannot reanimate a whole dead human, he likely also cannot reanimate a corpse's proper parts. Instead, he probably builds his monster out of homogeneous parts (bone, muscle, and skin) harvested from human and animal corpses—hence, the visit to the slaughterhouse—and shaped into proportionate proper parts—avoiding the need for minute work. When the monster later compares himself to Victor, he judges himself taller, more flexible, and more powerful than his maker.[93] When he compares himself to humankind in general, he judges himself *much* taller, more agile, more capable of eating coarse foods, more resistant to cold and heat—and perhaps even smarter.[94] So Victor fails to make a being like himself. Rather, he makes a being in many ways *better* than himself.

Although the monster seems not to feel sexual desire, Victor apparently intends his creation to reproduce. Anticipating success, he exults: "[a] new species would bless me as its creator and source; many happy and excellent natures would owe their being to me. No father could claim the gratitude of his child so completely as I should deserve their's."[95] Since Victor likely does not intend to make each member of his new species piecemeal, either he already envisions making his creation a fertile mate, or he expects the monster to reproduce with human females.

Accordingly, Victor does not neglect his creation's appearance. He tells Walton he made proportional limbs, and tried to select beautiful features.[96] But once his creation is animate, Victor's enthusiasm vanishes, and he sees the monster as horribly ugly. He details for Walton the monster's "dull yellow . . . watery [and] clouded" eyes, "his shriveled complexion, and straight black lips," his "yellow skin [that] scarcely covered the work of muscles and arteries beneath."[97] Victor certainly failed to harvest enough skin, but the deeper cause of the monster's ugliness is the contrast between his ugly parts and those Victor succeeded in making beautiful: his "lustrous black, and flowing" hair, his "teeth of a pearly whiteness."[98] Seeing the inanimate monster as a whole, Victor concedes to Walton, "he was ugly then."[99] But once the monster moves, "it became such a thing as even Dante could not have conceived."[100] Like the monster's beloved cottagers, Victor's enlightenment fails him at the sight of his animate creation. The natural philosopher who does not fear hell sees something worse than hell, and flees soon thereafter. Perhaps in his enthusiasm Victor hoped motion would beautify the monster's ugly matter, turning an "it" into a "he." But the opposite happens: once Victor sees him move, he starts calling his creation "monster."[101]

The monster's ugliness betrays the fragility of Victor's enlightenment, as it did with Felix, Safie, and Agatha; but it also reflects the vulnerability of enlightenment to chance. Victor's education grafted powerful modern techniques on to ancient alchemical goals, stitching them together into a project to cut form from matter, beauty from life, and ugliness from death. As a result, Victor believes he can fashion the ugly remnants of dissecting theatres, charnelhouses, and slaughterhouses into a beautiful living being. He expects to imitate by art a natural truth of metabolism: that the living shape themselves out of dead materials by eating them.[102] Just as the accidents of the monster's education offer him only the alternative of companionship or revenge, the accidents of Victor's education make for a monstrous enlightenment, which makes an ugly monster.

When Frankenstein returns to his laboratory, the monster is gone.[103] He does not see his monster again until after William's murder;[104] he speaks with him for the first time on the alpine sea of ice.[105] There, after Frankenstein tries and fails to kill the monster to avenge William's murder, the monster tells him his story, and secures Frankenstein's promise to make a female companion.[106] But this new project does not rekindle Frankenstein's enthusiasm. Instead, insane visions possess him, of animals torturing him continually, as if he were not conducting, but undergoing, his vivisections. It seems that now Frankenstein does fear hell. Collecting his new materials, he tells Walton, was horrible and disgusting; constructing the female monster was no better.[107] When his mind was fixed on success, he thinks, his enthusiasm for his first experiment blinded him to its horror. But now that he sees his work more clearly, he expects his second creation to be ugly.[108] Pride and emulation closed his eyes, Frankenstein now judges, to the true horror of his contest with death.

Qualms about his promise accompany Frankenstein's disgust. It is likely the female monster will reason; but what will her character be? The male monster became wicked, so a female might become "ten thousand times more malignant than her mate, and delight, for its own sake, in murder and wretchedness,"[109] something the male monster does not do. The male monster swore to quit human society, but a female might not keep a promise made by another before her creation.[110] Even if she is good, a female monster might not become the companion the male seeks. Since she will also be ugly, the male monster might find his own ugliness more abhorrent in female form; she might also be disgusted by him, and prefer the superior beauty of man. This fresh insult to the male monster might drive him back to human society. But if the monsters can stand one another, their intercourse will soon produce children—the beginnings of a new species to horrify and threaten humanity.[111] Without knowing exactly how his monsters would reproduce— whether piecemeal parents produce whole or piecemeal children—we can only guess that Frankenstein imagines a species horrifying by its ugliness, and threatening by its superiority.

So Frankenstein concludes his promise was wicked. Earlier he had dreamed of the blessings of mankind and of a new species[112]; now, he tells Walton, "I shuddered to think that future ages might curse me as their pest, whose selfishness had not hesitated to buy its own peace at the price perhaps of the existence of the whole human race."[113] Overcome by fear and disgust, Frankenstein looks up from his workbench to see the monster watching him. The monster grins, as he did on the night of his animation; as on that night, the ugliness of the expression shatters Frankenstein's enlightenment.[114] He sees betrayal in the monster's face, and destroys his female creation.

With the destruction of his Eve, and the path of Adam closed, the monster follows the path of Satan. "I shall be with you on your wedding-night," he promises, and disappears. Now Frankenstein thinks not of Dante, but of Milton: he is like the fallen Adam, kept from paradise, because the monster will kill him on the eve of his marriage to Elizabeth.[115] But the monster instead first kills Frankenstein's friend Henry Clerval, and then, on the night in question, Elizabeth herself. Alphonse Frankenstein dies from sorrow soon afterward.[116] This puts Frankenstein too on the Satanic path[117]: revenge, he tells Walton, became his sole passion.[118] Urged on by his monster, Franken-stein pursues him north to the arctic sea of ice, where Walton meets the monster and his shadow.

ROBERT WALTON'S STORY

What are we to make of Frankenstein's story of enlightenment? The mon-ster's ugliness both discovers a flaw in enlightenment—its vulnerability to chance—and is the result of this flaw. Does this mean we should avoid enlightenment, due to its dangers, or pursue it with more care, because it is not impossible to succeed? Robert Walton's story of enlightenment is a judg-ment on Frankenstein's. It begins with the accidental death of the young Walton's father, and Walton's desultory education by an uncle, who leaves him free to read, unsupervised, the tales of discovery that are the only books in his uncle's library. Above all, the young Walton loves tales of voyages to the Pacific over the North Pole. He reads them day and night. Poetry distracts him briefly from his dreams of discovery. But then another accident—per-haps the death of a cousin—leaves Walton with an inheritance sufficient to fund a career as an explorer.[119] Death shapes Walton's family, as it did Frankenstein's.

We read these details in Walton's letters to his sister. There he calls his self-education an evil, judging himself at twenty-eight "in reality more illiterate than many schoolboys of fifteen."[120] His thoughts and dreams are more magnificent and extensive than a fifteen-year-old's, but he finds them lacking in proportion. Walton's circumstances, like Frankenstein's, have made him an extravagant projector. But while Frankenstein had his friend Clerval to regulate his mind—though he fails to confide in him, and loses him to the monster—Walton has no friend, a lack he feels acutely.[121]

Walton imagines the North Pole as a beautiful region of perpetual sunlight—a land of both literal and figurative enlightenment.[122] There he expects to benefit humanity by making new discoveries that only a polar expedition can promise: discoveries in physics, by finding the cause of magnetism, and in geography, by finding a passage to the Pacific.[123] Walton adds a familiar personal ambition to these philanthropic ones: to be the first human to reach the pole.[124] Like Frankenstein and like Rousseau's wise man, Walton is also moved by pride and emulation.

Walton learns seamanship by day, and mathematics, medicine, and the physical sciences with naval applications by night. He inures his body to hardship. Then he travels to Archangel, in northern Russia, where he hires a ship, assembles a crew, and sails north into the ice.[125] He means to stake his life on discovery. Should he die in the north, he reassures his sister, he will not destroy her happiness, since she still has a husband and children.[126] And his crew will keep him from rashness in the face of danger, since he is cool, persistent, prudent, and considerate whenever charged with the safety of others.[127] Walton's prediction proves correct: his men do keep him from rashness. But they do so despite, not because of, Walton's efforts—and many of them die.[128]

When Walton happens on the monster and Frankenstein, and he brings the latter aboard, Walton sees in Frankenstein the friend he seeks. Were Frankenstein not crushed by his misfortunes, Walton tells his sister, he would be happy to have him as a brother.[129] Frankenstein praises Walton's desire for a friend, but rebuffs his overtures, saying his miseries prevent him from beginning his life anew.[130] Walton's overtures seem imprudent, since Frankenstein himself needed a friend to keep his projects in proportion, and failed to make good use of the one he had. And when Frankenstein nonetheless begins calling Walton "my friend" soon afterward, his first help is to encourage Walton's *crew* to persist at the risk of moral danger.[131] But the main help Frankenstein offers Walton is his story. "You seek for knowledge and wisdom, as I once did," he tells Walton, "and I ardently hope that the gratification of your wishes may not be a serpent to sting you, as mine has been."[132] Frankenstein promises to broaden Walton's understanding of natural possibility, but he rebuffs Walton's curiosity about the secret of the monster's animation, saying he wants to teach Walton about his own miseries, not to increase Walton's.[133] Walton transcribes Frankenstein's story, and Frankenstein corrects and augments the transcription, especially the passages containing his conversations with the monster. Frankenstein also leaves Walton the letters of Felix and Safie, received from the monster's own hand.[134] He seems to intend Walton to publish his story.

But what does Frankenstein mean his story to teach? After hearing him out, Walton does not lose his proud passion for exploration; rather, he tells his sister he would rather die than face the shame of failure.[135] And after concluding his story, Frankenstein tells Walton that he has reviewed his conduct, and found nothing blameworthy in it.[136] Perhaps he thinks he is a victim of chance. With his last breath he implores Walton, "[s]eek happiness in tranquility, and avoid ambition, even . . . the apparently innocent one of distinguishing yourself in science and discoveries"; but then he continues, "[y]et why do I say this? I have myself been blasted in these hopes, yet another may succeed."[137]

"Succeed" is a last word worthy of Victor Frankenstein's name. But it prompts us to wonder what he has learned from his own story. He seems as sensitive to glory at the brink of death as at the peak of life. And Walton, who hears Frankenstein's story, fails to reach the pole. His rebellious crew recovers from Frankenstein's encouragement and forces him to return home. Walton also fails to fulfill Frankenstein's last request: that he kill the monster, though not at the cost of his ship and crew. Walton does not even try to kill the monster, though he has the chance. When he finds the monster crouched over Frankenstein's corpse, on the night of Frankenstein's death, Walton sees the monster's horrible ugliness.[138] Yet unlike Safie, Felix, Agatha, and even Frankenstein himself, Walton neither faints, nor flees, nor attacks: instead, he listens. He seems persuaded by the monster's promise, to "seek the most northern extremity of the globe . . . collect my funeral pile, and consume to ashes this miserable frame, that its remains may afford no light to any curious and unhallowed wretch, who would create such another as I have been."[139] The monster will extinguish his light at the pole, in a blaze of light at the pole. Although the sight of Frankenstein's corpse angers Walton[140], he lets the monster go.[141] Perhaps the monster reaches the pole in Walton's place.

MARY SHELLEY'S STORY

Frankenstein has become for us a tale of technology run amok. Mary Shelley endorses this reading in the preface to the novel's third edition, writing "supremely frightful would be the effect of any human endeavor to mock the stupendous mechanism of the Creator of the world."[142] And her revisions to the third edition magnify the theme of enlightenment's vulnerability to chance into an outright assertion that Frankenstein is destined for destruction.[143] Our image of an inarticulate, lumbering, single-minded monster illustrates well our fear that certain technological achievements—like the creation of life—will inevitably have horrible consequences, if only because they violate a divine prohibition. This fear is already foregrounded in the title of the first stage production of *Frankenstein*, which Shelley loved: Richard Brinsley Peake's 1823 play *Presumption; or the Fate of Frankenstein*.[144] But in Shelley's original conception, in the novel's first edition, the monster is articulate, agile, and tormented. His story persuades Frankenstein, Walton, and us to ask whether a creator is obliged to make possible the happiness of his creation. And his ugliness forces us to go deeper, to ask whether *our* creator is not obliged to make *our* happiness possible. How can we be destined for an enlightenment that is so prone to go wrong, so horribly vulnerable to chance? If enlightenment is good, why does it make so many monsters?

In the preface to *Frankenstein*'s first edition, posing as the anonymous author, Percy Shelley writes that the novel's chief concern is "limited to . . . avoiding the enervating effects of the novels of the present day, and to the exhibition of the amiableness of domestic affection, and the excellence of universal virtue."[145] It is hard to imagine a more blandly misleading statement of purpose. True, at the novel's heart is a happy, wise, and good family; but the monster scares them away and burns down their home. The monster has no family, Frankenstein destroys his family, and Walton nearly abandons the little family he has. Enlightenment destroys family, friendship, and their attendant virtues. So when Percy Shelley continues, "no inference [is] justly to be drawn from the following pages as prejudicing any philosophical doctrine of whatever kind," we should think not of Milton, whose *Paradise Lost* chiefly provides errors that drive *Frankenstein*'s plot, but of Rousseau.

Frankenstein is strewn with allusions to Rousseau. Some are straightforward. Frankenstein is a Genevan who makes, and then fails to educate, what Rousseau imagines in *Emile*: a "man born big and strong."[146] Abandoned to himself, Frankenstein's man is like the savage in Rousseau's *Second Discourse*:[147] he first finds himself in a state of nature, where he judges himself to have been naturally good; but then circumstances force him into society, which enlightens him and makes him miserable and wicked. The monster is mistaken for a savage,[148] and longs to end his life with his mate[149]—and presumably with their offspring—in a state approaching the nascent society that Rousseau calls "the best for man."[150] *Frankenstein*'s subtitle is "The Modern Prometheus."[151] But Rousseau depicts himself as a modern Prometheus in the *First Discourse*,[152] where he argues that enlightenment causes moral corruption, making deformed human beings who loathe to be seen as they are[153]—that is, that enlightenment makes monsters.

Some allusions to Rousseau in *Frankenstein* are more recondite. In Shelley's time, the park outside Geneva, where the monster murders William and frames Justine, featured an obelisk dedicated to Rousseau, marking where the Genevans murdered their magistrates during the Revolution. [154] In a footnote in *Emile,* Rousseau mentions "another Prometheus" who made a tiny man "by the science of alchemy." [155] Shelley records in her journal that she read over two hundred books during the four years before *Frankenstein* was published, among which were Rousseau's *Confessions, Emile, Julie,* and *The Reveries of the Solitary Walker*—and that she read the first three of these twice. [156] Lastly, in his *Confessions* Rousseau claims to have abandoned his five children to a foundling hospital, where they very likely died. [157] Shelley went on to write an encyclopedia article about Rousseau, where she returned repeatedly to the subject of these children. [158] But in *Frankenstein*, the monster claims five victims from Frankenstein's family: William Frankenstein, Justine Moritz, Henry Clerval, Elizabeth Lavenza, and Alphonse Frankenstein. And *Frankenstein* itself consists of five stories of enlightenment.

So the "philosophical doctrine" most at issue in *Frankenstein* is Rousseau's doctrine, announced in the *First Discourse*, that enlightenment causes moral corruption, ruins families, and destroys virtue. [159] Shelley must have wondered whether this doctrine applies to her too. In Walton's sister, Mary Saville—but in Walton, Frankenstein, the monster, and Safie too—we see shadows of Mary Shelley herself, thinking through her fear that enlightenment has made her a monster. Perhaps the ambiguity of the novel's ending, with Frankenstein's "another may succeed," Walton's courageous audience with the monster, and Walton's unwilling, unrepentant return, nods to Rousseau's qualification that enlightenment necessarily corrupts morals only in peoples, because a few individuals can pursue it while keeping from vice. [160] Perhaps she understands that these individuals will look vicious to others, and still sides with enlightenment despite its risks. Perhaps she sees herself in the prediction of Frankenstein's creation: "we shall be monsters." [161]

But what about the other aspects of Rousseau's doctrine: that enlightenment causes moral corruption because enlightenment is fragile, dangerously vulnerable to chance; and that this fragility can perhaps be remedied if one learns with the guidance of a teacher, and yet "somehow by his own efforts"? This question prompts us to wonder how deeply Mary Shelley saw into Rousseau's thought. Death strikes us as the ultimate accident, the ultimate cause of enlightenment's dangerous fragility. But enlightenment teaches that causes are intelligible as necessary and sufficient. If the sphere of accident diminishes as enlightenment increases, and if the sphere of ugliness is coextensive with that of accident, then as enlightenment increases, ugliness diminishes too. Enlightenment might make monsters in the eyes of the partly enlightened, but it unmakes them in the eyes of those who really know. In the *Second Discourse* Rousseau laments humankind's accidental fall first from its original and then from its best state,[162] but he also teaches the causes of these accidents, so that in *Emile* he can avoid or mitigate them, in an education that "ought to be the history of my species."[163] He even presents his own enlightenment as the effect of a unique accident—like Frankenstein's, a sudden illumination[164]—and acknowledges that others see him as a monster.[165] Yet Rousseau insists that he is good.[166] It is true, after all, that by eating, we living things fashion ourselves out of dead materials. Perhaps it is an error to see ugliness in enlightenment.

NOTES

Thanks to Lise van Boxel, Michael W. Grenke, Timothy McCranor, Steven Michels, Katherine Melissa Watson, Brian Wilson, the members of the 2016–2017 Mellon Study Group on Digital Technology at St. John's College, Annapolis, and the faculty and students of St. John's College, Santa Fe, for their comments on earlier versions of this chapter.

1. Mary Shelley, *Frankenstein*, ed. J. Paul Hunter (New York: W.W. Norton & Company, 1996), 173.

2. Consider Shelley, *Frankenstein*, 302–313 and Jon Turney, *Frankenstein's Footsteps: Science, Genetics and Popular Culture* (New Haven, CT: Yale University Press, 1998), 28–29.

3. Jon Turney, *Frankenstein's Footsteps*, 3.

4. Jean-Jacques Rousseau, *Discourse on the Science and Arts (First Discourse) and Polemics*, trans. Judith R. Bush, Roger D. Masters, and Christopher Kelly, vol. 2, *The Collected Writings of Rousseau*, ed. Roger D. Masters and Christopher Kelly (Hanover, NH: The University Press of New England, 1990–2010), 4.

5. Shelley, *Frankenstein*, 7.

6. Shelley, *Frankenstein*, 83.

7. The secondary literature on *Frankenstein* is vast. In addition to countless writings focusing on Frankenstein's story and on the monster's, it includes excellent discussions of the story of the monster's beloved cottagers, such as Joyce Zonana's "'They Will Prove the Truth of My Tale': Safie's Letters as the Feminist Core of Mary Shelley's 'Frankenstein,'" in *The Journal of Narrative Technique* 21, no. 2 (Spring 1991), 170–184, and of Robert Walton's story, such as Rudolf Beck's note "'The Region of Beauty and Delight': Walton's Polar Fantasies in Mary Shelley's 'Frankenstein,'" from the *Keats-Shelley Journal* 49 (2000), 24–29. It also includes excellent discussions of the connections between Rousseau's thought and *Frankenstein*, including Lawrence Lipking's "*Frankenstein*, the True Story; or Rousseau Judges Jean-Jacques," in Mary Shelley, *Frankenstein*, ed. J. Paul Hunter (New York: W.W. Norton & Company, 1996), 313–330, and James O'Rourke's "'Nothing More Unnatural': Mary Shelley's Revision of Rousseau," in *ELH* 56, no. 3 (Autumn, 1989), 543–569. But this chapter is, to my knowledge, the only treatment so far of *Frankenstein* as a whole in the light of Rousseau's thought as a whole: that is, in the light of the concern—with the goodness of enlightenment rather than with the dangers of technology—that birthed Rousseau's philosophic system. Too many interpretations of *Frankenstein* begin from a concern with the dangers of technology, and thus rush straight to an interpretation of Frankenstein's and the monster's stories, neglecting the puzzling nested structure of the book as a whole.

8. Rousseau, *First Discourse*, 4.

9. Shelley, *Frankenstein*, 82.

10. Shelley, *Frankenstein*, 82.

11. Shelley, *Frankenstein*, 83.

12. Shelley, *Frankenstein*, 83.

13. Shelley, *Frankenstein*, 82.

14. Jean-Jacques Rousseau, *"Emile, or On Education." (Includes "Emile and Sophie, or the Solitaries")*, trans. Christopher Kelly and Allan Bloom, vol. 13, *The Collected Writings of Rousseau*, 598 and following.

15. Rousseau, *Emile*, 165–166.

16. Shelley, *Frankenstein*, 68.

17. Jean-Jacques Rousseau, *Discourse on the Origins of Inequality (Second Discourse), Polemics, and Political Economy*, trans. Judith R. Bush, Roger D. Masters, Christopher Kelly, and Terence Marshall, vol. 3, *The Collected Writings of Rousseau*, 27.

18. Rousseau, *First Discourse*, 12 note *; compare 179.

19. Shelley, *Frankenstein*, 69.

20. Shelley, *Frankenstein*, 70.

21. Shelley, *Frankenstein*, 72.

22. Shelley, *Frankenstein*, 77; compare 65.

23. Shelley, *Frankenstein*, 75.

24. Shelley, *Frankenstein*, 76; compare John Milton, *Paradise Lost*, 2nd ed., ed. Scott Elledge (New York: W.W. Norton & Company, 1993), book 4, lines 449–475.

25. Rousseau, *Second Discourse*, 44.

26. Shelley, *Frankenstein*, 76.

27. Shelley, *Frankenstein*, 77.

28. Rousseau, *Second Discourse*, 91.

29. Shelley, *Frankenstein*, 99; compare Rousseau, *Second Discourse*, 37.

30. Shelley, *Frankenstein*, 77.

31. Shelley, *Frankenstein*, 79.

32. Shelley, *Frankenstein*, 80; compare Rousseau, *First Discourse*, 9 note *.

33. Shelley, *Frankenstein*, 80; compare Rousseau, *Second Discourse*, 43 and 52.

34. Rousseau, *Second Discourse*, 27 and 44.

35. Rousseau, *Second Discourse*, 20; compare Rousseau, *Emile*, 504.

36. Shelley, *Frankenstein*, 81.

37. Rousseau, *Second Discourse*, 27.

38. Shelley, *Frankenstein*, 87.

39. Rousseau, *Emile*, 331–333.

40. Shelley, *Frankenstein*, 86.

41. Shelley, *Frankenstein*, 86–87.

42. Shelley, *Frankenstein*, 87.

43. Shelley, *Frankenstein*, 87–88.

44. Shelley, *Frankenstein*, 87; compare 68.

45. Shelley, *Frankenstein*, 88.

46. Shelley, *Frankenstein*, 88; compare Milton, *Paradise Lost*, book 4, lines 288–299.

47. Shelley, *Frankenstein*, 88; compare Milton, *Paradise Lost*, book 2, lines 477–495.

48. Shelley, *Frankenstein*, 85.

49. Shelley, *Frankenstein*, 89; compare 69.

50. Shelley, *Frankenstein*, 91.

51. Shelley, *Frankenstein*, 92; compare Milton, *Paradise Lost*, book 4, lines 73–75.

52. Shelley, *Frankenstein*, 94.

53. Shelley, *Frankenstein*, 96.

54. Shelley, *Frankenstein*, 76.

55. Compare Rousseau, *Emile*, 177–178.

56. Shelley, *Frankenstein*, 96–97.

57. Shelley, *Frankenstein*, 97.

58. Shelley, *Frankenstein*, 97.

59. Shelley, *Frankenstein*, 98.

60. Shelley, *Frankenstein*, 66.

61. Shelley, *Frankenstein*, 67.

62. Shelley, *Frankenstein*, 98.

63. Shelley, *Frankenstein*, 99; compare Milton, *Paradise Lost*, book 12, lines 641–649.

64. Shelley, *Frankenstein*, 100; consider Rousseau, *Emile*, 240 note *.

65. Shelley, *Frankenstein*, 98.

66. Shelley, *Frankenstein*, 76.

67. Shelley, *Frankenstein*, 114.

68. Shelley, *Frankenstein*, 19–20, 105.

69. Shelley, *Frankenstein*, 19, 24.

70. Shelley, *Frankenstein*, 19.

71. Shelley, *Frankenstein*, 147.

72. Shelley, *Frankenstein*, 18–19, 24.

73. Shelley, *Frankenstein*, 21.

74. Shelley, *Frankenstein*, 22.

75. Shelley, *Frankenstein*, 21.

76. Shelley, *Frankenstein*, 22; compare Rousseau, *First Discourse*, 19, 21–22, and Rousseau, *Second Discourse*, 63.

77. Shelley, *Frankenstein*, 22–23.

78. Shelley, *Frankenstein*, 23.

79. Shelley, *Frankenstein*, 24–25.

80. Shelley, *Frankenstein*, 25.

81. Shelley, *Frankenstein*, 26.

82. Shelley, *Frankenstein*, 27.

83. Shelley, *Frankenstein*, 27–28.

84. Shelley, *Frankenstein*, 28.

85. Shelley, *Frankenstein*, 29.

86. Shelley, *Frankenstein*, 29, 27.

87. Shelley, *Frankenstein*, 32.

88. Shelley, *Frankenstein*, 30.

89. Compare Jean-Jacques Rousseau, *"The Confessions,"* and *Correspondence, including The Letters to Malesherbes*, trans. Christopher Kelly, vol. 5, *The Collected Writings of Rousseau*, 575–576.

90. Shelley, *Frankenstein*, 30 and 32.

91. Shelley, *Frankenstein*, 31–32; compare 13 and 65.

92. Shelley, *Frankenstein*, 32.

93. Shelley, *Frankenstein*, 66.

94. Shelley, *Frankenstein*, 80; compare 89 and 79.

95. Shelley, *Frankenstein*, 32; compare Milton, *Paradise Lost*, book 4, lines 45–57 and Rousseau, *Emile*, 387–388.

96. Shelley, *Frankenstein*, 34.

97. Shelley, *Frankenstein*, 34.

98. Shelley, *Frankenstein*, 34.

99. Shelley, *Frankenstein*, 35.

100. Shelley, *Frankenstein*, 35; see also 48.

101. Shelley, *Frankenstein*, 35.

102. Consider Shelley, *Frankenstein*, 34.

103. Shelley, *Frankenstein*, 35 and 37.

104. Shelley, *Frankenstein*, 48.

105. Shelley, *Frankenstein*, 65.

106. Shelley, *Frankenstein*, 60 and 65–66.

107. Shelley, *Frankenstein*, 101.

108. Shelley, *Frankenstein*, 113.

109. Shelley, *Frankenstein*, 114.

110. Shelley, *Frankenstein*, 114; compare Milton, *Paradise Lost*, book 8, lines 333–343 and book 9, lines 758–760.

111. Shelley, *Frankenstein*, 114.

112. Shelley, *Frankenstein*, 32.

113. Shelley, *Frankenstein*, 114–115 and 118.

114. Compare Shelley, *Frankenstein*, 35 with 115.

115. Shelley, *Frankenstein*, 131.

116. Shelley, *Frankenstein*, 137.

117. Shelley, *Frankenstein*, 147.

118. Shelley, *Frankenstein*, 139.

119. Shelley, *Frankenstein*, 8.

120. Shelley, *Frankenstein*, 10.

121. Shelley, *Frankenstein*, 10, 16.

122. Shelley, *Frankenstein*, 7.

123. Shelley, *Frankenstein*, 8.

124. Shelley, *Frankenstein*, 7.

125. Shelley, *Frankenstein*, 8.

126. Shelley, *Frankenstein*, 148.

127. Shelley, *Frankenstein*, 11–12.

128. Shelley, *Frankenstein*, 149.

129. Shelley, *Frankenstein*, 15.

130. Shelley, *Frankenstein*, 16 and 147.

131. Shelley, *Frankenstein*, 17, 149.

132. Shelley, *Frankenstein*, 17.

133. Shelley, *Frankenstein*, 146.

134. Shelley, *Frankenstein*, 146; compare 83.

135. Shelley, *Frankenstein*, 150.

136. Shelley, *Frankenstein*, 151.

137. Shelley, *Frankenstein*, 152.

138. Shelley, *Frankenstein*, 152.

139. Shelley, *Frankenstein*, 155.

140. Shelley, *Frankenstein*, 154.

141. Shelley, *Frankenstein*, 156.

142. Shelley, *Frankenstein*, 172.

143. For a perceptive discussion of the thematic differences between the first (1818) and third (1831) edition texts of *Frankenstein*, see Anne K. Mellor, "Choosing a Text of *Frankenstein* to Teach," in *Approaches to Teaching Shelley's* Frankenstein (New York: Modern Language Association, 1990), 31–37, reprinted in Mary Shelley, *Frankenstein*, ed. J. Paul Hunter (New York: W.W. Norton & Company, 1996), 160–166, especially 164–166.

144. Turney, *Frankenstein's Footsteps*, 28.

145. Shelley, *Frankenstein*, 5–6; compare Jean-Jacques Rousseau, *Julie, or the New Heloise*, trans. Philip Stewart and Jean Vaché, vol. 6, *The Collected Writings of Rousseau*, 7–22.

146. Rousseau, *Emile*, 162, 189–190.

147. Rousseau, *Second Discourse*, 26, 41–42.

148. Shelley, *Frankenstein*, 13.

149. Shelley, *Frankenstein*, 99.

150. Rousseau, *Second Discourse*, 46–48.

151. Shelley, *Frankenstein*, 3.

152. Rousseau, *First Discourse*, 2 and 179.

153. Rousseau, *First Discourse*, 6.

154. Shelley, *Frankenstein*, 174.

155. Rousseau, *Emile*, 436 note *

156. Mary Shelley, *Mary Shelley's Journal*, ed. Frederick L. Jones (Norman: University of Oklahoma Press, 1947), 47–49, 55, 64, 72–73, 85–86, 89–90.

157. Rousseau, *Confessions*, 289, 299–301, 551–552.

158. Shelley, *Frankenstein*, 545.

159. Rousseau, *First Discourse*, 20.

160. Compare Rousseau, *First Discourse*, 7 with 9; consider Rousseau, *First Discourse*, 21, and Rousseau, *Second Discourse*, 63.

161. Shelley, *Frankenstein*, 99.

162. Rousseau, *Second Discourse*, 42, 48.

163. Rousseau, *Emile*, 599.

164. Rousseau, *Confessions*, 5 and 575.

165. Jean-Jacques Rousseau, *Rousseau, Judge of Jean-Jacques: Dialogues*, trans. Judith R. Bush, Roger D. Masters, and Christopher Kelly, vol. 1, *The Collected Writings of Rousseau*, 61–63.

166. Rousseau, *Confessions*, 5; compare Rousseau, *Dialogues*, 221.

BIBLIOGRAPHY

Milton, John. *Paradise Lost*. Second Edition. Edited by Scott Elledge. New York: W.W. Norton & Company, 1993.

Rousseau, Jean-Jacques. *The Collected Writings of Rousseau*. Edited by Christopher Kelly and Roger D. Masters. 13 Volumes. Hanover, NH: University Press of New England, 1990–2010.

Shelley, Mary. *Frankenstein*. Edited by J. Paul Hunter. New York: W.W. Norton & Company, 1996.

———. *Mary Shelley's Journal*. Edited by Frederick L. Jones. Norman: University of Oklahoma Press, 1947.

Turney, Jon. *Frankenstein's Footsteps: Science, Genetics and Popular Culture*. New Haven, CT: Yale University Press, 1998.

Chapter Four

Technology and Anxiety in Melville's "Lightning-Rod Man"

Tobin L. Craig

" . . . the Lightning-rod man still dwells in the land; still travels in storm time, and drives a brave trade with the fears of man." [1]

From its inception, modern science was advertised with the promise of making us safer, and so freer. It has succeeded, but in so doing it has only further inflamed the hopes and desires that propelled its advancement. Safe but insecure, at ease but uneasy, surely one of the most striking paradoxes of technological modernity is that, despite the tremendous advances in our ability to ward off danger, we are if anything more anxious about our bodily safety than were our grandparents and great-grandparents. As the late Peter Lawler wryly observed, "We live in a time when well-educated and prosperous Americans are nonjudgmental about everything but health and safety—about these we are increasingly paranoid, prohibitionist, and puritanical." [2]

In Herman Melville's short-story "Lightning-Rod Man" we encounter a charming and penetrating reflection on this counter-intuitive dynamic between science, technology, and anxiety, one that identifies and sheds considerable light on the shortcomings of the hope that increase in knowledge of causes with a view to predicting and intervening in the course of nature will make us less uneasy and more at home in the world. In what follows, I briefly summarize the story, emphasizing certain of the puzzling or noteworthy details of the narrative, and then, in reflecting upon these details, attempt to articulate the logic of Melville's argument that, so far from making us more at ease, the embrace of technological innovation as *the* rational response to our insecurity will actually tend to heighten anxiety and thereby frustrate our search for happiness.

I

"Lightning-Rod Man" is the tale of an encounter between an unnamed solitary mountain dweller and a travelling door-to-door salesman of lightning-rods. The tale begins with the musings of the mountain dweller on a tremendous thunderstorm booming through his mountainous environs.[3] He marks the thunder first, and only secondarily the "scattered bolts," "zigzag irradiations," and "swift slants of sharp rain." He reflects on how the mountains amplify the thunder, making it "more glorious." He is roused from his reflections by the sound of urgent fist-pounding on his door, wondering why the visitor doesn't, "man-fashion," use the knocker.[4]

The first exchange between the two characters establishes their divergent attitudes toward the storm: "'A fine thunder-storm, sir.' 'Fine?—Awful!'" In what will become a motif of the tale, the visitor, identified as "an entire stranger," again rejects the customary, declining the mountain-man's invitation to take a seat or stand with him by the hearth near the fire. Soaking wet, standing in the middle of the room, the "lean, gloomy figure" holds a strange trident-shaped pole of polished copper and green glass which his host apparently mistakes for a walking stick.[5]

Our country-dweller jovially inquires whether his visitor is Jupiter Tonans himself or his viceroy, and offers him occasion to delight in the majesty of a great peal of thunder. The stranger, wearing an aspect of wonder and horror, and, refusing for the second time an offer to take a chair near the hearth, solemnly warns his host, "stand with me in the middle of the room. . . . Are you so horridly ignorant, then, as not to know, that by far the most dangerous part of a house, during such a terrific tempest as this, is the fire place?" The mountain-man freely admits his ignorance, and "involuntarily" steps away from the stone hearth, but then, recognizing in his visitor "such an unpleasant air of successful admonition," the freedom-loving host defiantly returns to on the hearth.[6]

He then prods his visitor to announce his business, which he does, though interrupted by shudders of terror and exclamations of "Good heavens," "For heaven's sake," and "Merciful heaven!" at each sequent crash of thunder: "by nature there are no castles in thunder-storms; yet, say but the word, and of this cottage I can make a Gibraltar with a few waves of this wand."[7]

What ensues is a disorderly dialogue between the lightning-rod man and the solitary mountain dweller, repeatedly interrupted by the lightning-rod man's panicked exclamations on the peals of thunder and his attempts to gauge the proximity of the lightning. The lightning-rod man is on business, wandering abroad during the storm peddling his wares, apparently "deem[ing] it an hour peculiarly favorable to producing impressions favorable to [his] trade." But the mountain dweller is skeptical—the proverbial hard sell. This despite the fact that he reveals himself to be well-apprised of the dangers of lightning storms in his region and of recent news of fatal and destructive lightning-strikes. He presses the lightning-rod man to make his case, demanding that he adduce his reasons, and in particular that he respond to cases of lightning-rods failing to deliver the promised protection. But he is more struck by how terrified the salesman is, and the folly, given that terror, of his going abroad during such storms. "That I travel in thunder-storms, I grant; but not without particular precautions, such as only a lightning-rod man may know."[8] The mountain-man then presses the salesman to reveal his precautions and their basis.

The course of their conversation, however, is again deflected by the attempt on the part of the host—whose windows are still unbarred, indicating his delight or wonder at beholding the storm—to make his visitor more comfortable by closing and barring his windows. This too elicits a terrified response from the visitor, again connected to his special knowledge, "Are you mad? Know you not that yon iron bar is a swift conductor? Desist."[9]

The still half-amused host now asks, "Is there any part of my house I may touch with hopes of my life? . . . Tell me at once, which is, in your opinion, the safest part of this house?" But he refuses to modify his conduct until he hears the reasons behind the lightning-rod man's recommendations.

> "And now, Mr Lightning-rod man, in the pauses of the thunder, be so good as to tell me your reasons for esteeming this one room of the house the safest, and your own one stand-point there the safest spot in it."
>
> There was now a little cessation of the storm for a while. The Lightning-rod man seemed relieved, and replied:—
>
> "Your house is a one-storied house, with an attic and a cellar; this room is between. Hence its comparative safety. Because lightning sometimes passes from the clouds to the earth, and sometimes from the earth to the clouds. Do you comprehend?—and I choose the middle of the room, because, if the lightning should strike the house at all, it would come down the chimney or walls; so, obviously, the further you are from them, the better. Come hither to me, now."
>
> "Presently. Something you just said, instead of alarming me, has strangely inspired confidence."
>
> "What have I said?"
>
> "You said that sometimes lightning flashes from the earth to the clouds."
>
> "Aye, the returning-stroke, as it is called; when the earth, being overcharged with the fluid, flashes its surplus upward."
>
> "The returning-stroke; that is, from earth to sky. Better and better. But come here on the hearth, and dry yourself."[10]

Melville has left his reader to puzzle out for himself just what it is about the notion of the returning-stroke that reassures the mountain dweller.

The mountain dweller continues his querying of the lightning-rod man, returning to the earlier question of the salesman's precautions for travel abroad during a storm. He is treated to an enumeration: wet clothes are better than dry, walking slowly, not on horseback, avoiding pine trees, high houses, lonely barns, upland pastures, running water, flocks of cattle and sheep, a crowd of men, "[b]ut of all things, I avoid tall men." To which the mountain dweller responds, "Do I dream? Man avoid man? And in danger-time, too."[11]

The story reaches its climax when, as the storm abates, the lightning-rod man presses his host to make a purchase, urging him to consider himself "a heap of charred offal."[12] To this attempt to play upon his fears, the mountain-man responds sharply:

> "You pretended envoy extraordinary and minister plenipotentiary to and from Jupiter Tonans," laughed I; "you mere man who come here to put you and your pipestem between clay and sky, do you think that because you can strike a bit of green light from the Leyden jar, that you can thoroughly avert the supernal bolt? Your rod rusts, or breaks, and where are you? Who has empowered you, you Tetzel, to peddle round your indulgences from divine ordinations? The hairs of our heads are numbered, and the days of our lives. In thunder as in sunshine, I stand at ease in the hands of my God. False negotiator, away! See, the scroll of the storm is rolled back; the house is unharmed; and in the blue heavens I read in the rainbow, that the Deity will not, of purpose, make war on man's earth."[13]

Tellingly, the lightning-rod man regards such a view as a shocking form of impiety, and now, foaming with anger, "blackening in the face as the rainbow beamed," threatens to "publish" the mountain-man's "infidel notions," and ultimately attacks the mountain-man with his rod. His thrust is parried, his rod is dashed, and he is sent packing.

The story concludes with the mountain dweller commenting that despite his "dissuasive talk of him to my neighbors," "the Lightning-rod man still dwells in the land; still travels in storm time, and drives a brave trade with the fears of man."[14]

II

Now, as has been conclusively shown in an excellent essay by Allan Moore Emery, the clear targets of Melville's story are the hopes placed in the findings and fruits of modern technological science, and not, as a majority of scholars had previously argued, evangelical Christianity.[15] Emery directs our attention to source materials from which Melville clearly drew. Most importantly, Emery systematically lays out much of the best evidence that Melville was working from Franklin's *Experiments and Observations on Electricity*, and *A Treatise on Lightning Conductors; compiled from a work on Thunderstorms, by W. S. Harris and Other Standard Authors*, published in 1853 by one Lucius Lyon. The reflections that follow build upon Emery's work—

though I depart from his interpretation on one key point—with the intention of sharpening and generalizing his suggestion about what Melville is up to in the tale.

Like all great storytellers, Melville teaches his readers by means of the puzzles he weaves into his tales. "Lightning-Rod Man" is replete with such puzzles. The tale as a whole confronts the reader with the puzzle of just why the mountain-man is not buying what the lightning-rod man is selling. For the mountain-man is no mere primitivist, opposed to any and all efforts to artfully make oneself more secure and comfortable in a hostile environment. He lives in a house, a house that is full of other instruments and conveniences. Indeed, Melville has gone out of his way to point these out: the fireplace, the rug, the furniture, the shutters and their bars, the bell pull, the knocker on his door. And while some of these implements service his bare needs, living as he does somewhat alone in the mountains, others are clearly luxuries or comforts or conveniences. Moreover, it is clear that the mountain-man's enjoyment of the storm is made possible by the shelter afforded him by his house. However impressive the storm, it would be harder to admire while sopping wet and shivering (one of the precautions recommended by the lightning-rod man, taken from Franklin [who is almost surely jesting] and Lyon [who seems to be quite serious]).

Nor is he opposed in principle to the work of door-to-door salesmen. For most of the tale, he is a welcoming and curious, if slightly amused, host to the travelling peddler. Melville seems to present him as a potential customer, albeit a skeptical potential customer. He does not yet have a lightning-rod but is well aware of the dangers of lightning strikes and has attended in particular to stories of buildings with lightning-rods that were nevertheless destroyed. Above all, Melville's mountain-man is curious, even eager to learn from the lightning-rod man, offering occasion for and even insisting that the "expert" adduce his evidence and arguments before following his advice and buying.

Besides this skeptical curiosity and what we see and hear about his general attitude to nature, God, and mortality—about which we will have more to say below—the mountain-man's chief quality is his spirited concern for his independence. Consider his reaction to the lightning-rod man's "unpleasant air of successful admonition"—he moves back to the spot deemed more dangerous. An irrational response, to be sure, but one that is nonetheless revealing. Note, however, that on other occasions he does allow himself to be "commanded in his own house"—he neither bars the shutters nor pulls the bell-wire. Thus, while the mountain-man is willing to learn, and recognizes the claim of knowledge to rule, he also wishes to be his own master, and while not antisocial—indeed, quite the contrary (he has a knocker and expects his visitors to use it; he is repeatedly frustrated in his efforts to make his visitor more comfortable; he is especially shocked by the lightning-rod man's admission that he avoids his fellow man during lightning storms; he concludes by mentioning subsequent conversations with his neighbors that reveal a concern for them)—he lives alone and apart.

Summarizing, one could say Melville's mountain-man is or wishes to be as free and self-governing as possible. He is, to the extent possible, his own man, or an individual.[16] We are thus presented with a dialogue between a man, rather than, say, a citizen or even a father, and the lightning-rod man. Their exchange is thus as free of admixture or complications as possible. One could say Melville has presented us a model of who we understand ourselves to be as potential consumers of technological innovations: free individuals in an untamed wild, who ask simply whether the proffered innovation will improve or detract from our independence and happiness. Does the freedom-loving individual, alone in the wilderness, buy? And if not, why not?

The action of the story makes clear that a crucial part of the answer to this puzzle is to be found by addressing the second most conspicuous puzzle of the tale: the willingness of the lightning-rod man to venture out in the midst of the storm despite his manifest terror of lightning. At first blush, it would appear that he does so only because this is the best time to make sales. Note, he is silent when the mountain-man suggests as much. But while the lightning-rod man may be playing up his terror as part of his sales pitch, Melville clearly portrays him as genuinely panicked by the storm—compared with the mountain-man, he is utterly unable to retain his focus amid the thunder and lightning.[17] And yet, while he won't step onto the mountain-man's hearth "for worlds," he ventures into an unprotected house made of oak (apparently an especially conductive wood) in the hope of making a sale. Left at this, he is an amusing caricature of the confusions and follies induced by the capitalist spirit.

But there is, I think, something more to this puzzle, something pointed to by those critics who mistake the story for a critique of evangelical Christianity. For there is an unmistakably evangelical character to the lightning-rod man's zeal, and to the religious moralism of his language.[18] His vivid command, "Think of being a heap of charred offal," evokes a sacrificial victim or the torments of hell. Similarly, his response to the mountain-man's query about a story of a failed Canadian lightning-rod—"*Mine* is the only true rod"—and his angry final words, condemning the mountain-man for an "impious wretch" and threatening to "publish [his] infidel notions" reveal that he understands himself as something more than just a principled salesman of a particularly fine product. The lightning-rod man is not merely supremely confident in his rod and the knowledge that undergirds it, so that it would be simply irrational to fail to buy one, but he regards the rejection of his product as indicative of a kind of shocking impiety. He thus comes to sight as less a salesman than a proselytizer on a quasi-theological mission to win converts to a new creed or view of man and the whole.

It is in this light that we should understand the lightning-rod man's willingness to brave terrors and risk perdition by venturing out into the terrible wilderness at so dangerous an hour. He is a bringer of glad tidings, prophet or at least witness of the true hope, purveyor of knowledge vital to the happiness of his fellow man, and he comes to the vulnerable in their hour of utmost need. He desires and looks forward to the gratitude and honor that comes from instructing and so ameliorating the circumstances of his fellow men, introducing them to the truth about their vulnerability and presenting them with the only reasonable response to it. But as the concluding exchange makes clear, if his tremulousness did not, unlike a religious evangelist, the lightning-rod man lacks the security of faith in an afterlife or a providential order to the whole, and so he can't be calm in the face of the dangers he faces and the risks he runs on behalf of others. And because his awareness that others are still un-provided for and so needlessly at risk further undermines his own tranquility, he is propelled forth into the storm. When his willingness to run risks for the salvation of others is met with anything other than deferential gratitude, he is enraged, and not only on his own behalf—such infidel notions should be published.

What then is the character of the outlook on nature and the human situation that the lightning-rod man is peddling? On the one hand, the lightning-rod man clearly understands himself to be master of the relevant scientific findings about lightning and electricity and to have taken all possible precautions, as the mountain-man points out: "You stand in the safest possible place according to your own account."[19] On the other hand, he is the very picture of anxiety. Whence this curious combination of supreme confidence and irrepressible unease? We might be tempted to conclude that he is only fearful because he is in a house not yet equipped with one of his rods; that if we saw him outdoors, he would be boldness itself. But then why does he not suggest they step outside? Plainly, Melville means for us to see that the lightning-rod man's anxiety is not accidental or idiosyncratic, but belongs essentially to his outlook. To approach nature with a view to securing oneself to the extent possible against danger, even when accompanied by the best available science, so far from bringing calm, only serves to increase one's unease. *Even the certainty of having done all he can to avoid danger to himself does not put the lightning-rod man at ease.* But why should this be?

For starters, this science, while animated and oriented by a desire to improve our earthly condition, is not limited to discovering only phenomena and chains of causation[20] that can be interrupted or otherwise dealt with. Rather, the findings generated by this science will always outstrip our capacity to effectively intervene. We will be made aware of dangers that we cannot, at least at present, do anything about. Thus, precisely the most competent and up-to-date scientific expert cannot be anything but uneasy, at least insofar as, like the lightning-rod man, he is unreconciled to his ultimate vulnerability.

This line of reflection brings us to the central puzzle of the story: why the mountain-man is reassured by learning of the "return-stroke," or the possibility of lightning that "strikes" from earth to sky, or from the ground up. This is the most riddle-like of the story's many puzzles and when taken together with the lightning-rod man's anxiety, points the way to an answer to the most prominent puzzle of the story, namely, why the mountain-man isn't buying.

What is reassuring to the mountain-man about this idea of the return-stroke? Emery, our best guide, suggests that the return-stroke indicates that the earth can strike back against the heavens, and that the mountain-man takes comfort knowing that we here below are not altogether unarmed.[21] This won't do, however, for we learn too much of the mountain-man's outlook in the climax of the story to suppose that he harbors a Promethean anger at the gods or Nature, or even that he regards lightning as an instrument of divine wrath. Even his jocular identification of the lightning-rod man with Jupiter Tonans indicates a grateful admiration of the "Thunderer." Moreover, this account doesn't explain how the return-stroke inspires confidence as opposed to the alarm the mountain-man intuits that the salesman is trying to foster. Learning of the return-stroke reinvigorates the mountain-man's confidence in the outlook he already holds, and emboldens his skepticism toward the lightning-rod man's attempt to play upon his fears. How so?

In learning of the return-stroke, the mountain-man learns that even if the rod is mounted correctly and works as advertised, it cannot make of his house a Gibraltar, as the salesman boasts. His essential insecurity remains. Thus the device, which is offered with the promise of total security, cannot deliver on this promise.

For confirmation of this reading, we follow Emery's lead in returning to Melville's source material, and to Lucius Lyon's *Treatise*, which discusses the returning or ascending stroke at some length. In the course of the first section of the *Treatise*, wherein he reviews and summarizes contemporary theory about lightning, Lyon carefully documents the evidence for ascending lightning.[22] In the next section he repeatedly promises that "It is therefore demonstrable by physical facts, that *perfect security* is to be derived from an efficient conductor properly applied."[23] And yet, when Lyon returns, as he had promised to do, to the subject of the returning or ascending stroke, he acknowledges that even buildings with rods affixed to them, may be severely damaged, quoting the following story from a newspaper:

> Singular Freak of Lightning.—During the shower on Wednesday of last week, the house of A. J. Piatt, of Deep River, was struck, doing considerable damage. It appeared to be what is called an upward stroke, passing up the door-casing of the hall and parlor, and thence, through the hall, the side of the house, where

the wing connects, to the corner of the wing, passing down on a pillar; and also at another point into the sink, knocking off splinters, and loosening the clap-boards in various places.

A singular feature is, that the house was guarded by a lightning-rod at-tached to each chimney, running down the roof, and from thence to the ground; and there is abundant evidence that the electric current, in its progress, passed within some six or seven feet of this rod, and that the protection which it is claimed to give, was of no avail in this instance. The rod is one of those put up by Dr. Minor, who has also put up several in this village, and we would like to hear his explanation of their inefficiency in this he claims them as superior to any other.

That there is sure protection in a conductor, we believe, and it would be well for those about to procure this safeguard, to ascertain that they procure the best article, and have them rightly put up. It is a matter which is not lightly to be passed over, where the lives of people and property are at stake.

To which Lyon replies, "In so long a period as three-quarters of a century, it is not to be expected that no casualties should occur, either from a defective application of the conductor, or from an explosion falling on some part of the building at a distance from the conductor."[24]

Nevertheless, acknowledging that the lightning-rod man has thus been caught exaggerating, that he cannot promise complete security, and that such over-selling well might compromise a prospective buyer's confidence in the salesman, one still might ask, "Why object to partial security? Surely this is better than none?" And, why is the mountain-man *reassured* by learning of the returning-stroke? It is here that we reach the heart of the matter, for it is here that the mountain-man comes to understand the deepest root of the lightning-rod man's own fearfulness and the connection between "putting one's name down" for a lightning-rod and *becoming* a lightning-rod man.

For it is not only that the lightning-rod man's science discovers potential dangers we cannot at present address. But more importantly, by demonstrat-ing that the deployment of human reason *can* render us in some respect more secure, it invites us to doubt the necessity of other vulnerabilities. If we can do this, might we not be able to do that? Fears and hopes suppressed by the belief that things cannot be otherwise are reawakened and inflamed. No sooner do we address one inconvenience or threat than we are freed to become anxious about another. Repeated success leads us to regard *any* limit to our capacity to act as merely provisional rather than necessary. Thus precisely the *partial efficacy* of our technology undermines our efforts to reconcile ourselves to our essential vulnerability.

By contrast, as the mountain-man reveals in the climactic exchange, he has made his peace with the inevitability of his death, and so, "stand[s] at ease in the hands of [his] God." His calm good cheer, so impressive in the midst of the ferocious storm, is anchored by the conviction that he will die, that he is essentially and inescapably vulnerable: "The hairs of our heads are numbered and the days of our lives." What the mountain-man intuits is that grasping for the added but incomplete security provided by the lightning-rod risks unsettling this conviction, reawakening an unease or anxiety that his faith has helped him put to rest. And note, he is led to this insight *not* by doubting the science that undergirds the lightning-rod, but by learning from it (of the possibility of "the returning-stroke"). Thus his likening of the salesman to Tetzel, the infamous peddler of indulgences: under the cover of offering *additional* assurance, he is in fact sowing disquiet and anxiety. Indeed, his very presence has the effect of spreading unease, and when he is rebuffed, he calls those who turn him away the heretics.

While surely the most important, this is by no means the only cost. In being led to accept security as the chief good, one will adopt the lightning-rod man's outlook on nature, and then his precautions, thus breaking with long established customs—customs that comfort us and help us feel more at home in the world—whenever they contradict the dictates of safety. Upon review, one cannot help but admire how skillfully Melville has woven these into the tale.

The story begins with Melville inviting us to join his mountain-man in admiring the grandeur of nature as visible in the storm. To the mountain-man, the storm is "glorious," "noble," "majestic," "grand." It is not that he is indifferent to safety or comfort, or oblivious to the danger it presents. Rather, for him the storm's beauty and its fearsomeness are part and parcel. By contrast, to the lightning-rod man the storm is all fearsomeness and no beauty, terrifying, awful, inconvenient—requiring all sorts of provisions and accommodations that make one more uncomfortable. One could say that both the lightning-rod man and the mountain-man experience the storm as a reminder of our vulnerability, but whereas the former sees in that vulnerability only a curse, the mountain dweller intuits that this vulnerability is inseparable from experience of the grand and beautiful as such, and so is also a blessing.

Secondly, the mountain-man cherishes his independence, and the lightning-rod man demands deference and obedience. The lightning-rod man presents his device as essentially magical, which is to say, as effective but mysterious because not understood by its beneficiary. He has to be goaded repeatedly to disclose the basis for the claims he makes about his product. He would prefer that his customers simply take his claims on trust. But, as the mountain-man sees, coming to depend on the device without knowing how it operates and thus why it can be relied upon—or the extent to which it is reasonable to rely upon it—wouldn't assuage and may even exacerbate one's anxiety. Is it installed correctly? Did I buy the best model? Has a new and better rod been developed? Should I have it inspected again to ensure it is properly affixed to my house? At every stage we are dependent on the judgments and integrity of others—the expert knowers—which cannot but make us uneasy, the more so when we learn that they disagree among themselves and that rods sometimes fail or are improperly installed, etc.

Finally, the mountain dweller is hospitable, while the lightning-rod man is a poor guest. In the course of the tale we see over and over again that the lightning-rod man will accept no hospitality that does not accord with what he knows will make him more secure, and he will risk nothing for community with his fellows. He doesn't use the door knocker, he won't sit near the fire or in a chair. He forbids the pulling of the bell or the barring of the windows. He can no longer be comfortable when he knows he is at risk, or when he is aware that he hasn't taken every known precaution to make himself safe, and so he makes everyone he encounters uncomfortable as well. And of course, since taking *every* precaution would make going abroad at all impossible, he only goes abroad to correct and even command his fellow men in their own homes. Finally, to the express shock of the solitary mountain-man, the lightning-rod man confesses that he actively avoids his fellows during storms, at least if they are tall, but presumably also if they are not themselves following "best practices" with respect to health and safety during a lightning-storm. We are invited to wonder whether the lightning-rod man would refuse to help a particularly tall man in distress during a storm. He is opposed even to the ringing of church bells during a storm, presumably because doing so is dangerous for the one doing the ringing. We are thus brought to see that adopting the lightning-rod man's recommendations deprives we vulnerable beings of the comfort that comes from community with our fellows, whose community we seek not primarily for any contribution it makes to our security.

III

The primary value, one might even say the indispensability, of science fiction as a literary form is in depicting to us a world still recognizably human but somehow altered by the findings and fruits of modern science. It thus positions us to see the inadequacy of our characteristic tendency to consider technologies as merely neutral tools, the advantages or disadvantages of which are transparent and universal, and the beneficence of which depend upon the ends to which the users put them. Precisely in effecting manifest changes in our situation, technologies effect much subtler, easily overlooked changes in our thinking and therewith to our ways of life. Any truly adequate evaluation of a particular technology must always be with a view to the whole way of life into which it is introduced. Good literature of this kind thus helps us to make a reasoned judgment about technologies, to assess their value, to take their measure.

The peculiar value of Melville's "Lightning-Rod Man" derives from its stark simplicity and radicality. As the final sentence of the tale makes plain, Melville saw in this story a lesson of general applicability. We who tend to think of ourselves as individuals alone in a wild nature recognize ourselves in the mountain-dweller. Like him, we are burdened with the responsibility of plumbing the depths of each new innovation offered to us, and the obvious good it provides will always be clearer than the hidden costs or deprivations it brings. His deliberation with the lightning-rod man is thus a model for us to follow. And the lightning-rod is a peculiarly revealing instance or example to consider. By some reckonings, the lightning-rod is the first piece of modern technology. What makes modern technology distinctive is its being rooted in modern science. For one who wishes to make a reasoned choice about such devices, rather than to merely do the done thing, there is no evading the effort to understand the device's basis in the findings of modern science. Thus the exchange between the mountain-man and the lightning-rod man ostensibly about whether to buy a lightning-rod becomes a dialogue into the understanding of lightning that informs the lightning-rod man's own actions. He is pressed to disclose more and more of what he knows and the reasoning that underlies his comportment. And in being so pressed, the limitations of that understanding reveal themselves, together with the limitations of the lighting-rod itself.

But as the final sentence also indicates, Melville was under no illusions that the mountain-man's example would become the rule rather than the exception. Furthermore, by presenting the mountain-man's defiant refusal to leave the hearth and his clarity about the threat posed by the promise of greater safety to his way of life as anchored by belief in the revealed word of God and therewith a hidden providential order to the whole, Melville would appear to suggest that such was the only promising basis from which the lightning-rod man's appeal to the fears of men could be generally refused. That such was the basis of Melville's own thinking about this matter, however, must remain an open question.

NOTES

In memory of Peter Augustine Lawler. Thank you to Charlie Rubin for inspiring and encouraging my interest in science fiction and science policy; to my father, for pointing me to Melville; to my dear friend Eric Petrie, for the many helpful conversations and editorial suggestions.

1. I will cite by page number from the original edition of *The Piazza Tales* (New York: Dix and Edwards, 1856), 285.

2. Peter Augustine Lawler, "Restless Souls," *The New Atlantis* Number 4 (Winter 2004): 42.

3. "The Acroceraunian hills." Of course, there are no such mountains in the United States. The name means, "Thunder-heights" or "lightning-peaks."

4. Melville, 271.

5. Melville, 272.

6. Melville, 274.

7. Melville, 275.

8. Melville, 278.

9. Melville, 279.

10. Melville, 280–81.

11. Melville, 282–83.

12. Melville, 284.

13. Melville, 284–85. It is worth comparing the mountain-man's view of the rainbow to that of Ishmael in *Moby-Dick* (chapter 85 end).

14. Melville, 285.

15. Allan Moore Emery, "Melville on Science: 'The Lightning-Rod Man,'" *New England Quarterly* 56, no. 4 (December 1983): 555–568. On prior critics, see n.1 on p. 555. See also Sean Silver, "The Temporality of Allegory: Melville's 'The Lightning-Rod Man,'" *Arizona Quarterly* 62, no. 1 (Spring 2006): 1–33; Douglas L. Verdier, "Who is the Lightning-Rod Man?" *Studies in Short Fiction* 18, no. 3 (1981): 273–279.

16. One is tempted to see the mountain-man as a distinctly American type. The mention of Taconics and Hoosics makes clear that we are in New England, though so far as I have been able to discern, there is no town of Criggan. The scornful tone of the lightning-rod man's "Those Canadians are fools" sounds very American, as does the suggestion that everyone knows that Kentuckians are abnormally tall.

17. As the mountain-man quips, "For one who would arm others with fearlessness, you seem unbeseemingly timorous yourself." Melville, 278.

18. See in this connection, Steven Frye, "Melvillean Skepticism and Alternative Modernity in 'The Lightning-Rod Man," *Poe Studies* 39, no. 1 (2006): 120.

19. Melville, 280.

20. More precisely, knowledge of provisional claims of constant conjunction. If it was genuine knowledge of cause then it would, presumably, have some calming effect.

21. Emery, 564, n. 25. I think Marvin Fisher's reading of this moment equally implausible, "'The Lightning-Rod Man': Melville's Testament of Rejection," *Studies in Short Fiction* 7, no. 3 (1970): 436.

22. Lucius Lyon, *A Treatise on Lightning Conductors; compiled from a work on Thunderstorms, by W. S. Harris and Other Standard Authors* (New York: Putnam, 1853), 59–66. Note further that the conclusion of this section relates a number of stories of lightning in or on mountains.

23. Emphasis added.

24. Lyon, 168–169.

BIBLIOGRAPHY

Emery, Allan Moore. "Melville on Science: 'The Lightning-Rod Man.'" *New England Quarterly* 56, no. 4 (December 1983): 555–68.

Fisher, Marvin. "'The Lightning-Rod Man': Melville's Testament of Rejection." *Studies in Short Fiction* 7, no. 3 (1970): 433–38.

Franklin, Benjamin. *Experiments and Observations on Electricity Made at Philadelphia in America*. London: Newberry, 1769.

Frye, Steven. "Melvillean Skepticism and Alternative Modernity in 'The Lightning-Rod Man.'" *Poe Studies* 39, no. 1 (2006): 114–25.

Lawler, Peter Augustine. "Restless Souls." *The New Atlantis* 4 (Winter 2004): 42–6.

Lyon, Lucius. *A Treatise on Lightning Conductors; compiled from a work on Thunderstorms, by W. S. Harris and Other Standard Authors*. New York: Putnam, 1853.

Melville, Herman. *The Piazza Tales*. New York: Dix and Edwards, 1856.

Silver, Sean. "The Temporality of Allegory: Melville's 'The Lightning-Rod Man.'" *Arizona Quarterly* 62, no. 1 (Spring 2006): 1–33.

Verdier, Douglas L. "Who is the Lightning-Rod Man?" *Studies in Short Fiction* 18, no. 3 (1981): 273–79.

Chapter Five

The Head, the Hands, and the Heart

Political Rationalism in Fritz Lang's Metropolis

Damien K. Picariello

I. "THE SILLIEST FILM"

At the time of its release, Fritz Lang's 1927 silent film *Metropolis* met with what are politely called mixed reviews. Writing for *The New York Times*, the science fiction writer H. G. Wells pronounced it "the silliest film." "I do not believe," he continued, "it would be possible to make one sillier. . . . It gives in one eddying concentration almost every possible foolishness, cliché, plati-tude and muddlement about mechanical progress and progress in general, served up with a sauce of sentimentality that is all its own."[1] Fritz Lang himself would later say that he thought *Metropolis* "silly and stupid," and that he "detested it after it was finished."[2]

Metropolis, one of the first science fiction films, is the story of Freder Fredersen, son of the ruler of a futuristic city in which subterranean workers and surface-dwelling managers are both governed by an unforgiving and impersonal scientific method of rule. Freder falls in love with Maria, a beau-tiful and good-hearted advocate for the workers, and the city undergoes a calamitous workers' revolt; after much trial, the revolt ends and the spirit of love and human brotherhood carry the day.

As this brief description makes plain, Wells's charge of sentimentality, at least, is accurate. But it is this same "sauce of sentimentality" that makes the film a profoundly interesting place to explore the theme of political rational-ism, that is, the "attempt to govern political society in the light of reason alone," or the idea that politics is best and most fruitfully approached "on the basis of abstract, calculating reason alone. . ."[3] In its depiction of life in a scientifically managed city of the future, *Metropolis* asks us to examine the notion that the application of reason alone, as embodied in the correct formula or technique, is the best way to approach—and to resolve—the problems of political life.[4]

Wells himself points us squarely, though unintentionally, in this direction. In the film's future city, Wells observes: "the workers are spiritless, hopeless drudges, working reluctantly and mechanically. But a mechanical civilization has no use for mere drudges; the more efficient its machinery the less need there is for the quasi-mechanical minder." Referring to one of his own works, he continues:

> It may indeed create temporary masses of unemployed, and in "The Sleeper Awakes" there was a mass of unemployed people under the hatches. That was written in 1897, when the possibility of restraining the growth of large masses of population had scarcely dawned on the world. It was reasonable then to anticipate an embarrassing underworld of underproductive people. We did not know what to do with the abyss. But there is no excuse for that today.[5]

Wells's blithe embrace of eugenics as a solution to the difficulties created by automation is precise and perfectly responsive to the problem. And yet it is also deeply unsettling. That this latter consideration would not occur to Wells—and, more, that he would overlook the myriad other considerations having to do with family, faith, feeling, dignity, love, etc., that might make his readers recoil from such a suggestion—makes one think that *Metropolis* may be on to something after all. The film's focal phrase—"THE MEDIATOR BETWEEN HEAD AND HANDS MUST BE THE HEART!"—is certainly sentimental.[6] And yet there may be something in this sentimentality that cuts to the core of the approach to human and political questions exemplified by Wells's proposal. As its action progresses, *Metropolis* suggests that political life is—to borrow the language of the film—a matter just as much of the "heart" as of the "head."

Metropolis's critique of political rationalism—its case for "the heart" as opposed to, or in addition to, "the head"—points in two different and yet connected directions. Firstly, this critique, as Wells recognizes, has an economic or class component: the "mechanical civilization" depicted in the film looks a great deal like "the great factory of the industrial capitalist" as described by Marx; its workers—Wells calls them "spiritless, hopeless drudges"—are, in Marx's words, "organized like soldiers . . . daily and hourly enslaved by the machine. . ."[7] This, indeed, is the case made by Maria, who attacks the great city's unequal and unjust living conditions—workers toil below while the rulers administer above—in the name of human brotherhood. But *Metropolis* is not, or is not only, a critique of industrial capitalism. The film goes further, suggesting that a rationalist approach to human organization—which, as we'll see below, is characteristic of but certainly not limited to industrial capitalism—may not be well-suited to political life.

This suggestion, in turn, points us away from the "abstract, calculating reason" from which political rationalism takes its bearings and toward what Aristotle calls "prudence": a virtue that enables us to "deliberate nobly" about "the human things"—how we should live, and how we should organize our communities. But these kinds of questions, which are the kind "the political art examines, admit of much dispute and variability."[8] Unlike political rationalism, which promises precise answers to the questions of human life and human community, prudence delivers its conclusions "roughly and in outline": it "admits of no precise answers."[9] Further, the conclusions of prudence are situational: they depend on circumstances and on the particulars of a given community. For Aristotle, "prudence is not concerned with the universals alone but must also be acquainted with the particulars: it is bound up with action, and action concerns the particulars."[10] This contrasts sharply with the rationalist approach to politics, according to which "the function of reason is precisely to surmount circumstances," to yield conclusions that are universal and exact rather than situational and provisional.[11] The action of *Metropolis* points toward a vision of political life as resistant to rationalist rule, and toward an approach to political life that takes full account of irreducible human complexity—encompassing the sometimes contradictory demands of the head, hands, and heart—and is therefore prudently humble in the conclusions it draws.

II. THE "SCIENTIFIC MANAGEMENT" OF THE CITY

Metropolis opens with the title illuminated on the screen as if projected by lights. As the text fades away, the skyline of a great city comes into focus, a twisting, turning, awe-inspiring and architecturally astounding festival of structure and shadow, radiating majesty and beauty.

The skyline darkens into an outline, and we see in front of us the image of a steel piston, pumping rapidly up and down and flanked by two others. Now the skyline fades as the action of the machines assumes center stage. Lights move across the screen—this time in rapid and orderly lines—and the pistons are replaced by spinning wheels, by rotating cranks and whirling disks, by the turning of monstrous gears and the never-ending back-and-forth motion of metal pumps. The machines are endless, and their motion is unceasing; their kinetic force is both entrancing and disturbing.

The implications of this fatigueless and steel-strong motion are emphasized by the transition onscreen from the sequence of machines to the movement of a giant clock, the twitching hands of which seem to underscore the machines' unrelenting demands. The inner ring of the clock is open, exposing its gear-driven core and reinforcing the affinity between the regular motion of the machines and the relentless advance of measured time.

In 1927, the year *Metropolis* was released, Dexter Kimball, dean of Cornell University's engineering school, declared, "At no time has the influence of Fred Taylor been so great or his memory so secure as at this moment."[12] If "Fordism" and the mass production of automobiles on the assembly line are often said to characterize that era, we might counter that Fordism was "simply 'an application of the Taylor system to mass production': Fordism was the special case, Taylorism the universal." As one engineer put it, "All that the rest of us have done . . . is simply to take [Taylor's] basic ideas, refine them, and adapt them to big-scale modern production."[13] At the heart of things are Frederick Taylor's ideas about the relation between human beings, materials of production, and time—as well as his sense of what is, and what is not, important to take into account when organizing and directing groups of human beings.

These ideas, in Taylor's words, constitute a "true science" of management, "resting upon clearly defined laws, rules, and principles, as a foundation."[14] These laws, rules, and principles are discoverable by systematic investigation into human capacities—investigation that, throughout Taylor's lifetime, often involved the repeated execution of timed tasks.[15] These tasks could then be broken down into sub-tasks—even into individual motions—and the optimal time for executing each component of each task could be determined, as well as the optimal motion at each stage of each task's execution. Each task could then be resolved into the single most efficient series of timed movements, which could be made standard for—and required of—all workers. This emphasis on measurement and standardization also indicates what Taylorism excludes: the initiative and intuition of individual workers, the kind of "craft knowledge" that is acquired through practice, the judgment or prudence that often comes with hands-on experience and is resistant to—indeed, compensates for the shortcomings of—standardization, and the innumerable variations between human beings that makes what is appropriate for one inappropriate for another.[16] The purpose of Taylor's approach, to borrow from the title of a book on Taylor and his system, is to discover and implement "the one best way," to resolve complexity into perfectly efficient simplicity in the organization of human beings.

Metropolis introduces us to a city organized according to the Taylorist conception of human beings, based on principles derived from the Taylorist sense of what is and isn't important to know.[17] It is a city in which those who labor are reduced to their function in, and their utility to, the city; it is a city in which those who rule need not ever actually see their workers, since all necessary information can be gleaned from a finite set of measurements and metrics. It is a city in which "the plan" is first, and the purpose of governance is to ensure that the plan is kept. In its depiction of such a city, *Metropolis* does nothing more than follow out the implications of Taylor's own remarks, which end the "Introduction" to *The Principles of Scientific Management*:

> The illustrations chosen [here] are such as, it is believed, will especially appeal to engineers and to managers of industrial and manufacturing establishments, and also quite as much to all of the men who are working in these establishments. It is hoped, however, that it will be clear to other readers that the same principles can be applied with equal force to all social activities: to the management of our homes; the management of our farms; the management of the business of our tradesmen, large and small; of our churches, our philanthropic institutions, our universities, and our governmental departments. [18]

In other words, the principles of scientific management are applicable to all fields of human endeavor, and promise—unlike Aristotelian prudence—to resolve disputes about "the human things," not "roughly and in outline," but perfectly, precisely, and entirely. [19]

In this sense, scientific management speaks to one of the primary concerns of modern political thought, which is to "guarantee the actualization of wisdom"; that is, to bring life into conformity with thought. [20] This requires that we take our bearings from the distance Machiavelli identifies between "how one lives" and "how one should live." [21] Turning our thoughts away from "how man ought to live" and toward the sustained and methodical examination of "how men actually do live," we may attain "certain or exact or scientific knowledge" of the right way to order any field of human social endeavor: as Taylor would have it, homes, farms, businesses, churches, and governments. [22] This mastery of "the positive science of Nature and history," in Friedrich Engels's words, will allow us to subject both "social forces" and "natural forces . . . more and more to our own will, and by means of them to reach our own ends." [23] Through the attainment of scientific or technical knowledge of human life, we may bring human affairs under the control of reason alone; we may "guarantee the actualization of wisdom." Taylorism and the scientific management of human beings in the name of efficiency embody this drive to master human life and to force it into conformity with the conclusions of reason.

Metropolis shows us the enactment of the principles of scientific management, and also dramatizes these principles being undermined. The film suggests that to claim technical or scientific knowledge of human beings and human society is the height of destructive arrogance; it shows us the awful consequences that follow from reducing human beings to pieces in a plan, and the incoherence of a regime that shuns human complication in favor of mechanical simplicity. If the famous industrial scene in Chaplin's *Modern Times* can be said to depict the merging or melding of man and machine, *Metropolis* can be understood as an exploration of—and, ultimately, a warning against—the Taylorist analogy between machine and man, or the Taylorist reduction of man to machine. The film shows us a political community in which the city and the factory are one, and in which both are arranged according to the same total and totalizing principles. It also shows us this community undermined by the aspects of human existence—love, friendship, family, curiosity, sex—that help to differentiate men from machines, and that are resistant to, and destructive of, standardization and planning.

III. HUMAN BEINGS AND MACHINES

We return to the never-ending motion of the machines, and then to the unceasing advance of the clock, and as the hands converge the words "Shift Change" appear on the screen. Two identical columns of workers stand stock-still as a giant gate slowly opens at the mouth of a tunnel; one column faces toward us, the other away from us.

As the camera pulls back, we begin to realize just how many men are involved in this operation, all dressed identically in dirty coveralls and dark caps, one column returning from work while the other begins its shift. The whistle blows again, and the spent workers file into a giant elevator and descend, motionless, as the intertitles explain:

> Deep below
> the earth's surface
> lay the workers' city [24]

Our first view of the city below the earth shows the endless rectangular light fixtures by which it is illuminated, affixed to a ceiling that meets the tops of numberless blocky buildings. This is the workers' skyline and the workers' sky. As the men file out, we realize that the elevator in which we travelled is flanked by two others, and that the three elevator loads of workers have been preceded by three more—and, presumably, will be followed by more still. The mournful resonance of the score continues as the camera lingers on the workers, still moving in formation toward drab, identical buildings.

The scene fades slowly into darkness.

Support for and reaction against Taylorism were both adamant and vigorous. Scientific management, for Taylor and his supporters, would end the antagonism between workers and owners by removing disputes from the realm of opinion and submitting them to the cool and impartial judgment of science. Disputes over rates of pay would become irrelevant, since such rates were not "a subject to be theorized over," but rather to be settled according to the conclusions of scientific experiment. [25] Under this system, "'collective bargaining . . . becomes of trifling importance.' Should some injustice arise, workers had only to protest and receive 'a careful scientific investigation' into the case."[26] In Taylor's own words, "What constitutes a fair day's work will be a question for scientific investigation, instead of a subject to be bargained and haggled over."[27] The greatest good for employers, employees, and "the whole people," will be brought about through "scientific management, which has for its sole aim the attainment of justice for all . . . parties through impartial scientific investigation of all the elements of the problem."[28] In this rendering, scientific management holds out the prospect, not of settling disputes between classes of men, but of *solving* them, of determining—impartially, scientifically—the correct hours, rates of pay, methods, and conditions of any given field of human activity. Political disputes between men are to be resolved into the scientific administration of things.[29]

For critics of Taylorism, precisely this propensity to resolve all questions into matters of scientific investigation and administration—to relentlessly observe, measure, time, set, and standardize, and to exclude anything that is resistant to measurement and standardization—was its most destructive quality. For Taylor, this was scientific management's philosophical core and greatest promise; for his opponents, the effects of Taylorism on human beings were ominous in the extreme. They complained that it would reduce the worker to an "automaton," a "*factotum* or machine," and that "workers [were] now 'nothing more nor less than human machines to carry out . . . instructions.'"[30]

At bottom, this was a complaint about the way scientific management conceived of human beings, the way it understood the men and women it sought to arrange. Testifying in front of Congress, one proponent of Taylorism was asked "whether he would 'class a man in the same category that you would an ordinary machine.'" He understood a man, he responded, "'as a little portable power plant . . . a mighty delicate and complicated machine. . . . The physical body of the man is constructed on the same mechanical principles as the machine is, except that it is a very much higher development.'" Asked how he knew how hard to drive the human machine, he replied: "'Specialists . . . We employ the specialist who knows what the machine can stand, and we should use the specialist who knows what the human frame can stand.'"[31] Like the Taylorist conception of useful knowledge, this understanding of human beings is conspicuous for what it excludes: the attachments and relationships—familial, romantic, friendly—that bind men to one another above and beyond the demands of utility or function; the multiplicity of roles that human beings take on, which includes but is not limited to—and, crucially, has unavoidable bearing on—a given function in an organizational scheme; and the curiosity that drives human beings to seek out personal experience, face-to-face understanding, and familiarity with that which resists measurement and standardization.

Leaving the workers' city, we move upward and outward. Our ascent brings us to the Club of the Sons and the Eternal Gardens, the liveliness and variety of which force an immediate and sharp contrast with the workers' city below. Here we meet Freder Fredersen, son of the city's master, who thrives and frolics among the "lecture halls and libraries . . . theaters and stadiums."[32] We are struck by the richness, the vigorousness, and the enthusiasm of Freder's existence—and then Freder is struck by Maria.

The doors to the Eternal Gardens open, and framed in the middle of the shot is Maria, a young woman of about Freder's age, surrounded by threadbare children. The camera moves closer, and Maria is never anywhere other than the center of the screen, the focus of Freder's—and our—attention.

We move back and forth between Freder and Maria, as if to emphasize the intensity of the connection that all of a sudden exists between the two, and then Maria speaks to the children. "Look," she says to them, "These are your brothers!"[33] She gestures as if to display the immaculately dressed Freder and his companions to her dirty and barefoot young charges, but it seems as though she more clearly intends the children as display. She looks directly at Freder and repeats: "These are your brothers!"[34] We again alternate between Freder and Maria gazing at one another before Maria and the children are hustled out the door. Freder runs after her, and the music quickens—and becomes both tense and ominous—as we next see him amid the whirling, pulsing machines at the heart of the city.

This encounter between Freder and Maria provides the starting point for—and the driving force behind—the action of *Metropolis*. In this encounter are also found several of the themes that bring the film into contact with the principles of scientific management. Firstly, the encounter between Freder and Maria is a powerfully visual and personal encounter, as indicated by the degree to which the camera lingers on their mutual gaze. Maria's intent in bringing the children to the Eternal Gardens is to display them, to show them to the sons of the city's masters; for Freder, this display is intensely affecting, and prompts the desire for more "face-to-face" encounters, more experience as seen from close up, with his own two eyes. This contrasts sharply with the visual schema according to which Joh Fredersen, Freder's father and the city's "brain," operates: the panorama, the skyline, the undifferentiated block of workers performing the impersonal task.[35] If Freder desires to see for himself, Joh prefers to receive information—to see—via the sequence of signs and figures on a monitor, or through lighted boards indicating function or non-function. It is striking when we learn later in the film that Joh Fredersen—whose plan governs the movements of every worker on every machine—has never actually seen much of what is below the surface of Metropolis.[36]

The encounter between Freder and Maria also brings to our attention different kinds of human roles and relationships, some of which are unaccounted for in Joh Fredersen's governing scheme. In displaying her young charges in the Eternal Gardens, Maria employs familial language—"these are your brothers"—that complicates the relationship between the sons of the rulers and the children of the workers. For Joh, the relation between workers and rulers is based entirely on function: both parties are defined by their function in the city, and relate to one another in terms of this category. The language of family complicates this relationship, in the sense that a familial relation involves bonds of affection and obligation that Joh's emphasis on function elides. Freder's interest in Maria is also—indeed, is primarily—romantic: the relationship he envisions with Maria is based on spontaneous feeling, on desire, rather than on the performance of tasks toward a planned end. As the film continues, Freder will also experience strong feelings of kinship and friendship, both with one of the workers he encounters and with Josaphat, his father's soon-to-be-dismissed functionary. The relationships Freder explores in the film—familial, romantic, friendship—all challenge Joh's function-centric understanding of human beings, just as the roles with which Freder experiments—brother, lover, friend—transcend the bounds of function and are spontaneous rather than planned.

The dichotomy that undergirds these thematic examples is that between simplicity and complexity: a complexity that takes full account of the "tangle and variety" of human experience, and a simplistic rationalism that seeks to abstract from this fullness.[37] This dichotomy points back to Taylorism, and to the Taylorist understanding of human beings. Thus *Metropolis* offers, to repeat, a case against Taylorism that acknowledges but extends beyond the economic or class critique raised above: The most powerful charge against scientific management is not that it may lead to poor working conditions, but rather that it abstracts from the full human being in order to conceive of the "little portable power plant" perfectly defined by its function. The Taylorist analogy between man and machine is based upon this abstraction, as is the particular brand of political rationalism according to which *Metropolis*'s city is governed. Joh Fredersen's rationalist approach to political rule, like Frederick Taylor's approach to management, eschews or elides a great portion of human life: it deals with people as though they were less than what they are.

IV. THE HEAD AND THE HEART

Wandering about in the machine halls below the city, Freder is struck by the relation between the movements of the machines and the movements of their minders, who jerk from left to right in sharp, unsettling unison. Facing toward their work and away from Freder—their faces as if glued to the metal and glass in front of them—each appears bound or joined to his great machine, or perhaps part of it.

Then there is an explosion, caused by a worker unable to keep up with his machine, and the aftermath of this disaster—workers fleeing, falling, injured or dead—prompts Freder to a vision: he looks back at the machine, and its center is transformed into a hideous face, dominated by a gaping, hungry mouth, into which masked overseers feed chained slaves. The image is fantastical, but it also captures a truth about the awful cruelty of the workers' existence, a truth that cannot be captured by the lifeless reports and readouts that will reach Freder's father.

We move now to the new Tower of Babel, where we have our first encounter with Joh Fredersen, the master of Metropolis and the brain of the city. The music turns imposing, as if to convey the weight of the activities taking place, as Joh paces a gigantic office issuing instructions. Behind him, an endless stream of information appears on a large, manned monitor; to the side, a collection of well-dressed clerks attend diligently to a tremendous stack of documents. His massive desk sits in front of a window that seems to take in the entire city.

The office attendants here work as single-mindedly as the laborers below; their rhythm, like that of the machine-workers, emerges from the demands of their work—from the flow of information they attend—rather than from within themselves. But not all the men share Joh's discipline, his absolute focus: Josaphat, employed in attending to the stream of information appearing on the monitor, is distracted by Freder's arrival and approaches the young man. As Freder shares what he's seen with the concerned Josaphat, Joh refocuses his attention on his son—and then swiftly, angrily, on Josaphat, who had not informed him of the accident at the machine. When Joh asks Freder why he entered the "machine halls," Freder responds:

> "I wanted to look into the
> faces of the people whose little
> children are my brothers,
> my sisters. . ."

Sensing Freder's distress, but clearly not sharing his familial feelings, Joh steps over to his massive window and gazes out; Freder approaches and appeals to his father:

> "Your magnificent city,
> Father—and you the brain
> of this city—and all of us
> in the city's light—"[38]

And the city is indeed magnificent: the music turns majestic, and we are presented with shot after shot of towering buildings, futuristic skyline, and architectural feats. But these views, like those from Joh's window, are detached, imposing but not intimate, alive with majesty but devoid of humanity.[39] When Joh explains to Freder that "the depths" are simply "Where [the workers] belong," Freder recoils from his father's coldness. He is affected more by the up-close experience of human misery—by his look "into the faces" of the workers—than by the commanding, distant view from the tower.[40] For Joh, Freder's focus on the personal, the intimate, blinds him to the big picture; for Freder, Joh's big thinking obscures things that are smaller but more important.

The relentless movement of the wall clock catches Freder's eye and sends a shiver down his spine, but Joh is more interested in the arrival of Grot, the foreman of the "Heart Machine," who has discovered plans for a worker uprising. Appalled that Josaphat has again failed to transmit crucial information, Joh dismisses him from service. Freder is horrified at Josaphat's dismissal, reminding his father that his now former clerk will be sent to "the depths"—will become, in other words, one of the workers. But for Joh, this is appropriate: Josaphat's performance proved him unsuited to his function in the office, which means that his abilities would be put to better use below. The bonds of friendship that are soon to form between Freder and Josaphat—sparked by Freder's horror at Josaphat's dismissal—are either alien to Joh or simply irrelevant.

Now, Freder goes below once again, and he is greeted—and frightened—by smoke, motorized carts, and teams of workers trudging along amid the heat and iron. He finds himself mesmerized by the frantic movements of a worker operating—or being operated by—a machine that looks like nothing other than a giant clock.

The symbolism is inescapable: this man is literally joined with the clock, bound to the rhythm of the machine and hostage to its movements. He embodies the relation between time, machines, and the human body upon which Joh Fredersen's city is based, and from which Taylorism takes its bearings: the human being is indistinguishable from the machine. Freder addresses the exhausted man as "Brother," cradles him in his arms, and insists that he wants to "trade lives" with him, manning the machine while the other makes his way up to the surface. Georgy, the worker, obliges, but Freder swiftly finds himself out of step with his mechanical dance partner, unable to operate the machine.

While Freder grapples with the consequences of his rashness, Joh goes to visit Rotwang, the mad inventor. Rotwang has created a robot that can take the form of a human being, a project that Joh wishes to employ for his own purposes.

Rotwang's project seems to confirm his insanity—and yet it fits almost perfectly with the city that Joh Fredersen oversees. Rotwang has created "the man of the future," he says, "The Machine-Man."[41] In his madness, the inventor has captured the city's ideal subject: a fusion of human being and machine, or a being that is human in form but mechanical—perfectly functional, and nothing other than functional—at its core. "Give me another 24 hours," Rotwang promises, "and . . . no one will be able to tell a Machine-Man from a mortal—!"[42]

Turning away from the subject of the Machine-Man, Joh offers the reason for his visit: He needs to learn the truth about the planned workers' rebellion, and he cannot learn it from his office in the tower, nor from his information stream, his lighted indications, and his commanding view. Examining the plans Joh has intercepted, Rotwang identifies them as maps of the catacombs below the city, and the two descend into the depths in order to ascertain the workers' intentions. It becomes clear that Joh has never been to the catacombs before; we are forced to question whether he has ever even seen the workers' city with his own eyes, or observed their strenuous work in person. Both of the things Joh needed to know in order to learn what the workers intend to do—the meaning of the plans, and how to follow them to the destination indicated—are well beyond the means at his disposal: curiosity and firsthand experience would have served him better than endless streams of data. The workers, by virtue of their station beneath the city, know something—something important—that Joh does not. And Rotwang, by virtue of his arcane interests, has information about the mysteries of the city that Joh lacks; indeed, Joh Fredersen's city should not *have* mysteries. What Freder is doing—following his curiosity and seeking out firsthand experience—may provide him with a better education in the workings of the city than his father ever could.

Meanwhile, Freder finds himself increasingly unable to manage his machine, the hands of which, in his imagining, have turned into the hands of a giant clock, the motion of which he cannot control.

Just as he collapses in exhaustion, a new shift of workers arrives, leaving him staggering away from his ill-conceived adventure in substitution. He had recoiled earlier at his father's impersonal attitude toward the workers—he had wanted to understand them as individuals, as unique human beings, rather than as undifferentiated and perfectly replaceable (because perfectly identical) lumps of flesh and bone. But here the truth of his insight has been brought home to him in a powerfully physical way: he is not identical with his "brother," and so cannot substitute himself in his place. Freder, like his father, had failed to differentiate properly: his father between workers, Freder between worker and surface-dweller. Neither man has taken full account of difference and its implications; if Joh relies too much on his head, Freder seems to lean too strongly on his heart.

Following the workers, Freder makes his way down into the catacombs, and arrives at the meeting place just as Joh and Rotwang begin their surveillance. Entering the hall, Freder is shocked and overjoyed to discover Maria standing at the center. Many of the workers have knelt, and Maria begins to speak: "Today I will tell you the legend of THE TOWER OF BABEL . . ." We are then shown the legend, the brief film-within-the-film capturing the tale of "a tower whose top may reach unto the stars!"[43]

Maria's telling emphasizes the tower as a plan, an image in the "minds" of those who "conceived" of it. She also draws our attention to the separation between the minds in which the tower was conceived and the "hands" who were assigned the task of building. Clearly, Maria's tale has significance both for the old and the new Towers of Babel:

> "But the *hands* that built
> the Tower of Babel knew
> nothing of the dream of the
> *brain* that had conceived it."[44]

The theme here is the stark disjunction between the beauty of the plan of the Tower and the harshness and cruelty involved in the actual building. This is powerfully captured by the appearance of the word "BABEL," which both drips blood and glimmers with light and promise. The point of the story, for Maria, is not that one tongue was scattered into different languages, but rather that "mind" and "hands" could not communicate, even in their common tongue: "People spoke the same language, but could not understand each other. . . ."[45] The Tower is destroyed by the very hands that built it, and here we return to an angelic Maria, who shares the moral of her tale, which is also the focal phrase of the film: "THE MEDIATOR BETWEEN HEAD AND HANDS MUST BE THE HEART!"[46] When one of the workers asks the identity of the mediator, Freder is immediately thrust before our eyes.

The score now changes tone and becomes harsher: some of the workers are impatient, and this impatience makes an impression on Joh Fredersen. As Freder and Maria embrace, and Freder offers to act as mediator, Joh instructs Rotwang to "give the Machine-Man the likeness of that girl."[47] Joh intends to turn the workers against Maria, and therefore to render them leaderless and—presumably—unable to act. But here, too, Joh is missing something important: Rotwang alone has seen the embrace between Maria and Freder. The plan Joh formulates to perform his function as the city's "brain"—to decapitate the workers' rebellion and therefore ensure that they continue to peacefully and dependably attend the machines—will do great violence to the happiness of his son; Joh's role as "brain" is in direct conflict with his role as father.

Rotwang puts Joh's plan into action, and in one of the most visually arresting sequences in the film, the Machine-Maria is created.

This is in many ways the climactic moment of *Metropolis*. Perhaps the governing theme of the film—the distinction between men and machines, and the blurring of this distinction—is enacted before our eyes, as machine and human being are merged into what Rotwang has identified as "the man of the future." This new being would seem the ideal subject of Joh Freder-sen's city, the perfectly functional entity that Joh imagines when he plans and directs. That the Machine-Man will eventually undermine the city for which it is perfectly suited—that Joh's ideal subject will prove his undoing—speaks to the incommensurability or disharmony between human being and machine. Joh's dream is unnatural; his ideal subject is the herald of his doom.

V. "KILL THEM—THE MACHINES—!!"

Some brief time has passed, and the Machine-Maria has sown discord and despair among the men of the city's upper classes, drawing them away from their duties with a seductive nightclub floor show and provoking them into rivalry with one another. This is something Joh Fredersen had not counted on: the power of sexual desire did not figure into his function-centric ideal of human behavior. In fact, the Machine-Maria has thrown the city's upper classes into disorder precisely because of their inability to act as Machine-Men, because of the human desires that pull them away from what Joh considers their proper place.[48] But this has not distracted Joh from his broad-er aim, and we are now shown Joh's plan in action, as the Machine-Maria incites rebellion among the workers. Her movements as she speaks are rapid and provocative, her expression both inviting and challenging, and she seems to all but pull the workers into her with her outstretched hands.

As Machine-Maria speaks to the workers, we find her using Joh's own ideas—and one of the tropes of Taylorism—against him. In his governance of the city, Joh had conflated human beings with machines; he had arranged things as though a human being was no more than "a little portable power plant . . . a mighty delicate and complicated machine."[49] Now the Machine-Maria exposes the dysfunction at the heart of this analogy, the inadequacy of this conflation, by turning the mechanical into the organic in her rhetoric. "Who is the living food for the machines in Metropolis?" she asks.

> Who feeds the machines
> with their own flesh—?!
> Let the machines starve,
> you fools—! Let them die—!!
> Kill them—the machines—!![50]

The Machine-Maria urges the workers to destroy the "Heart Machine," over-seen by Grot himself, who protests: "If the Heart Machine is destroyed, the entire workers' city will be flooded—!!"[51] Grot is overpowered and the

Machine-Maria sets in motion the Heart Machine's destruction—but the workers, in their frenzy, have forgotten their children in the city below. Luckily, Maria—the real Maria—reunites with Freder in the workers' city, and with Josaphat's help they herd the children out of the city and make the arduous climb up the airshafts, the only available means of escape.

Meanwhile, the frenzied workers continue to dance around the destroyed Heart Machine, as if rejoicing at the death of a hated god. In his office, Joh Fredersen is consumed by worry, his once proud and erect bearing giving way to hunched and agitated concern. "I must know," he howls at his assistant, Slim, "Where is my son?!!!"[52] Slim responds, and in his response is made clear the fullness of Joh's obtuseness and the magnitude of its consequences: "Tomorrow, thousands will ask in fury and desperation: Joh Fredersen, where is my son—!"[53] Joh, helpless, can only close his eyes and cover his ears; it is too late for him to put right his mistakes. He had overlooked, or disregarded, the familial roles and relationships of others; now his own family is being taken from him.

We return to Grot, the foreman of the Heart Machine, who cries out to the workers: "Where are your children??!"[54] When Grot details the destruction of the city below, the workers are thrown into violent mourning; when he asks who incited them to such folly, their sadness turns to anger: "It's the witch's fault," one cries out, by which she means the Machine-Maria.[55]

But it isn't the Machine-Maria's fault, of course; the Machine-Maria was merely a spark, a catalyst, exposing the workers' own destructive oversimplifications. The workers had narrowed their vision in the same fashion as had Joh Fredersen: they reduced themselves to their function in the city—they saw themselves as workers alone—and failed to account for their roles as husbands, wives, fathers, mothers, aunts and uncles, and so forth. In abandoning their children in order to destroy the machines—in forgetting that they were familial in addition to laboring beings—the workers have acted as though Joh's reductive understanding of their lives were true. Maria—the real Maria—had spoken to the workers of family, of affection, of relationships animated and characterized by more than functional utility; she had spoken of the need for the "heart," and in the language of brotherhood. She had taken the richness and variety of their lives as her starting point, even amid the crushing monotony of their work. The language of the Machine-Maria, on the other hand, had blurred the lines between machine and human—had imagined machines that carry out organic processes: eat, live, die—and had therefore undercut the crucial differences between human beings and machines, which differences consist precisely in the richness, variety, and complexity of human, as distinct from mechanical, existence. Thus roused and tempted, the workers forgot their children—forgot the physical manifestations of their complex humanity—and went to destroy the machines as though setting after a living, breathing, human enemy rather than an artfully arranged pile of iron.

The workers eventually seize the Machine-Maria and burn her at the stake, melting away the "skin" that had covered her steel skeleton and revealing her true form. A sequence in which Rotwang is killed leads to a final scene at the entrance to an old church, around which the workers are assembled. Joh, Freder, and Maria emerge from the church, and Grot walks to greet them. Grot extends his hand to Joh, and Joh, at Maria and Freder's prompting, begins to extend his—then hesitates. Maria approaches Freder, and reminds him of his role: "Head and hands want to join together, but they don't have the heart to do it. . . . Oh mediator, show them the way to each other."[56] Freder speaks encouragingly to his father, then takes both men's hands in his own and joins them together. As the score concludes triumphantly, the two men clasp hands, and the film's focal phrase appears again onscreen: "THE MEDIATOR BETWEEN HEAD AND HANDS MUST BE THE HEART!"[57]

VI. POLITICAL RATIONALISM AND POLITICAL RULE

Metropolis is nakedly, unashamedly sentimental: in its staging of the three-sided battle between the "head," the "hands," and the "heart," it makes no secret of where its sympathies lie. It is a story of plans gone awry, order overtaken by chaos, human beings shattered, and human relationships torn asunder—all mended and redeemed by the power of fellow-feeling and love. It aligns us with Freder's naïveté and guides us toward what is ostensibly the most naïve of approaches to the problems of social and political organization. Taken as a set of literal recommendations, or as a model for how we should make decisions about political life, the suggestions that emerge from the film—reason and its technical fruits are inherently odious, the wisest insights emerge from the unreflective emotional lives of childlike people, the impulses that follow from love are more reliable than the conclusions derived from calculation, one should at all costs avoid making robots that look like humans—seem to confirm Wells's judgment that *Metropolis* is, in fact, "the silliest film."[58]

But taken less programmatically, as a set of provocations for thinking about the place of reason in social and political organization, the film helpfully illuminates some of the blind spots of a rationalist approach to politics. These blind spots are evidenced by Wells's blithe suggestion that we explore "the possibility of restraining the growth of large masses of population," or that we use reason and the tools provided by science to accommodate human reproduction to projected societal need.[59] These blind spots also appear in Joh Fredersen's rule in the city, in which the techniques of the scientifically managed workplace are applied to the whole of social and political organization. The city's destruction emerges from these blind spots, and the film is most interesting not as a spur to total reorientation away from the "head" and toward the "heart," but rather as the strongest possible case in favor of the "heart," which points ultimately to the need for Joh's rationalism and Freder's sentimentalism—and, of course, Grot's powerful "hands"—to mediate with one another, or for the considerations that emerge from each to be taken into account. On this reading, the film prompts us not to exchange one sort of simplicity for another, but rather to embrace the kind of complexity that can only be negotiated by an entirely human—not mechanical, and never precise—prudence.

This, in turn, points us toward what Aristotle calls "political rule," the sort of rule proper to a political community made up of complex human beings with layered and interlocking sets of roles, obligations, and relationships, "in accordance with which one rules those who are similar in stock and free."[60] If Joh Fredersen's rule applies the techniques of scientific management to governance, and in so doing attempts to resolve politics into administration, Aristotle's understanding of political rule recognizes that the kinds of things that "the political art examines, admit of much dispute and variability," and are therefore not susceptible to perfect or complete resolution.[61] In this understanding, politics can never be administered or scientifically managed away, and prudence is always prudently aware of its own limitations.

NOTES

This chapter is a revision of one of the chapters of my dissertation, "Political Rationalism in Unlikely Places." Thanks are due to the members of my dissertation committee: Arlene Saxonhouse, Don Herzog, Mika LaVaque-Manty, and Michael Makin. I'm also grateful for comments provided by my fellow panelists at the 2014 meetings of the Southern and Western Political Science Associations. The Earhart Foundation, the University of Michigan Department of Political Science, and the Rackham Graduate School at the University of Michigan generously provided funding during the course of this project. I owe special gratitude, as always, to Erin.

1. H. G. Wells, "Mr. Wells Reviews a Current Film," *The New York Times Magazine*, April 17, 1927, 4 and 22. Reprinted in Michael Minden and Holger Bachmann, eds., *Fritz Lang's* Metropolis: *Cinematic Visions of Technology and Fear* (New York: Camden House, 2000), 94.

2. Holger Bachmann, "Introduction," in Minden and Bachmann, 3. Though Lang had said much earlier: "[E]verything I have to say and will never be able to express in words is written down in the black and white film writing of 'Metropolis,' and if I did not succeed in expressing myself there, I will certainly not find the expression here [in words]" (45).

3. Peter J. Ahrensdorf, "The Limits of Political Rationalism: Enlightenment and Religion in Oedipus the Tyrant," *The Journal of Politics* 66, no. 3 (August 2004): 773; Arlene W. Saxonhouse, "The Tyranny of Reason in the World of the Polis," *The American Political Science Review* 82, no. 4 (December 1988): 1272.

4. I'm drawing on Michael Oakeshott, "Rationalism in Politics," in *Rationalism in Politics and Other Essays* (Indianapolis, IN: Liberty Fund, 1991).

5. Wells, in Minden and Bachmann, 96.

6. *Metropolis*, directed by Fritz Lang (1927; Germany: Kino International, 2010), DVD.

7. Karl Marx, *The Communist Manifesto* (New York: W.W. Norton & Co., 1988), 61–62. I've adjusted the spelling slightly.

8. *Aristotle's Nicomachean Ethics*, trans. Robert C. Bartlett and Susan D. Collins (Chicago: University of Chicago Press, 2011), Book 6, Chap. 5, 1140a24–26; 6, 7, 1141b9; 1, 3, 1094b15–16.

9. Arlene W. Saxonhouse, *Fear of Diversity: The Birth of Political Science in Ancient Greek Thought* (Chicago: The University of Chicago Press, 1992), 207.

10. *Aristotle's Nicomachean Ethics*, 6, 7, 1141b15–17.

11. Oakeshott, "Rationalism in Politics," 10.

12. Kimball, of course, is not talking about the film *Metropolis*. Robert Kanigel, *The One Best Way: Frederick Winslow Taylor and the Enigma of Efficiency* (New York: Viking, 1997), 494. In Weimar, Germany, according to Kanigel, the embrace of Taylorist principles was known as *Rationalisierung*—rationalization. As Kanigel also notes, "By 1927, a scholarly bibliography on scientific management in Germany was forty pages long" (527). Others have commented on the link between *Metropolis* and Taylorism, including Ludmilla Jordanova, "Science, Machines, and Gender," in Minden and Bachmann.

13. Kanigel, 498.

14. Frederick Winslow Taylor, *The Principles of Scientific Management* (Easton, PA: Hive Company, 1985), 7.

15. The following description of Taylor's process is drawn from Kanigel. See also Taylor, 117–118.

16. Kanigel says of Taylor's early efforts at standardization: "Traditional craft know-how was being reduced to scientific data and passing from workman to manager, from shop floor to front office" (179). Taylor himself refers to this same process as "the gradual substitution of science for rule of thumb throughout the mechanic arts" (25).

17. I'm not aware of any evidence that Lang was familiar with Taylorism, but see note 12 above for more on the subject.

18. Taylor, 8.

19. *Aristotle's Nicomachean Ethics*, 6, 7, 1141b9; Saxonhouse, *Fear of Diversity*, 207.

20. Leo Strauss, *Natural Right and History* (Chicago: University of Chicago Press, 1953), 171.

21. Niccolò Machiavelli, *The Prince*, trans. Harvey C. Mansfield (Chicago: University of Chicago Press, 1998), 61.

22. Strauss, 178–179.

23. Friedrich Engels, "Socialism: Utopian and Scientific," in *The Marx-Engels Reader*, ed. Robert C. Tucker (New York: W.W. Norton & Co., 1978), 712.

24. *Metropolis.*

25. Kanigel, 213.

26. Kanigel, 476; the quotations are Taylor speaking.

27. Taylor, 143.

28. Taylor, 138–139.

29. Engels, 689.

30. Kanigel, 444–445; 462.

31. Kanigel, 460.

32. *Metropolis.*

33. *Metropolis.*

34. *Metropolis.*

35. In the version of the film released in the United States, Joh Fredersen was known as "John Masterman"; see the American film reviews found in Minden and Bachmann.

36. This way of understanding vision and perspective owes much to James Scott, *Seeing Like a State* (New Haven, CT: Yale University Press, 1998).

37. Oakeshott, "Rationalism in Politics," 6.

38. *Metropolis.*

39. Again, this way of understanding vision and perspective owes much to Scott, *Seeing Like a State.*

40. *Metropolis.*
41. *Metropolis.*
42. *Metropolis.*
43. *Metropolis.*
44. *Metropolis.*
45. *Metropolis.*
46. *Metropolis.*
47. *Metropolis.*
48. For more, see Jordanova, "Science, Machines, and Gender," and Andreas Huyssen, "The Vamp and the Machine," in Minden and Bachmann.
49. Kanigel, 460.
50. *Metropolis.* I've condensed multiple intertitles into a single quotation here.
51. *Metropolis.*
52. *Metropolis.*
53. *Metropolis.*
54. *Metropolis.*
55. *Metropolis.*
56. *Metropolis.*
57. *Metropolis.*
58. H. G. Wells in Minden and Bachmann.
59. H. G. Wells in Minden and Bachmann.
60. Aristotle, *The Politics*, trans. Carnes Lord (Chicago: University of Chicago Press, 1985) Book 3, Chapter 4, 1277b7–9.
61. *Aristotle's Nicomachean Ethics*, 1, 3, 1094b15–16.

BIBLIOGRAPHY

Ahrensdorf, Peter J. "The Limits of Political Rationalism: Enlightenment and Religion in Oedipus the Tyrant." *The Journal of Politics* 66, no. 3 (August 2004).
Aristotle's Nicomachean Ethics. Translated by Robert C. Bartlett and Susan D. Collins. Chicago: University of Chicago Press, 2011.
Aristotle. *The Politics*. Translated by Carnes Lord. Chicago: University of Chicago Press, 1985.
Bachmann, Holger. "Introduction." In *Fritz Lang's* Metropolis: *Cinematic Visions of Technology and Fear*, edited by Michael Minden and Holger Bachmann. New York: Camden House, 2000.
Engels, Friedrich. "Socialism: Utopian and Scientific." In *The Marx-Engels Reader*, edited by Robert C. Tucker. New York: W.W. Norton & Co., 1978.
Huyssen, Andreas. "The Vamp and the Machine." In *Fritz Lang's* Metropolis: *Cinematic Visions of Technology and Fear*, edited by Michael Minden and Holger Bachmann. New York: Camden House, 2000.
Jordanova, Ludmilla. "Science, Machines, and Gender." In *Fritz Lang's* Metropolis: *Cinematic Visions of Technology and Fear*, edited by Michael Minden and Holger Bachmann. New York: Camden House, 2000.
Kanigel, Robert. *The One Best Way: Frederick Winslow Taylor and the Enigma of Efficiency.* New York: Viking, 1997.
Lang, Fritz, dir. *Metropolis.* 1927; Germany: Kino International, 2010. DVD.
Machiavelli, Niccolò. *The Prince*. Translated by Harvey C. Mansfield. Chicago: University of Chicago Press, 1998.
Marx, Karl. *The Communist Manifesto*. New York: W.W. Norton & Co., 1988.
Oakeshott, Michael. "Rationalism in Politics." In *Rationalism in Politics and Other Essays*. Indianapolis, IN: Liberty Fund, 1991.
Picariello, Damien. "Political Rationalism in Unlikely Places." PhD diss., University of Michigan, 2014.
Saxonhouse, Arlene W. *Fear of Diversity: The Birth of Political Science in Ancient Greek Thought*. Chicago: The University of Chicago Press, 1992.

———. "The Tyranny of Reason in the World of the Polis." *The American Political Science Review* 82, no. 4 (December 1988).

Scott, James. *Seeing Like a State*. New Haven, CT: Yale University Press, 1998.

Strauss, Leo. *Natural Right and History*. Chicago: University of Chicago Press, 1953.

Taylor, Frederick Winslow. *The Principles of Scientific Management*. Easton, PA: Hive Company, 1985.

Wells, H. G. "Mr. Wells Reviews a Current Film." *The New York Times Magazine*, April 17, 1927. Reprinted in Minden and Bachmann.

Chapter Six

Technology and Human Nature in Aldous Huxley's *Brave New World*

Nivedita Bagchi

Written in 1931 and published in 1932, Aldous Huxley's *Brave New World* conceptualized a world where bureaucracy and science have melded together to form a new type of dystopia. Unlike Yevgeny Zamyatin's *We*, which was published in 1924, Huxley did not depict a political system which controlled its citizens through restrictions of their desires. Rather, *Brave New World* depicts a state of plenty, where the citizens behave in any licentious way they please. Set six hundred years in the future in London, it depicts an industrialized and standardized world called the World State. Babies are bred in hatcheries. They are genetically sorted into one of five specific hierarchical classes. Each class fulfills clear class roles. These roles are then reinforced through conditioning by the state. Each caste is made aware of its own importance and how it is different from, and its life superior to, the lives of other classes. The World State is controlled by a bureaucratic, scientific elite called Controllers and exemplified by the character of Mustafa Mond. This state seeks to promote total stability in order to encourage continuous consumption. In the process, the Controllers attempt to exert complete control over the society by eliminating history and controlling human nature.

As we shall see, Huxley believed that the World State portends a new form of dictatorship that would be made possible through scientific and technological developments combined with the power of the state. *Brave New World* warns that new technologies, combined with a scientific and administrative bureaucracy, would lead to the formation of a new world where the ultimate god would be a capitalist one—and where stability would be ensured at all costs in order to promote consumption. Unlike previous dystopias which repressed its inhabitants, this world is one in which people are allowed to indulge their desires. The World State creates people, trains them to consume more, and shortens the gap between desiring something and fulfilling it. In fact, the relationship between desire and its fulfilment in this world is deceptive since the state tells the people what to desire and then provides the means to fulfill these desires. While the people appear to get what they want, it is also true that they only desire what they can have; they never desire what they cannot have. The people in this dystopia never resist their servitude; they love their lives and never understand that they are not free. This form of dictatorship can be established in any state and therefore, according to Huxley: "rulers will re-establish democratic forms, quite confident that the sovereign people will always vote as they themselves intend it to vote. And the sovereign people will go to the polling booths firmly believing itself to be exercising a free and rational choice, but in fact absolutely predestined by a lifelong course of scientifically designed propaganda."[1] Dictatorship now allows licentiousness, promotes instant gratification of desires, and makes people believe that they are free and happy while undermining their individualism and freedom. Through science and technology, the World State eliminates independent thought, destroys the concepts of family and love, and aims at promoting complete stability in an attempt to increase consumerism. At the same time, Huxley shows that every society attempts to condition its people to a certain extent and that it is not possible for any state to completely suppress all elements of individuality.

The reader may draw three main conclusions from these elements of the book. First, Huxley shows the power of science and technology, especially when combined with the power of the state, to condition people. Second, he shows the ways in which human nature resists the conditioning applied through science and technology. Third, he shows that those twin forces can be a force for both good and evil—lack of science and technology is as much of an evil as using it to its full potential for the wrong reasons. As we shall see in Huxley's description of the Savage Reservations, life without science and technology can be as limiting as a life which is entirely dependent on it. Huxley, therefore, posits that a new type of dystopia is both possible and yet susceptible to resistance and reform.

THE ROLE OF TECHNOLOGY IN THE WORLD STATE

Huxley's World State is based on the principle that the secret to happiness and virtue is liking what you do. At the same time, the state wants to ensure that its citizens do what the state wants them to do. These two principles are harmonized by technology and pharmacology. Technology and pharmacology are used by the state to create human beings in the image that would aid the state the most. The state ensures that the people are designed for certain jobs and like the jobs they are designed to do. It ensures that people do not desire what they cannot get. In fact, the Controller defines happiness as follows: "People are happy; they get what they want, and they never want what they can't get."[2] Therefore, the World State believes that lack of true freedom and choice is, in fact, what ensures that people are happy. The World State promotes stability in order to ensure instant gratification of most physical desires which, they claim, will make people happy by fulfilling their desires. It also provides escapes such as soma which would minimize the impact of unfulfilled desires.

The book opens in the hatcheries which is where babies are decanted in the World State. Babies are decanted as one of five classes—Alphas, Betas, Gammas, Deltas, and Epsilons. The first two classes do not have embryos multiplied, but the last three classes go through the Bokanovsky's Process which multiplies eggs to create sets of twins. In some cases, ninety-six human beings are created out of one egg, which this world touts as progress. This process of decanting babies serves multiple purposes for the state. First, the babies go through a process which "predestines" them to certain characteristics which are needed by their particular class. The language of predestination is Huxley's nod to the human capacity to play God using technology. Epsilons, for instance, are deprived of oxygen in order to ensure that they lack intelligence. Those that are meant to work in the tropics are taught to love heat and hate cold. Second, it creates "standard men and women; in uniform batches" which is "mass production applied to biology."[3] Third, it eliminates the possibility of individuality which is the source of instability in society—eliminates it, at least, in the lower three classes.

After decanting these human beings, all babies are then put through a rigid process of conditioning. This conditioning is meant to make "people like their unescapable social destiny."[4] Babies are taught to associate books and flowers with electric shocks and therefore to avoid both books and nature. The explanation given for this is simple: at first, love of nature was fostered to make people travel to the countryside and consume transportation. But it soon became obvious that love for nature does not increase consumption of anything other than transportation. Therefore, the state changed the goal to making the people hate nature but travel to the countryside for sporting events which allowed greater opportunities for consumption. As for reading books, books can be the gateway to revolutionary ideas which destroy the conditioning of the classes and destabilize society.

The second method of conditioning is sleep-teaching or hypnopaedia. Huxley makes it clear that hypnopaedia is for moral teaching and not intellectual development. Each class is taught to feel superior to the lower classes and given reasons why it is best not to be in the classes higher than the class they are in. For instance, Betas are taught that Alphas work too hard and wear grey—and this is why they do not want to be Alphas. This method consists of reciting axioms to the children while they sleep and repeating the same axioms over and over again. This is done till "at last the child's mind is these suggestions, and the sum of the suggestions is the child's mind. And not the child's mind only. The adult's mind too—all his life long."[5] The fact that they are successful is seen throughout the book in the fact that, at crucial moments, key characters explain their world to outsiders through these axioms.

The final means of ensuring stability is through the use of soma. Soma is a drug which allows the people to take a holiday from reality. Taken in small doses, this drug erases the past and the future, allowing one to live solely in the present. It makes people happy with their immediate circumstances. In the book, soma is presented as a substitute for religion, in general, and Christianity, in particular. In other words, those who take soma are able to let go of guilt, anxiety, and fear, and live in one's immediate moment. It allows people to escape self-consciousness. The effectiveness of combining hypnopaedic teachings with soma is seen in Lenina's attempt to comfort herself during her trip to the Savage Reservations where she repeats mindlessly, "Was and will make me ill. I take a gramme and only am" while taking soma.[6] In other words, hypnopaedia has taught her to take soma in order to block out the past and the future and to live contentedly in the present.

NATURE FIGHTS BACK

In spite of the success of the World State in producing human beings who fit the system, Huxley demonstrates that it may not be entirely possible, or even desirable, to condition all individuals within the state. The first reason that this may prove impossible is that the World State needs intelligent workers who can independently carry on the business of administering the state, leading the state to breed classes differently based on their status within society. Since the Alphas and Betas need to administer the state, they do not go through the Bokanovsky Process, which leads to a proliferation of one egg into multiple individuals. This ensures that Alphas and Betas are the most intelligent classes within the state. Yet, Huxley makes it clear that the fact that Alphas and Betas go from one egg to one adult is a problem. As we will see, it is the Alphas and the Betas who are prone to resisting their decanted natures and their conditioning. While Alphas and Betas go through the same conditioning as the lower three classes, their conditioning alone proves to be inadequate to suppress individuality. In this sense, readers are shown that conditioning alone cannot control all individuals completely. It is made clear that Alphas have gone against the conditioning of the system in the past and these Alphas had to be relegated to distant islands as a punishment.

The World State is clearly aware of the potential problem that Alphas and Betas may pose. As the Director says, intelligent Alphas should consciously accept the conditioning of the state. In other words: "Alphas are so conditioned that they do not have to be infantile in their emotional behavior. But that is all the more reason for their making a special effort to conform. It is their duty to be infantile, even against their inclination."[7] It is their moral responsibility to play a part, to pretend to be what they are not. Unorthodox behavior is a threat to society and it is the responsibility of the upper classes to demonstrate conventional behavior at all times. This is displayed in the character of Mustafa Mond who makes it clear that he rejected science to take the position of the Controller, even though he finds the demands of the job wearying. Therefore, the stability of the state has to be preserved, not only through scientific and technological advancements and conditioning, but also through social pressure to fit in, regardless of one's personal feelings.

The second reason for the remnants of individuality in the World State is the possibility that there may be human error in using technology. The cause for human error may vary. At one point in the story, Lenina is so distracted by her feelings for John that she makes a mistake while working with the embryos. This mistake results in the death of a young Alpha-Minus, who dies of a disease which had been eradicated in the World State. Thus, in this example, Lenina's emotions cause her to make a mistake.

Finally, Huxley shows that nature may inexplicably assert itself. The fact remains, as Henry Foster says, that some people "don't respond properly to conditioning."[8] This is true for a minor character, Benito Hoover, who is so good-natured that he does not need to take soma to get away from the reality of his life.

The influence of these factors in resisting the conditioning of the state is seen throughout the book. The characters who act outside of the expected norms of this World State are all Aphas and Betas—Bernard Marx, Helmholtz Watson, and Lenina. Bernard Marx is a member of the Alphas whose job is to help condition the children after they are decanted. There is one striking physical fact about him: he is significantly shorter than other Alphas. Since height is related to intelligence and command in this society, Bernard Marx is always acutely aware of his lack of physical stature. Emotionally, he feels himself to be different from other Alphas. He likes being alone, he rejects the continuous changing of sexual partners, and he dreams of being an individual. Bernard Marx wants to be free of his social conditioning. The rumor is that human error is at fault for these differences—that Bernard Marx mistakenly had alcohol put into his blood-surrogate, a process of treatment which is reserved for Gammas. Therefore, at least his physical difference is blamed on human error in using technology, and the implication is that the physical difference leads to emotional differences.

Helmholtz Watson, also an Alpha, is a lecturer at the College of Emotional Engineering, in the Writing Division. He, unlike Bernard Marx, looks every bit an Alpha-Plus but is perceived by others as having almost "too much ability." Watson is friends with Bernard Marx; both men are acutely aware of their individuality. Readers are made aware that a "physical shortcoming could produce a kind of mental excess. The process, it seemed, was reversible. Mental excess could produce, for its own purposes, the voluntary blindness and deafness of deliberate solitude, the artificial impotence of asceticism."[9] Too much intelligence in Watson and lack of height for Marx (as compared to his class) lead to feelings of individuality and an inability to meld effortlessly in the social body. Being different from others (in both positive and negative ways) makes it difficult to fit in.

Lenina, a Beta and the subject of Bernard Marx's desire for most of the book, desires to be monogamous from the start of the book. In a world where everyone is supposed to belong to everyone else, this is shocking and considered unsocial. When her character is introduced to the readers, she has been sleeping exclusively with Henry Foster for four months, a fact which is shocking to her friend. However, aware that her desires violate the norms and conditioning of the World State, she routinely uses the axioms learnedt through hypnopaedia and soma to escape from this desire and from all other realities of her life which she wishes to escape. Lenina's desire for monogamy may be Huxley's way of demonstrating that nature may be inescapable.

While Helmholtz Watson embraces his difference from the other Alphas, the characters of Lenina and Marx show intense tension between their conditioning and their desires. Both characters are aware of the conflict between their desires and their conditioning and both attempt to periodically act as their state wants them to act in order to fit in. Lenina, for instance, desires monogamy and yet, aware of how that desire violates the norms of this society, forces herself to act non-monogamously in order to fit in. Both act outside the mold dictated by the state and both dislike the consequences of breaking out of the mold.

Thus, these characters show that the decanting and conditioning are not always 100 percent successful. In addition, it is also made clear that these are not isolated incidents. At the end of the book, the Controller, Mustafa Mond, reveals that there are islands where those individuals who "have got too self-consciously individual to fit into community life" are exiled.[10] Thus, it is clear that the possibility of individuality always exists. This possibility is demonstrated through moments of individuality shining through, even for the most well-adjusted Alphas. The Director of the Center where Bernard Marx works, for instance, gives in to momentary weakness and tells Bernard the story of how he had gone with a girl to the Savage Reservations and lost her there. The storytelling itself is a break with the traditions of this state which discourages discussion of the past. Similarly, Henry Foster, who seems to be a model citizen, has moments where he emphasizes individuality rather than social cohesion. Watching the switchback where the dead are dispersed, he muses that the puff of smoke was once a person and wonders which caste they were a part of. Thus, he points to the individual life of the dead instead of simply accepting their social contributions in life and death. However, he quickly reverts back to the state's position that individuality is irrelevant because these people were all happy when they were alive, because everybody is happy in this world.

Finally, Huxley shows that definitions of "natural" are based on conditioning. In other words, what we assume to be "natural" may depend on our experiences, our education, and our social and political conditioning. In a letter to Mustafa Mond, Marx, writing about John's attachment to his mother, Linda, writes about how it is an "interesting example of the way in which early conditioning can be made to modify and even run counter to natural impulses (in this case, the impulse to recoil from an unpleasant object)."[11] Thus, Marx makes the point that it is natural to "recoil" from something which is ugly but he completely discounts the possibility that affection may be natural too. Since this world has eliminated mothers and motherhood, he is unable to understand that relationship and assumes that it is "unnatural." He assumes that it is John's early conditioning which attaches him to Linda. Like Mustafa Mond, Marx makes it clear that he believes that instinctual beliefs can be overcome through conditioning, in spite of his own struggle against his conditioning.

ESCHEWING TECHNOLOGY FOR A RETURN TO NATURE?

Does Huxley's position that science and technology can be used to suppress human individuality and freedom imply that he thinks that human beings should discard all technological progress and return to nature? Is he advocating a version of life as led by Rousseau's natural man? While Rousseau clearly understood that human beings could not permanently live in the state of nature, he believed that the best stage of development for the human species would be an intermediary stage between the state of nature and civil society. Huxley depicts no such intermediate stage in this book. In the book, the World State is juxtaposed against the "Savage Reservations." These are the uncivilized parts of the world, guarded by electrified fences, and populated by tribes who bring up their children based on their own beliefs and without access to the comforts of the World State and its technology. Bernard Marx invites Lenina to visit the Savage Reservations with him. Before he leaves, he hears the story of his Director's visit to the Savage Reservations where he lost the woman whom he went with. During the course of their visit, Lenina and Marx find the woman, Linda, and her son, John. Marx decides to bring them both back to the civilized world with him.

The depiction of the Savage Reservation shows a world which harbors some of the institutions which no longer exist in the World State. However, Huxley equivocates on the value and positivity of these institutions as they are depicted in the Savage Reservations. In other words, the Savage Reservations are no golden age for humankind nor do these more traditional ideas create an ideal state. Huxley acknowledged that neither the World State nor the Savage Reservations were meant as depictions of the kind of world human beings would want to live in. Babies are born, not decanted. Religion exists in many different forms. Families live together. Human beings grow sick and old. There is no soma, no way to escape the present. They do have alcohol but this has undesirable side-effects, unlike soma. In juxtaposing these depictions of the Savage Reservations and the World State, Huxley simultaneously shows how institutions like a family may be both desirable and problematic. In the World State, people age but they do not look old. They are able to carry on the same activities till death. This is not true of the Savage Reservations. Lenina is shocked by what old age looks like. Similarly, the idea of Linda as a mother is repulsive to Linda herself, to Lenina, and to the citizens of the World State. In fact, the description given of families loathingly by Mustafa Mond seems to be replicated in the Savage Reservations: "Home, home—a few small rooms, stiflingly over-inhabited by a man, by a periodically teeming woman, by a rabble of boys and girls of all ages. No air, no space; an understerilized prison; darkness, disease, and smells."[12] He goes on to discuss the psychically stifling atmosphere of families, where people cannot fulfill their desires, people are emotional, and there is a stifling sense of ownership over each other. Certainly, some of these problems are replicated in Linda's life. Unused to the idea of a family, she sleeps with the men of the tribe, leading to social ridicule and reprimand for herself and for her son, John. She resents growing older and sicker—especially without soma. Both mother and son feel cast out of the tribe but while John tries to fit in, Linda makes no such attempt.

In the character of John, Huxley shows that all people are products, to a certain extent, of their socialization. John has been taught about the World State by his mother. However, because Linda is a Beta, she is not able to teach John adequately. That, combined with his desire to be accepted by the tribe, leads John to adopt both Shakespeare and the religious views of the tribe. Ultimately, therefore, Huxley makes two points in describing the Savage Reservations: first, that natural is not always better and that technology and modernity are not always evil; and second, every person is a product of socialization to a certain extent and this is as true of the Savage Reservations as it is of the World State.

Ultimately, Huxley shows that both the World State and the Savage Reservations are equally flawed. The former used technology to erase nature, promote stability and consumerism, and establish a system which is controlled by the Controllers. The Savage Reservation also conditions its inhabitants (though without the use of technology) while showing the problems of life without any access to science and technology—sickness, old age, poverty, etc. Science and technology are, therefore, shown to be both a blessing and a curse, a necessity and a peril, while nature is shown to be both open to massive amounts of manipulation and resistant to such manipulation.

THE COMPLICATED RELATIONSHIP
BETWEEN FREEDOM AND HAPPINESS

Liberalism as conceptualized by philosophers like John Locke has argued for freedom on the grounds that it best allows individuals to conceptualize their own versions of happiness. Therefore, liberalism has been premised on the assumption that freedom is a prerequisite for happiness. While Huxley does not challenge this argument, he eschews the simple argument that freedom is necessary for happiness. Huxley challenges this idea in two ways: first, through the World State itself, and second, by challenging the notion that anyone is truly free—to the extent that they are products of their circumstances and upbringing. The World State's logic is that people do not actually want the consequences of true freedom. Yet, the reader's emotional response to the World State is to see the positives of freedom. Huxley also shows that both the Savage Reservations and the World State condition people to make sure that they fit the norms and requirements of these societies. The difference in the conditioning the people of the two societies receive is highlighted through John's responses to the World State and their reactions to him. John's experiences do not match his expectations of the World State. Seeing the ways in which the people are conditioned, John makes the case for freedom and individuality. However, in putting the demand for the freedom and individuality in the mouth of John, a person who is deeply flawed, Huxley undercuts the possibility that freedom and individuality alone will yield a good state or happiness for individuals. What, according to Huxley, does freedom allow you to do? As Controller Mustafa Mond says, "Liberty to be inefficient and miserable. Freedom to be a round peg in a square hole."[13] In this section, through John's reaction to the World State, we shall see both the argument for freedom and the complicated relationship between freedom and happiness that emerges from a portrayal of the World State and the Savage Reservations.

John is horrified by the promiscuity of women in this world since he has lived through the impact of his mother's promiscuity in the Savage Reservations. Having learned from the various tribes that women and men commit to each other, John, who is attracted to Lenina, is shocked by her behavior and repelled by his own attraction to her. Taught by the tribe, learning from Shakespeare, and repelled by his mother's behavior, he expects chastity from both himself and Lenina, which the latter is simply unable to understand. He rejects the sexual freedom of the World State.

John is equally repelled by soma and its effects. Linda starts taking copious amounts of soma when she returns to the World State. The result is that she is alive but not alert or aware of the world around her. In fact, it is Linda's death which precipitates John's revolt against this world. He tells the lower classes that he intends to "teach you; I'll make you free whether you want to or not."[14] This statement is reminiscent of Rousseau's belief that people will be "forced to be free" through the general will. However, Rousseau's meaning, presumably, is that people in the state would be forced to be the best versions of their moral selves by following the general will. By throwing out the soma which is rationed out to the lower classes, John, on the other hand, seems to imply that freedom simply means experiencing true feelings and indulging in whatever actions one wants—both pleasant and unpleasant. Therefore, while the citizens of the World State view soma as a way to be free of pain (both physical and emotional), John views freedom as an opportunity to experience both pain and pleasure. John's definition of freedom seems more simplistic than that of Rousseau.

It is John who called the World State a "brave new world." He got this language from Shakepeare's *Tempest*. After he spends some time in this world, he makes it clear that this phrase is a call to arms, a call to overthrow the system and free the people within it. This rebellion lands both Marx and Watson, along with John, in front of the Controller, Mustafa Mond. Mond explains the system and the logic behind it to John, who is horrified by it all. In his conversation with Mustafa Mond, John makes it clear that he does not want to live a life like those lived by the citizens of the World State. Their happiness is not true happiness because it is defined and orchestrated by the World State. They are not really free. John says that freedom means the ability to be sinful, unhappy, to grow old, to get sick, etc. This statement suggests that Huxley is opposed to the materialistic and limited happiness which is the result of conditioning.

However, Huxley also shows that he is concerned with the ramifications of freedom. He is aware that freedom can lead to a life which may be insecure or imperfect in some way. While people may crave freedom, they would not want that freedom to actually result in sin or sickness (as in the Savage Reservations). Unable to adjust to the social norms of this world, John retreats to an isolated lighthouse where he attempts to rid himself of his desires through praying and voluntary crucifixion. The sight of him beating himself with knotted cords attracts both reporters and crowds. He physically attacks reporters and finally attacks Lenina when she comes to see him at his retreat. After a night of uncontrolled frenzy, he kills himself. Therefore, he does get the freedom that he wanted, the freedom to be sinful, unhappy, sick, etc. as he had mentioned to Mond. However, the consequences of that freedom were the kind of behaviors that he had been conditioned to believe was sinful and he seemed unable to accept that in himself. Huxley shows that freedom can sometimes lead to consequences antithetical to the desires of people. Simply speaking, be careful what you wish for.

PESSIMISM OR WARNING?

Given Huxley's tendency to show the advantages and disadvantages of nature and technology and the suicide of John as the ending of the story, one is left to wonder whether this story is meant to be a pessimistic look at humankind's future or whether there is any hope that a warning like this would prevent such a future.

In the 1930s, Huxley wrote that history "makes it fairly clear that most people will accept reason only in small doses and (except in matters which do not touch them very closely) only on irrational grounds, generally of a religious nature."[15] In other words, Huxley believed that people are more likely to make decisions based on emotion rather than reason. Huxley believed that if fascism did win, it would win by emotional appeal. One could then surmise that the emotional appeal of a book could serve as a warning against fascism and all forms of dictatorship. Thus, while one can make an argument against fascism based on reason, that argument would be more effective based on an emotional portrayal in a book. Indeed, the power of emotion is highlighted in Huxley's dystopia itself. The World States knows that emotion is destabilizing and can lead to the overthrow of a political system. This is why it eliminates emotion or blunts its force. The World State eliminates family and love through its principle that everyone belongs to everyone else. Even death is made routine and unemotional. In other words, there is no place for love of the particular in this state. The use of soma and the system of instant wish fulfillment is put into place to make sure that any remaining emotion is not a threat to the system.

The book's appeal is, therefore, an emotional one. This emotion is rendered through the aversion to the World State and to the tragic ending to the story. In *Music at Night*, Huxley theorizes on the value of tragedy against what he terms the "whole truth." Both truth and tragedy need to be a part of human life. However, tragedy can produce a deep emotional catharsis because it highlights certain features of the truth. The whole truth is not capable of producing the same type of emotion because it does not highlight certain aspects of the story. This ability of tragedy to elicit strong emotions is also why tragedy is discarded in the World State. John, who has read Shake-speare, asks why, instead of the sensuous senseless "feelies," the people are not given something meaningful to watch. The Controller responds: "you can't make tragedies without social instability. The world's stable now."[16] This world eliminates tragedy because he eliminates emotion.

This assertion, that emotion, and concomitantly, tragedy, is antithetical to the sort of happiness promoted by the state, is seen in the Controller's claims that you have to make a conscious choice "between happiness and what people used to call high art."[17] This is because: "actual happiness always looks pretty squalid in comparison with the overcompensations for misery. And, of course, stability isn't nearly so spectacular as instability. And being contented has none of the glamour of a good fight against misfortune. . . . Happiness is never grand."[18] It is important to note again that the Controller defines happiness as getting what one wants and never wanting what one cannot get. The truth of tragedy and emotion being antithetical to this form of happiness is seen in the fact that Lenina feels unhappy when she is denied her wish to sleep with John. She does not want to feel rejection and is not used to being denied her wishes. Marx feels unhappy even when his wish to be an individual and face adverse circumstances is granted. Thus, while the World State makes it clear that tragedy is neither desirable nor inevitable and there-fore, has nothing to teach, John rejects the possibility of being happy while abandoning freedom and individuality. While the World State prioritizes its limited version of happiness at all costs, John prioritizes freedom over happi-ness.

Yet, *Brave New World* ends with the tragic suicide of John. On one hand, this can be seen as a condemnation of John's position that individuality and freedom should trump all other values and desires. The readers are shown that individuality and freedom may have very tragic endings. John's suicide can be seen as his atonement for being unable to live the life of purity and chastity which he desired in the World State. John felt that this was the only way to escape the corrupting influence of the state. Even the World State's limited version of happiness seems easier on human beings than facing the consequences of freedom and individuality.

On the other hand, this ending can be seen as an assertion of his own individuality against the power of the state. After all, John did say, "I'm damned if I'll go on being experimented with."[19] One could interpret this action as John's assertion that this society cannot control a person's death, in spite of their attempts to do so. In this sense, John flouted the norms of the state through his action. Horrified by the actions of the state and his inability to escape it by living alone, John takes the ultimate action which removes him from this state. Man "is heroic in his capacity for committing himself to a tragic choice, and then accepting its full consequences. His pitiable or awful fate is less significant than the mere fact of his existence."[20] Seen in this way, tragedy serves to undermine the system.

One could also make the case that the fates of Marx and Watson mitigate the tragic ending to the book. Being relegated to an island that allows individuality seems to be the preferred option between the World State and the Savage Reservations. Indeed, this is the outcome that Watson hopes for. Watson is a writer, but he feels as if he is writing meaningless drivel. The point Huxley makes here is that there is nothing in the World State which is worth writing about. The activities which the Aphas and Betas partake in—constant materialism and sexuality—has none of the drama that Watson hopes to capture. Thus, he is against a system which prevents him from writing something meaningful by depriving him of meaningful experiences. For Watson, the elimination of emotion, tragedy, the personal impact of family life, love, etc. makes this a state not worth writing about.

Ultimately, therefore, the fact that the death of John makes this book into a tragedy does not mean that it is pessimistic. Hope may be found in the fact that one is able to overcome the conditioning of the state and escape its restrictions. Hope may also be found in the fact that an individual can undermine the system, even if it is through a desperate individualistic act.

CONCLUSION

Brave New World received mixed reviews. To some, it was unserious, undeveloped, and superficial. It was excoriated by H. G. Wells who saw it as defeatist, pessimist, and an affront to the possibilities of science. However, it did receive praise from some scientists like Joseph Needham who praised the work but thought that it would only gain the appreciation of scientists and philosophers. While some read it as a dystopia, others read it as a joke. Some read it as despairing of the future of mankind while others saw it as a warning.[21] The arguments against it varied, with some criticizing its lack of character development and others criticizing its conception of the dictatorial state.

Yet, as we have seen, *Brave New World* has some complex messages. Huxley's views of the impact of science on human nature is intricately linked to his views on the state. In fact, Huxley traces this connection back to utopias, making it clear that utopias often link the perfect arrangement of the state with a harmonious human nature: "Many definitions of the ideal human society have been attempted. That which, I suppose, the majority of modern men and women would find most acceptable is what, for want of a better name, I will call the 'humanistic' definition. The humanist is one who believes that our human nature can, and should be, developed harmoniously as a whole."[22] Unlike H. G. Wells in *Men Like Gods*, Huxley did not believe that this was either possible or desirable. He did not believe that human beings could use science to create a scientific utopia because: "the complexity of society and of human nature is such that it is often very difficult to foresee all the results of a given social change. Reformers frequently discover that, along with much good, they have unintentionally done harm."[23] A harmonious human nature needs to be created by the state in order to achieve utopia. But Huxley was fearful of this argument on two grounds. First, he feared the possibility that this could depersonalize human beings and to "depersonify human beings and to personify abstractions are complementary errors which lead, by an inexorable logic, to war between nations and to idolatrous worship of the State, with consequent governmental oppression."[24] Second, and in a related argument, Huxley argued that creating utopias was a product of the human "Will to Order," where the state attempted to wipe out individual differences among people. As Huxley pointed out, if the individual differences among people "were trifling and could be completely ironed out by appropriate conditioning, then, obviously, there would be no need for liberty and the State would be justified in persecuting the heretics who demanded it. For the individual termite, service to the termitary is perfect freedom. But human beings are not completely social; they are only moderately gregarious."[25] In other words, human beings are not all born to fit perfectly into any unit and any attempt to make them do so reduces their status as free human beings. The differences among human beings are vast, not trivial, and therefore, a perfect state acting perfectly in sync with all its people may not be possible. Therefore, Huxley's *Brave New World* can be read as his attempt to show how the state can use technology to manipulate conceptions of nature to create an oppressive state—with the understanding that, thankfully, this is not completely possible.

Huxley takes a position that is opposed to that of many utopias which posit that science and technology can make utopia possible. For instance, Francis Bacon in his *New Atlantis* makes the claim that science and knowledge can better the human condition and create and maintain utopia. His island of Bensalem is based on the premise that knowledge and science can cure all human ills—sickness, war, material want, etc. Bacon asserts that having the knowledge to eradicate such evils is key; humankind, he assumes, would use this knowledge wisely. But, for Huxley, science and technology are amoral. They are the means to an end, and it is that end which determines the morality of the technology and science used. It is clear, however, that technology and science can be used by both scientists and bureaucrats to create a system which distorts human nature and makes a mockery of freedom. In other words, stability in order to increase consumption becomes the rationale for the manipulation of human nature and technology can severely restrict human freedom and rename it happiness.

In another sense, Huxley can be seen to be amplifying some aspects of Bacon's thought. While Bacon assumed that science and knowledge can be used to better the human condition, he also acknowledged that human beings had certain weaknesses and characteristics that prevented them from benefiting from the knowledge of science. These human characteristics and tendencies had to be acknowledged and compensated for, if there ever was to be an ideal state. Huxley also acknowledges that human beings have certain characteristics which are difficult to erase through scientific and technological advancement, but he sees this as a strength and refuses to enumerate what those specific tendencies are.

In his preface to a later version of the book, Huxley made it clear that his goal was to show a world where social stability is meant to facilitate consumption, and where man is made to be used by science and technology. In the book, he shows a juxtaposition between an industrialized World State which promotes instant gratification of all desires and a primitive state which lacks technology and the basic comforts of life. However, the book offers no good alternative—no alternative where technology and the state are used for good. They are either absent as in Huxley's "Savage Reservations" or developed against individual freedom as in the World State. In his preface, Huxley stated that

> If I were now to rewrite the book I would offer the Savage a third alternative. Between the utopian and the primitive horns of his dilemma would lie the possibility of sanity—a possibility already actualized, to some extent, in a community of exiles and refugees from the *Brave New World*, living within the borders of the Reservation.[26]

As it is, no such alternative exists within the story itself. Therefore, the story depicts a world where the only alternatives are a world where human beings are controlled by technology and where human beings' lives are made worse by the complete absence of technology. In painting this picture, he warns of a world which can neither do without technology nor prevent it from eroding personal freedoms. In this sense, one can find a foreshadowing of works such as Kurt Vonnegut's *Player Piano*, which shows technology as both necessary to human life and destructive of human freedom. In doing so, Huxley makes two concomitant points. First, a life without any access to science and technology is not always desirable or freer. Both the Savage Reservations and the World State conditions their members; one merely uses more traditional and less technological methods than the other. Second, science and technology cannot entirely overcome the power of nature. So while human conditioning cannot be avoided, this does not entirely eradicate the possibility of individual freedom. Rather, the possibility of freedom exists in the spaces left open by human conditioning. As a result, Huxley's book can be read as both a warning about the combined power of the state and technology and the possibility that their power is not absolute or inevitable. Huxley reiterates this point in *Brave New World Revisited* where he insists that human beings can "refuse to co-operate with the blind forces that are propelling us."[27] Huxley makes the case for the value of freedom based on the fact that "Every individual is biologically unique and unlike all other individuals."[28] Ultimately, therefore, Huxley opines that individuals must be taught the value of human uniqueness, charity, compassion, love, and intelligence. Only then can human beings use science and technology without giving into their oppressive possibilities.

NOTES

1. David Bradshaw, *The Hidden Huxley: Contempt and Compassion for the Masses*, (London: Faber and Faber, 1994), 110.
2. Aldous Huxley, *Brave New World* (New York: HarperCollins Publishers, 1969), 198.
3. Huxley, *Brave New World*, 18–19.
4. Huxley, *Brave New World*, 26.
5. Huxley, *Brave New World*, 36.
6. Huxley, *Brave New World*, 101.
7. Huxley, *Brave New World*, 96.
8. Huxley, *Brave New World*, 88.
9. Huxley, *Brave New World*, 72.
10. Huxley, *Brave New World*, 204.
11. Huxley, *Brave New World*, 148.
12. Huxley, *Brave New World*, 43.
13. Huxley, *Brave New World*, 51.
14. Huxley, *Brave New World*, 193.
15. Bradshaw, *The Hidden Huxley*, 40.
16. Huxley, *Brave New World*, 198.
17. Huxley, *Brave New World*, 199.
18. Huxley, *Brave New World*, 199.
19. Huxley, *Brave New World*, 217.
20. Herbert J. Muller, *The Spirit of Tragedy* (New York: Alfred A Knopf, 1968), 22.
21. John Wain deems Huxley a "pseudo-novelist" who uses novels for the purposes of writing tracts against materialism. *Aldous Huxley: A Collection of Critical Essays*, ed. Robert E. Kuehn (Englewood Cliffs, NJ: Prentice Hall Inc, 1974), 26. Peter Firchow also agreed that Huxley cannot create real characters. *Aldous Huxley: Satirist and Novelist* (Minneapolis: University of Minnesota Press, 1972).
22. Bradshaw, *The Hidden Huxley*, 107
23. Bradshaw, *The Hidden Huxley*, 147–148.
24. Aldous Huxley, *Collected Essays* (New York: Harper and Brothers Publishers, 1959), 255.
25. Aldous Huxley, *Brave New World Revisited* (New York: HarperCollins Publishers, 1958), 326.
26. Huxley, *Brave New World*, 7.
27. Huxley, *Brave New World Revisited*, 257.
28. Huxley, *Brave New World Revisited*, 321.

BIBLIOGRAPHY

Bradshaw, David. *The Hidden Huxley: Contempt and Compassion for the Masses.* London: Faber and Faber, 1994.

Firchow, Peter. *Aldous Huxley: Satirist and Novelist.* Minneapolis: University of Minnesota Press, 1972.

Huxley, Aldous. *Collected Essays.* New York: Harper and Brothers Publishers, 1959.

———. *Brave New World.* New York: HarperCollins Publishers, 1969.

———. *Brave New World Revisited.* New York: HarperCollins Publishers, 1958.

Kuehn, Robert, ed. *Aldous Huxley: A Collection of Critical Essays.* Englewood Cliffs, NJ: Prentice Hall Inc, 1974.

Muller, Herbert J. *The Spirit of Tragedy.* New York: Alfred A Knopf, 1968.

Chapter Seven

An Exhortation to Secure Humanity against the Buggers

Ender's Game

Steven Michels and Danielle Sottosanti

Ender's Game, a 1985 novel by Orson Scott Card, tells the story of Andrew "Ender" Wiggin, who is recruited when he is six years old by the government's International Fleet to defend humanity against the "buggers," an alien race. While at Battle School, Ender demonstrates superior tactical ability, despite mistreatment by many of the other cadets. During what is said to be his final test, Ender employs an aggressive maneuver that sacrifices his entire fleet but also eliminates the entire bugger race. Only then is Ender told that his simulations were related to an actual battle, which he has won and committed unwitting xenocide—that is, the extinction of another species.

Ender's Game resonates with fans because of the young and fearless protagonist who saves humanity. The same impulse is at work in the first pages of *Harry Potter*, when young Harry learns after an unexpected knock on the door that he is to be trained as a wizard, and with Luke Skywalker, who after the murder of his aunt and uncle by the Empire, declares his intent to follow in his father's footsteps and become a Jedi. Democracy might be founded on the belief in political equality, but modern democracy does not seem to have rooted out the desire to be exceptional and honorable in a grand way.

The invention of "the other" as an otherwordly threat is a powerful literary device. Alien invasions and threats are a common motif in science fiction, with *The War of the Worlds* being the most well-known for its real-world reaction in 1938. The same thing happens in *Independence Day*, the 1996 film by Roland Emmerich. In *Ender's Game*, all of humanity is united by the fight against the buggers, although it is more than a simple us-vs.-them narrative. It seems especially relevant in a post-9/11 world dealing with a rising tide of nationalism and immigration crises.

As a piece of science fiction, *Ender's Game* has also benefited from Card's ability to foresee important technological developments—specifically, a communications platform that resembles the internet and screened tablets that work like iPads. Not surprisingly, the book has impacted military recruitment and training, education, and political discourse. Throughout the early 2000s, the U.S. Army released versions of the game technology platform *America's Army*, which helps recruitment by giving players a chance to "experience" being a soldier. More recently, all branches of the military are using virtual reality technology to train soldiers in a realistic but safe environment.[1]

The novel is remarkable for its combination of realist and idealistic or moralistic elements. Even so, Card's politics are not obvious, and there are reasons why progressives and conservatives would cheer on the book. Card, a Mormon and long-time Democrat, has supported Republicans and has said disparaging things about gays. But what political lessons did Card intend with the text?

In the first section, we analyze the manner in which Ender is selected to lead the forces against the buggers. It raises questions of human nature and the equality or inequality of individuals. The tension between rights and duties in a political community are also at issue. The second section turns to the question of the training Ender receives and the role that cooperation and competition ought to have in education. We then explore international relations and the ethics of war, which includes ethnocentrism and the psychology of the other that serve as the story's moral foundation. Finally, we will look at democratic discourse and propaganda by Ender's brother and sister, as they seek to influence events on Earth.

We will focus on *Ender's Game*, the novel that expands on Card's initial story, despite the novel's many sequels. We will also draw from *Ender's Shadow*, the 1999 sequel that takes Bean as its main character. It roughly tracks the same period and serves as a parallel book to the original story. Throughout, we will be turning to foundational thinkers to situate Card in the tradition of political philosophy and to make an argument about the book's overall teaching.

I. MASTER OF WAR

The bulk of the story focuses on the virtues of great leaders, particularly in a strategic military sense. The International Fleet (IF) seems to be in many ways platonic, although, as we will see, it's infused with a heavy dose of Niccolò Machiavelli.

Selective breeding in the perfect city of *The Republic* is intended to improve the soul-pool (as it were) as much as possible. In *Ender's Game*, despite a government-imposed two-child limit, the Wigginses are allowed to have a third child (Ender) because of their genetic potential to have another child as skillful as their first two (Peter and Valentine). The hope is that the third will not share the same vices as the other ones. In both books, the children there are kept from their families and held in common to focus their duties on the common good. As with *The Republic*, the Fleet commanders focus on finding an individual who has the natural capabilities that the training will bring to light.

In *The Republic*, people are divided according to the ordering of their soul. Philosophers are governed by the wisdom-loving part of the soul; the guardians or auxiliaries are governed by the courage-loving part; and the craftspeople, the bulk of a city, are governed by the pleasure-loving part. Both the just city and Fleet training are extreme meritocracies of sorts. The just city is an aristocracy of philosophers, but it is not a hereditary aristocracy. Socrates acknowledges that it is possible for philosophers to be born to craftspeople, and the other way around, we should assume.

It is also possible for women to be philosophers, as we see at Battle School, albeit in fewer numbers. *Ender's Game* reveals a view more aligned with Plato, Mary Wollstonecraft,[2] and John Stuart Mill.[3] Like Plato, who imagines female philosopher kings,[4] and Mary Wollstonecraft, who points to the lack of educational opportunities for any differences between the sexes, the ultimate leader could have just as easily been a woman. Their numbers are vastly fewer, but they are not shut out from the possibility that one of them, especially, Petra, could be the leader of the whole offensive.

In *The Republic*, every person must do his part, consistent with the ordering of the soul.[5] We might be tempted to place Ender atop Plato's schema, as a philosopher-king. Indeed, from the opening page of *Ender's Game*, we are told that Ender is: "the one. Or at least as close as [humanity is] going to get."[6] Ender and his siblings, Peter and Valentine, have all been recognized as having superior intelligence since birth, but only Ender is accepted into the prestigious Battle School. Ender is always thinking, but he is hardly a philosopher. To the extent that his abilities correspond to Plato's typology, Ender is the timocratic soul par excellence.

The smartest character is Bean, which Ender himself recognizes. In *Ender's Shadow*, we learn that Bean, who was the product of genetic engineering, possesses the greatest amount of pure intelligence. Like Colonel Graff, Bean is also aware that he is not the person to lead the forces. But it is not because of any deficiencies in intellect. Bean's talents are in many ways superior; his abilities of perception and analysis are without equal, even by the most established commanders at Battle School. Bean is able, for example, to discern that the final simulation was a real battle well before it began, which he reveals to Graff.[7] Bean's discovery might have been a liability were it not also matched with the practical intelligence to keep that knowledge from Ender. Bean sometimes makes mistakes, but they are because the leaps he is able to make are so long.

Bean is also too smart to be courageous in the way that Ender is, which is one of the reasons *Ender's Shadow* is such a compelling and essential companion to the original novel. Bean's mastery of military history confirms the lesson he learned on the streets as a youth: force matters. David slew Goliath, but most times Davids are killed, he observes.[8] As Bean sees it, there is no moral arc to the universe; outcomes are only the temporary product of those who are strong enough to bend it in their favor. Ender might be an exceptional strategist, but strategy is usually not enough to overwhelm force.

Bean does not possess Ender's moderation or restraint. Bean would side with Machiavelli in appreciating the role that force plays in ruling and self-preservation. Bean, like Machiavelli, also would not have done what Ender did in saving the buggers from extinction. Instead, he spends the wake of the war thinking about the next one,[9] which, given the likelihood of a future battle, Ender has all but made inevitable. From Machiavelli's perspective, Ender's rescue is suspect.

More to the point, Bean is not a leader in the way that Ender is. The other students could have been respectful and obedient to Bean, but they would not have viewed him in the same light. Given the magnitude of their task, it might have meant the difference between victory and defeat. Ender possesses the true mark of all great leaders: the fierce devotion of those under his command. Moreover, since Bean is not entirely human, he admits to not having the same loyalty to the species that Ender does and sees Ender as a proper savior.

The relationship between Ender and Bean resembles what we see in Captain Kirk and Mr. Spock from *Star Trek*. The strengths of each—Kirk's boldness and courage and Spock's interminable rationality—compensate perfectly for the other man's flaws, which are their virtues in the extreme. "Sometimes a feeling is all we humans have to go on," Kirk says in "A Taste of Armageddon." Ender could have said the same thing to Bean in defense of his irrational confidence and aggressive tactics.

This lesson comes not from Plato, but from Machiavelli. Machiavelli focuses on the young because they are bold. As he writes, fortune "is a friend of the young, because they are less cautious, more ferocious, and command her with more audacity."[10] Like Machiavelli, who recommends recruiting soldiers no older than seventeen to fill the ranks, Battle School targets the very young to use their impetuousness and creativity to actually lead the forces, albeit under the tutelage of the experienced commanders who would watch from on high. Ender is six years old when he leaves for Battle School, nine when given his own command, and eleven at the time of the final battle. It is also remarkable that none of the existing commanders thinks him- or herself capable of leading the attack, including Mazer Rackham, the hero of the original invasion. Ender is passed along sooner than are other students, but the focus is on the youth, with several established and prominent military figures eschewing, seemingly voluntarily, their opportunity to lead the fleet.

That said, Machiavelli cautions against recruiting soldiers who "will be a scandal to an army, and who not only become mutinous and ungovernable themselves, but sow the seeds of corruption among others."[11] Indeed, although most of Machiavelli's examples are Roman, he makes some modifications related to making soldiers "gentler and more practicable."[12] An effective army is an army that works as a whole and is able to look past certain harsh behaviors, so long as the common objective is not compromised. In Peter's case, his flaw is his lust for power. It makes him unfit for Battle School, but it's a classic example of the disposition that Machiavelli associates with true rulers. If asked the classic Machiavellian question of whether it is better for a ruler to be feared or loved, Peter would most likely say feared, which appears to be the case. That said, Peter runs the real risk of making himself hated, which Machiavelli cautions against.

In many ways, Peter is what the International Fleet wants: he's intelligent and crafty, with a drive to assert power. Although Peter, like his brother, at first seemed like "the one" who would save humanity from the buggers, he ultimately "tested out impossible," but not for his ability.[13] The private dialogue between commanders reveals that the IF found Peter to be too dangerous.[14] Unlike Peter, who would enjoy being a soldier for the power to kill others, Ender has a cerebral approach to training and winning. This also explains why the IF is able to tolerate Ender's killing of Bonzo, which did nothing to undermine the effectiveness and morale of the Fleet. If anything, it merely made victory more likely.

For Machiavelli, people are divided into one of two "diverse humors": those who want to rule and those who do not. Those who do not want to rule simply want to be left alone. In *Ender's Game*, we see more of a continuum. Valentine is "too mild" for Battle School, based on the International Fleet's analysis.[15] Her more emotional, compassionate nature enables her to provide the important moral perspective and empathy that grounds Ender in the war and after. And from the IF, we learn that Peter is "one of the most ruthless and unreliable human beings we've laid hands on."[16] The IF ultimately proves correct in their hope that Ender would be a third way between the extremes of his siblings.

In a sense, Ender could be seen as the least prince-like among the three Wiggin children.[17] People who want to rule can benefit from chance (*fortuna*) but must possess a great deal of virtue (*virtù*), Machiavelli instructs.

Fortune will inevitably turn against you; virtue is the ability to do what is necessary to preserve yourself for as long as possible, especially given that human nature is so fickle. Unlike Peter, and also Bean, Ender does not crave perpetual war. And when total victory is given to him, he is horrified enough to risk his reputation and give up his spoils.

Yet Ender is violent, and even deliberately so, in order to prevent future conflict. Ender has the ability to adjust his manner of behavior to meet what the circumstances require. He spends a great deal of the book bothered by how much he is like his brutal brother. But unlike Peter, and the other bullies we encounter, Ender's violence is always done with the recognition that justice sometimes requires something other than force, which is why he is so bothered by his massacre of the buggers: it was disproportionate and unnecessary. For Ender, the fact that Peter saved millions while he himself killed billions is perhaps the most difficult pill to swallow because, throughout his journey to adolescence, Ender most fears being or becoming like his violent brother. To take violence as an end unto itself, as Peter does, would make every peace tenuous or altogether impossible. Ender is smart enough to be a strategist, naive enough to be bold, and human enough to be empathetic and revered. In Machiavelli's parlance, Ender is both the lion and the fox. [18]

At this point, we could be tempted to conclude that Card is simply blending these ancient and modern perspectives. From Plato, we find the focus on virtue and the proper breeding and ordering of citizens in a city, especially the place for women. From Machiavelli, there is the division of human nature and reliance on force, and certainly Ender's motivation for victory is more in line with Machiavelli than what we find in Plato regarding truth and virtue.

Yet the training Ender receives, the focus of the next section, and how Ender conducts himself after the war reveals something more complicated at work.

II. GUARDIANS AND THE GALAXY

The selection of recruits and how they are trained are not distinguishable processes. As Bean observes, the greatest problem with the education at Battle School is that it is given by teachers, who themselves are limited. Graff's talent lies not only in his ability to stray from accepted practice, but to also doubt that he knows what he is doing. In that sense, he is trying to find a leader without knowing for certain what the qualities of a leader are—a rather modern enterprise, to say the least. The selection is successful not because it resulted in the discovery of a true leader, but because it discovered a recruit who could reshape the system into one that prepared him for his role.

As much as Ender grows to resent his training and his teachers with it, he still works hard to win, gathering skills however and from whomever he can. As Ender progresses through Battle School, he becomes somewhat of an autodidact, but out of sheer necessity, it seems. "But where could Ender go to learn new things?" The omniscient narrator asks.[19] Ender learns all he can from his instructors; to learn more, he turns to the "vids," watching footage of the Formic Wars over and over.

As Machiavelli writes, "to exercise the intellect the prince should read histories, and study there the actions of illustrious men, to see how they have borne themselves in war, to examine the causes of their victories and defeat, so as to avoid the latter and imitate the former; and above all do as an illustrious man did."[20] As someone who scrutinizes military history and footage, it's a proposition Ender would wholeheartedly endorse. As he does in *The Prince*, in *The Art of War* Machiavelli emphasizes the importance of preparations for great undertakings. It is possible, Machiavelli contends, to revere the strategy and habits of the ancients without imitating them.

A military leader should first master these general rules, Machiavelli counsels, but "even those are not sufficient, unless he has the qualities to strike out something new of his own occasionally. For no man ever excelled in his profession who could not do that."[21] This is true of every endeavor, especially war, and it is a trait that Ender no doubt possesses. This is a question of qualities but also of training, insofar as proper training would allow for and develop the kind of boldness required of successful military commanders. Ender was constantly making adjustments to his battle plans for every simulation. And after those innovations were adopted, he found himself having to create countermeasures to his own strategies, after they were adopted by the other platoons.

When Battle School is first described, it has a clear and formal hierarchy, which exacerbates the competitive nature of the curriculum and activities. The school is Machiavellian, but in the crudest sense. The students are also informally sorted based on physical prowess and a willingness not to be constrained by ethics. None of the students are particularly capable in a strategic sense. They seem to have earned their position out of the force of their will and the lack of a recognized or superior alternative. That changes when Ender arrives on the scene. He is by no means the strongest or the toughest, but he is able to take his rightful place at the top of the formal and informal structure based on his boldness and cunning. This makes Ender immediately detested by the students who had been at the top of the pecking order. In upending the power dynamic, Ender also challenges the principles upon which that dynamic had rested.

Even though the mission to find the best military strategist succeeded, the education in Battle School is unusual if not cruel. From the very first pages of the novel, it's clear that military command does not have Ender's best interests in mind, even though he's only a child. Each chapter begins with a dialogue between members of military command, allowing readers to witness the behind-the-scenes maneuvering from which Ender feels the effects. "'So what do we do? Surround him with enemies all the time?' 'If we have to,'" the opening dialogue reads.[22] In the days and years to come, Ender is purposefully surrounded with enemies all the time—from Peter and Stilson on Earth, to Bernard and later Bonzo in Battle School. He is simultaneously separated from those who are close to him, so much so that he is surprised that Bean, Alai, Petra, Dink, and all of the best students are part of his command team for the final battle.

Given what we know about how they used technology and what the commanders knew of Ender, we have to assume they observed (and thus encouraged or permitted) everything that went on at the school. Their letters to and from home are censored or intercepted, but even more insidious and pervasive is how their digital lives are monitored. Ender especially is constantly surveilled and manipulated. He and Bean are smart enough to occasionally use it to their advantage, but the overall consequences, especially the final battle, are chilling.

Lance Belluomini notes how children appear as the most moral creatures of the novel. They might not always do the right thing, but they are capable of controlling their actions.[23] Indeed, the children have a more sophisticated moral compass than the adults, whose ethics are more transactional and flexible. Belluomini also contends that Card's own morality emphasizes intentions above all else. Consider, for example, how Card waits to tell us about the deaths of Stilson and Bonzo until the reader has an opportunity to see the outcomes of those actions.[24] In that view, being well intentioned allows us to escape responsibility for the bad that we do. It's a position that Ender would endorse after his victory over the buggers. That said, to the extent that ethics is learned, the child soldiers will likely experience a degree of "moral damage" to their development. There is also the related consequence of making them less likely to become well-adjusted members in a peaceful and ordered society, after the conflict has ended.

As with nearly everything in Battle School, Ender's perpetual outsider status is orchestrated by the adult commanders for the ostensible goal of training Ender as a leader. The administrators are complicit in nearly everything that goes on during the training, including Bonzo's death. By routinely praising Ender, calling him better than the other children, even as early in their training as their journey to Battle School, the commanders make Ender the one to beat. "You made them hate me," Ender tells Graff, who is without remorse.[25] "There's only one thing that will make them stop hating you. And that's being so good at what you do that they can't ignore you. I told them you were the best. Now you better damn be," he tells Ender.[26] Ender, of course, does just that; by the end of the novel, he is the most celebrated student to ever come through Battle School, a hero not only among his peers, but also considered a hero by adults on Earth, even if his prowess also now makes him feared.

Card includes elements from John Dewey and Plato in his description of the training at Battle School. From Dewey, Card takes the emphasis on experience. There is a great deal of teamwork and active learning in the training that takes place there, and as a matter of life and death, what is being taught could not be more relevant to the politics of the times. There is a clear curriculum of exercises, but students are able to distinguish themselves and their roles are adjusted accordingly. Emotions are certainly welcome and even encouraged, to the extent that they advance the learning and the mission. In addition to the formal studies and activities, there is also the interpersonal relations and communications among the students. Ender's obvious abilities and genuine decency makes him attractive to a handful of other students who had been shut out of or victim to the status quo. This is almost as important as the battles in determining which of them gives humanity the best chance at victory. It is, as Dewey would have understood, the development of the whole person and for the sake of making a contribution. [27]

That said, it's unlikely that Dewey would endorse what goes on at Battle School. The schooling is rooted not in cooperation, but in a serious and even deadly competition. It would be hard to excuse an educational environment in which an older boy, Bonzo, has the opportunity to gather a group to ambush a younger boy, Ender, alone and naked in the shower. Ender wins in the end, resulting in the death of not only Bonzo but also of any innocence that Ender had left, even though the commanders keep him ignorant of the fatal outcome.

Ender does not receive the kind of education Socrates details in *The Republic*—that is, one that is steeped in arithmetic, geometry, astronomy, and music. [28] Indeed, what Ender studies is more fit for guardians than philosophers. What both curricula have in common, however, is that they are founded on a falsehood. The city Socrates describes in *The Republic* uses the myth of metals to justify the hierarchy of the city. What Graff told Ender about his "Final Exam" could be considered a noble lie because it is used by a knowing elite for the purposes of winning the war, just as the lie in *The Republic* is told for the preservation of the city.

As Graff later explains to Ender, they needed a commander with "so much empathy" to be able to think like the buggers, [29] a disposition Ender understood and relished. This is, of course, to assume that, unlike Bean who, as we learn in *Ender's Shadow*, is on to the rouse long before the Final Exam, Ender was indeed unaware of the truth behind the simulation. In Matthew Brophy's reading, Ender is a "willing pawn," for letting himself be conned by Graff to have his victory and keep his conscious clear. Brophy, for whom "Ender's greatest talent is to know his enemy," cannot imagine how Ender would not catch on.[30] Apart from being eleven years old and exhausted by his training, the best argument against this interpretation is that Ender devotes the rest of his life to undoing the consequences of his victory. Although the argument is not entirely convincing, it does emphasize the extent to which the willingness to suspend judgment of political decisions can be necessary to military command.

Card makes individuals into tools for the government, with some as better tools than others. The bugger threat has affected how people are treated and how people are willing to be treated, as they are seemingly satisfied with giving up some individual freedoms to keep the buggers at bay. As Graff puts it, "Human beings are free except when humanity needs them."[31] For as much as humanity is united in the novel to defend itself and its freedom, it does not always concern itself with what is required for that defense.

Jeffrey L. Nicholas observes how none of the characters in the novel appear to be happy.[32] Everyone is too preoccupied with the training and interpersonal posturing brought about by the situation with the buggers to consider such a luxury. In admitting his lack of happiness to Ender, Rackham rejects it as important: "Humanity does not ask us to be happy. It merely asks us to be brilliant on its behalf." Rackham's doctrine resembles what Socrates says about the happiness of the philosophers in Book IV of *The Republic*. It's possible that philosophers could be the happiest of all, but their goal is the good of the city.[33]

The process of selecting cadets for Battle School would not occur as it does in a democracy were it not for the interstellar threat. It's designed to save the species. Battle School does not offer the kind of education that would be proper for citizens who could exercise their freedoms or participate in political life. Instead, the focus is on military history and practical strategies through simulated combat. Ender, the other child soldiers, and arguably all of humanity face a relative lack of freedom due to the felt need to defend itself against the buggers. It is not a liberal education of ancient Athens, but a military one more akin to Sparta.

III. JUST AND UNJUST WARS

Apart from the questions of how students should be selected and how they should be trained, there's also the question of the ethics of the war and whether it is justified. Card clearly does not advocate for a strict pacifism that we see in Thoreau and Gandhi.[34] But he does insist that there ought to be limits placed on the how and why war is conducted.

For Machiavelli, war is the essential activity. Those who want to lead will need to know how to defend a city with an army against others who want the same thing. In that respect, Graff offers a fairly standard Machiavellian defense for the attack on the buggers. Earth defeated the buggers once, but there is a great likelihood of them returning with greater forces and veracity. The only rational decision is to attack them at our choosing, rather than wait for the time when the buggers have an advantage. As Machiavelli counsels, "[W]ar is not to be avoided, but is only to be put off to the advantage of others."[35] The buggers were not an immediate threat, but they were a threat, and had to be handled accordingly. Military prowess is an intrinsic good for those who by their natures desire to rule, in that it is good for what it can provide for the city.

Graff is unconcerned about the need to use Ender and lie to him or even the possibility that a total victory might lead to the annihilation of an entire species. Like Machiavelli, Graff is more concerned with doing what is required of necessity in the moment. "[L]et a prince have the credit of conquering and holding his state, the means will always be considered honest, and he will be praised by everybody," Machiavelli writes.[36] Machiavelli asserts that *virtú* contains military but also political skill. Ender, however, is used for strictly military purposes. He ends the war and almost ends the buggers, but he is the ultimate "means."

Even Plato's much-touted idealism leaves room for the defense of an aggressive war. In *The Republic*, Socrates lets the discussion of taking someone else's land to satisfy Glaucon's wants come and go without comment.[37] War is permitted, but it has to be for the sake of peace or justice: lower is for the sake of higher. Note also how the view that justice is a dedication to the good of the city and is at odds with the interests of those beyond the city, begun by Cephalus and developed by Polemarchus, is preserved at the end of the book.[38]

A greater issue is how the war ends, which only Ender stops from becoming a xenocide by chance. Indeed, Aquinas's theory of just and unjust wars has established the framework for normative evaluations of conflict.[39] The war against the buggers would seem to be consistent with some of its principles, especially how war needs to be waged by a legitimate authority. The same could be said for the cause of the invasion, which was done in response to the attack on Earth by the buggers. Certainly, the International Fleet was a just authority to defend humanity. That said, there is an open question as to whether the war was a last resort, which is the first of Aquinas's criterion. Graff certainly makes the case that the war needs to be waged, but an equally strong case could be made for a less aggressive posture. The chief, and very serious, obstacle to diplomacy would be the inability to communicate with the buggers. It is not until the final pages that we learn that such communication is even possible, which begs the question of how much this had been tried during the previous conflict.

Although the war may be suspect with regard to *jus ad bellum*, or the conditions in which war may ethically be undertaken, the war with the buggers would run afoul of just war theory to the extent that total war was the goal—that is, *jus in bello*, or the manner in which war ought to be conducted. The creation of and reliance on a weapon of mass destruction reveals that to be a part of the calculation. Ender, too, was motivated by the desire to not only end this war but to end all wars. The war also conflicts with the requirement of just war theory that success ought to be probable. Even so, the ultimate judgment on the morality of the conflict is decided by the disproportionality of the outcome and the extent of civilian casualties, which is what so disturbed Ender. There was no attempt to discern military versus civilian targets and the near-xenocide was certainly disproportionate to the level of the threat.

Even Hobbes might take issue with the attack on the buggers. From a Hobbesian perspective, humanity exists in a state of nature with the alien race—that is, there is not an interstellar league of species to make laws and establish justice. That would seem to suggest that anything is permitted. Yet absent a galactic contract, this state of nature should not be a total state of war. Even though the right of nature grants us the moral authority to do whatever is necessity to defend ourselves, which would seem to include an aggressive war of choice, we are inclined to "endeavor peace" whenever possible.[40] Nature has its own laws, which we can discern through reason. Given the absence of any prevailing and recognized legal authority, the war against the buggers is neither just nor unjust. But what might be ethically permissible is not necessarily consistent with reason. The war might be outside the parameters of the law, but that does not mean that it is not at odds with a higher authority.

IV. THE CLASH AND CIVILIZATIONS

In addition to the ethics underlying the attack on the buggers, there is also the more general question of politics on Earth, especially what will happen after the conflict with the buggers is resolved. Humanity had adopted a somewhat Hobbesian view of government after the First Formic (Bugger) War, forming the Hegemony as a central government with power over every country on Earth. It was only the emergence of a mutual enemy that could unite the sovereign nations, which formed into a League and created the International Fleet.

Card uses Peter and Valentine to examine political rhetoric and how communications technology can alter discourse in a democracy. Though still children themselves, Ender's brother and sister use the relative anonymity of "the nets" to participate in the debates related to what will happen after the end of the bugger conflict. The nets seem to be vast but independent communications networks, which function like list-serves or communities on Reddit.

As the political events unfold on Earth, Peter and Valentine, writing as the moderate "Locke" and radical "Demosthenes," respectively, become increasingly influential. As Kenneth Wayne Sayles III notes, the practice of using pseudonyms to write political discourse is not new or foreign to American politics.[41] Of course, Alexander Hamilton, James Madison, and John Jay wrote *The Federalist Papers* using the pseudonym Publius. But Hamilton, Madison, and Jay also were not twelve years old.

It is Peter who develops the idea to use their father's citizen access to go on the nets. "You're just what the world needs," Valentine responds, "A twelve-year-old to solve all our problems."[42] Looking at the patterns of historical change, however, Peter has an answer to her rebuke:

> It's not my fault I'm twelve right now. And it's not my fault that right now is when the opportunity is open. Right now is the time when I can shape events. The world is always a democracy in times of flux, and the man with the best voice will always win. Everybody thinks Hitler got to power because of his armies, because they were willing to kill, and that's partly true, because in the real world power is always built on the threat of death and dishonor. But mostly he got to power on words, on the right words at the right time.[43]

In evoking Adolf Hitler, Peter seems to do his argument an injustice, as Valentine aptly points out. But Peter is correct insofar as the speech and the conversation that ensues (the "right words at the right time") bring him to power. As much as Valentine fears helping Peter, whom she knows to have tortured Ender and animals, to acquire power, she fears a future of world wars and the Warsaw Pact to a greater extent. And Peter knows this.

The only solution is a powerful and centralized government that will keep things peaceful and ordered—as Hobbes would advise. Yet as soon as Ender puts an end to the buggers, the League War begins. "It's crazy down there," Rackham tells Ender, who is still in space. "Americans claiming the Warsaw Pact is about to attack, and the Russians are saying the same thing about the Hegemon. The bugger war isn't twenty-four hours dead, and the world down there is back to fighting again, as bad as ever."[44] Absent a common threat and a common power, the sovereign states put themselves back into a state of nature with one another almost immediately.

The League War is somewhat anticlimactic in that it lasts only five days. What matters more, for the Ender but also for the other novels in the *Ender* series, is the War's resolution. It is Peter, still writing as Locke, who proposes the solution to the war. In this way, Peter fulfills his lust for power, but also incidentally avoids more war. The Locke Proposal calls for the continuation of the International Fleet, but without the involvement of the Warsaw Pact, an alliance of nations dominated by Russia. Here, Card is drawing from the Soviet Union's post-World War II power grab to demonstrate how realpolitik is humanity's default setting. Nations will always compete for power, with aliens or with each other.

The Locke Proposal seems to quell the conflict between nations, as it "forestalled a really vicious war that could have lasted for decades."[45] The proposal, however, only does so by maintaining the Hegemony as a centralized power. Ender learns of the impetus for the Locke Proposal from Valentine, who leaves Earth to go with the first colony to space. In Peter's "cynical moments, of which there are many, he pointed out to me that if he had allowed the League to fall apart completely, he'd have to conquer the world piece by piece. As long as the Hegemony existed, he could do it in one lump," Valentine explains.[46]

If Peter and Valentine's father had not agreed to let them use his citizen's access, and if they did not have the ability use pseudonyms, their age would have barred them from engaging in public political debate, even as children younger than them are being trained as soldiers. In other words, in post-Formic War Earth, children are young enough to fight but too young to participate in the decision-making process that leads to or stops wars. This distinction is part of what makes the future portrayed in *Ender's Game* so troubling. It's a future in which childhood is prized for the ability that children have to think creatively and hence solve problems in ways that adults cannot. But it's also a future in which children are not afforded the rights that come with those duties.

Friedrich Nietzsche, like Machiavelli, sees humanity as fundamentally divided into two: masters and slaves. It is almost entirely a function of power. Nietzsche blames the Jews for the inversion of values that turned weakness (formerly a bad) into good and turned strength into something evil.[47] Civilizations, or at least any civilization worth its name, are founded by strong individuals who can impose their wills on others and establish the values (politics, religion, art) for society as a whole. It is not a question of whether people are free, but whether a people are great.[48] Nietzsche would not like the idea that such a large centralized bureaucracy had been created to educate the youth.[49] He would agree with Bean (and also with Plato) that the fundamental problem with Battle School is the question of who teaches the teachers. But he would endorse the extent to which individual students are able to distinguish themselves and exert their will to power.

Nietzsche sees the necessity of great individuals as value creators in founding and protecting civilizations. Nietzsche, who cared more for civilizations than for the people in them, would likely approve of Peter, even if most readers do not. After all, Peter is at his core a world historical individual who imposes his will on others and sets the values for society—the very type of person whom Nietzsche believes establishes a civilization. Ender saves humanity from the bugger threat, real or perceived, but Peter provides the framework on which humanity will thrive. Peter might be a Caesar, but he hardly has the soul of Christ. Neither Peter nor Ender are Nietzschean: Peter lacks the Christ part and Ender has no desire to rule.

CONCLUSION

The appeal of *Ender's Game* stems from the ability but also the fundamental goodness of its main character. Whether it is preserving his planet or saving another species, Ender does the *right* thing. In that sense, he is a platonic figure in a Machiavellian universe.

Even so, Card leaves the reader to answer to the question of whether Ender's victory compensates for the suffering he experiences. The fact that he potentially saves humanity is no consolation for him. The guilt he experiences after eliminating the buggers is what drives his actions at the end of *Ender's Game*, paving the way for the novel that follows, *Speaker for the Dead* (1986), part of the expansive universe Card has created.

After the war, we learn that Ender goes with Valentine and other colonists to the empty bugger worlds. Ender's motivations here are knowledge and guilt, not the adoration of the colonists. "I'm going because I know the buggers better than any other living soul, and maybe if I go there I can understand them better," he tells Valentine. "I stole their future from them; I can only begin to repay by seeing what I can learn from their past."[50]

And repay them Ender does. When he and an eleven-year-old boy from the human colony go to find a place for another colony to settle, he sees an environment that he is very familiar with—the playground and cliff from the Giant's Drink video game that he played in Battle School. He instantly realizes that the buggers built it for him and, sure enough, he finds the fertilized pupa of the queen bugger waiting for him. She can communicate with him through his mind—remember that these were the creatures who created the ansible after all—and he sees himself carrying the pupa to a safe place and helping her find a nesting place. At first, he resists, but then she convinces him: "We could live with you in peace. Believe us, believe us, believe us."[51]

Ender believes her. He carries away her cocoon and conveys "all the good and all the evil that the hive queen knew" in *Speaker for the Dead*, a book he publishes with no author.[52] The book starts a new "religion among many religions" that calls for a Speaker for the Dead to speak at funerals, saying "what the dead one would have said, but with full candor, hiding no faults and pretending no virtues."[53]

Ender emerges not as a war hero, but as the originator of a religion that focuses on speaking the truth—the whole truth, good and bad—about loved ones. It is not only that war is for the sake of peace, but that peace is for the sake of truth and justice. It is a kind of teaching that has its home not in the realpolitik of Machiavelli and other moderns, but in the moral realism of ancient philosophy.

NOTES

1. David Kushner, "Ender's Game is Already a Reality for the U.S. Military," *IEEE Spectrum*, Oct. 31, 2013, https://spectrum.ieee.org/computing/software/enders-game-is-already-a-reality-for-the-us-military.

2. Mary Wollstonecraft, *A Vindication of the Rights of Men and A Vindication of the Rights of Women*, ed. Sylvanna Tomaselli (New York, NY: Cambridge University Press, 1995).

3. John Stuart Mill, *On Liberty and On the Subjection of Women* (New York, NY: Penguin Press, 2006).

4. Plato, *The Republic*, trans. Allan Bloom (New York, NY: Basic Books, 1991), 451c–457b.

5. Plato, *Republic*, 435b–441e.

6. Orson Scott Card, *Ender's Game* (New York, NY: Tom Doherty Associates, 1991), 1.

7. Orson Scott Card, *Ender's Shadow* (New York, NY: Tom Doherty Associates, 1999), 443.

8. Card, *Shadow*, 346.

9. Card, *Shadow*, 459.

10. Niccolò Machiavelli, *The Prince*, trans. Harvey Mansfield (Chicago, IL: University of Chicago, 2010), 101.

11. Niccolò Machiavelli, *The Art of War*, trans. Ellis Farneworth (New York, NY: Library of Liberal Arts, 1965), 34.

12. Machiavelli, *War*, 12.

13. Card, *Game*, 1.

14. Card, *Game*, 122.

15. Card, *Game*, 24.

16. Card, *Game*, 122.

17. Jason P. Blahuta, "Peter's Game," Ender's Game *and Philosophy: Genocide is Child's Play*, eds. D. E. Wittkower and Lucinda Rush (Chicago, IL: Open Court, 2013), 171.

18. Machiavelli, *Prince*, 69.

19. Card, *Game*, 187.

20. Machiavelli, *Prince*, xiv.

21. Machiavelli, *War*, 205–6.

22. Card, *Game*, 1.

23. Lance Belluomini, "'I Destroy Them': Ender, Good Intentions, and Moral Responsibility," *Ender's Game and Philosophy: The Logic Gate is Down*, ed. Kevin S. Decker (Malden, MA: Wiley Blackwell, 2013), 139.

24. Belluomini, 140.

25. Card, *Game*, 35.

26. Card, *Game*, 35.

27. John Dewey, *Experience and Education* (New York, NY: Touchstone, 1997).

28. Plato, *Republic*, 526c–534c.

29. Card, *Game*, 298.

30. Matthew Brophy, "War Games as Child's Play," *Ender's Game* and Philosophy: The Logic Gate is Down, ed. Kevin S. Decker (Malden, MA: Wiley Blackwell, 2013), 74–75.

31. Card, *Game*, 35.

32. Jeffrey L. Nicholas, "Of Gods and Buggers: Friendship in *Ender's Game*," Ender's Game and Philosophy: The Logic Gate is Down, ed. Kevin S. Decker (Malden, MA: Wiley Blackwell, 2013), 128.

33. Plato, *Republic*, 420b.

34. See *Civil Resistance and Power Politics: The Experience of Non-violent Action from Gandhi to the Present*, eds. Adam Roberts and Timothy Garton Ash (New York, NY: Oxford University Press, 2009).

35. Machiavelli, *Prince*, 12–13.

36. Machiavelli, *Prince*, 71.

37. Plato, *Republic*, 373d–e.

38. Leo Strauss, "Plato," *An Introduction to Political Philosophy: Ten Essays by Leo Strauss*, ed. Hilail Gildin (Detroit, MI: Wayne State University Press, 1989), 172.

39. For a summary of Aquinas' view, see Thomas L. Pangle and Peter J. Ahrensdorf, *Justice Among Nations: On the Moral Basis of Power and Peace* (Lawrence, KS: University Press of Kansas, 1999), 80–88.

40. Thomas Hobbes, *Leviathan*, ed. Edwin Curley (Indianapolis, IN: Hackett Publishing, 1994), 80.

41. Kenneth Wayne Sayles III, "Locke and Demosthenes: Virtually Dominating the World," *Ender's Game and Philosophy: The Logic Gate is Down*, ed. Kevin S. Decker (Malden, MA: Wiley Blackwell, 2013), 190.

42. Card, *Game*, 130.

43. Card, *Game*, 130–31.

44. Card, *Game*, 299.

45. Card, *Game*, 311.

46. Card, *Game*, 312.

47. Friedrich Nietzsche, *On the Genealogy of Morals and Ecce Homo*, trans. Walter Kaufmann (New York, NY: Vintage Books, 2010), 33–34.

48. Nietzsche, *Genealogy*, 52–54.

49. Friedrich Nietzsche, *Anti-education: The Future of Our Educational Institutions*, trans. Damion Searls (New York, NY: New York Review Books Classic, 2015).

50. Card, *Game*, 314.

51. Card, *Game*, 321.

52. Card, *Game*, 322.

53. Card, *Game*, 322–23.

BIBLIOGRAPHY

Belluomini, Lance. "'I *Destroy* Them': Ender, Good Intentions, and Moral Responsibility." In *Ender's Game and Philosophy: The Logic Gate is Down*, edited by Kevin S. Decker, 139–150. Malden, MA: Wiley Blackwell, 2013.

Blahuta, Jason P. "Peter's Game." In *Ender's Game and Philosophy: Genocide is Child's Play*, edited by D. E. Wittkower and Lucinda Rush, 171–179. Chicago, IL: Open Court, 2013.

Brophy, Matthew. "War Games as Child's Play." In *Ender's Game and Philosophy: The Logic Gate is Down*, edited by Kevin S. Decker, 66–77. Malden, MA: Wiley Blackwell, 2013.

Card, Orson Scott. *Ender's Shadow*. New York, NY: Tom Doherty Associates, 1999.

———. *Ender's Game*. New York, NY: Tom Doherty Associates, 1991.

Dewey, John. *Experience and Education*. New York, NY: Touchstone, 1997.

Hobbes, Thomas, *Leviathan*. Edited by Edwin Curley. Indianapolis, IN: Hackett Publishing, 1994.

Kushner, David. "*Ender's Game* is Already a Reality for the U.S. Military." *IEEE Spectrum*, Oct. 31, 2013, https://spectrum.ieee.org/computing/software/enders-game-is-already-a-reality-for-the-us-military.

Machiavelli, Niccolò. *The Prince*. Translated by Harvey Mansfield. Chicago, IL: University of Chicago, 2010.

———. *The Art of War*. Translated by Ellis Farneworth. New York, NY: Library of Liberal Arts, 1965.

Mill, John Stuart. *On Liberty* and *On the Subjection of Women*. New York, NY: Penguin Press, 2006.

Nicholas, Jeffrey L. "Of Gods and Buggers: Friendship in *Ender's Game.*" In Ender's Game *and Philosophy: The Logic Gate is Down*, edited by Kevin S. Decker, 124–135. Malden, MA: Wiley Blackwell, 2013.

Nietzsche, Friedrich. *Anti-education: The Future of Our Educational Institutions.* Translated by Damion Searls. New York, NY: New York Review Books Classic, 2015.

———. *On the Genealogy of Morals* and *Ecce Homo.* Translated by Walter Kaufmann. New York, NY: Vintage Books, 2010.

Pangle, Thomas L. and Peter J. Ahrensdorf. *Justice Among Nations: On the Moral Basis of Power and Peace.* Lawrence, KS: University Press of Kansas, 1999.

Plato. *The Republic.* Translated by Allan Bloom. New York, NY: Basic Books, 1991.

Roberts, Adam and Timothy Garton Ash, eds. *Civil Resistance and Power Politics: The Experience of Non-violent Action from Gandhi to the Present.* New York, NY: Oxford University Press, 2009.

Sayles III, Kenneth Wayne. "Locke and Demosthenes: Virtually Dominating the World." In Ender's Game *and Philosophy: The Logic Gate is Down*, edited by Kevin S. Decker, 189–201. Malden, MA: Wiley Blackwell, 2013.

Strauss, Leo. "Plato." *An Introduction to Political Philosophy: Ten Essays by Leo Strauss.* Edited by Hilail Gildin. Detroit, MI: Wayne State University Press, 1989.

Wollstonecraft, Mary. *A Vindication of the Rights of Men* and *A Vindication of the Rights of Women.* Edited by Sylvanna Tomaselli. New York, NY: Cambridge University Press, 1995.

Chapter Eight

Seeing and Being Seen in the Kingdom of Ends

On Immanuel Kant, Adam Smith, and Star Trek: The Next Generation

Daniel J. Kapust

Star Trek holds a central place in American science fiction and popular culture. As evidence, we might point to all of the series that followed the original series (1966–1969)—*The Next Generation, Deep Space Nine, Voyager, Enterprise, Discovery* and even an animated series—along with fourteen feature films, a vibrant convention culture, and even a now-defunct multimedia tourist attraction at the Las Vegas Hilton. But its place in the science fiction imagination also has to do with its deep philosophical engagements, engagements evident in a substantial scholarly literature on *Star Trek* and philosophy.[1]

Star Trek's philosophical engagement is especially clear when it comes to political thought, as the United Federation of Planets is the political backdrop of the series. Founded in San Francisco in 2161, the United Federation of Planets is an interstellar confederated republic that is at the center of the *Star Trek* Universe. With laws enacted by the Federation Council, enforced by the president of the United Federation of Planets, and adjudicated at the final level by the Federation Supreme Court, the Federation's civilian government is based in two documents: the Constitution of the United Federation of Planets and the Federation Charter. Joining the Federation requires that a planet be invited or formally request admittance, and being able to join requires the capacity for interstellar travel and something like a planetary republic featuring "respect of the rights of the individual."[2] The latter principle, along with others, is evident in the text of the Federation Charter, as displayed on a computer screen in the series *Voyager*:

> We the lifeforms of the United Federation of Planets determined to save suc-
> ceeding generations from the sources of war, and to reaffirm faith in the
> fundamental rights of sentient beings, in the dignity and worth of all lifeforms,
> in the equal rights of members of planetary systems large and small, and to
> establish conditions under which justice and respect for the obligations arising
> from treaties and other sources of interstellar law can be maintained, and to
> promote social progress and better standards of living on all worlds, and for
> these ends, to practice toleration and live together in peace with one another,
> and to unite our strength to maintain interstellar peace and security, and to
> ensure, by the acceptance of principles and the institutions of methods, that
> weapons of destruction shall not be used, save in the common interest, and to
> employ interstellar resources for the motion. [3]

As an interstellar republic made up of planetary republics predicated on dignity, equality, peaceful coexistence, and fundamental rights, the Federation is a decidedly Kantian enterprise rooted fundamentally in the rights of all sentient beings. Though the Federation Charter does not flesh out the content of the term "sentient," the context suggests its connection to both the dignity and worth of all lifeforms. Crucially, for my purposes, the document does not differentiate between individuated and non-individuated lifeforms.

While the formal structures of the Federation are recognizably Kantian, this does not tell us very much about how individual citizens of the Federation or members of Starfleet animate their moral choices within this Kantian structure. In other words, what actually motivates the members of Starfleet to act on Kantian principles as they carry out their roles within the organization? Do they act from Kantian duty, obeying the dictates of reason, unmoved by the passions? Or do they act in a different way, taking their bearings from the concrete and affective? I will argue that the latter does more to explain a prominent episode in which Star Fleet's principles—and the Federation's principles—are put to the test: "I, Borg" (season 5, episode 23). [4] While all episodes are distinct, I argue that this one is representative of both the Kantian underpinnings of the Federation and the challenges that members of Starfleet face in engaging in moral judgments. In this episode, the Enterprise crew is presented with what seems to be a classical ethical dilemma, pitting deontology (Kantian respect for persons) against consequentialism of a realist sort (normally immoral deeds, such as the extermination of an entire collectivity of beings, become moral through their massively good consequences). I will argue that the action and cinematography of the episode are best explained not by recourse to Kantian human rights, but to Adam Smith's moral psychology as described in *The Theory of Moral Sentiments*. The episode, I suggest, is less a showcase of how to apply a larger

Kantian set of principles than it is a depiction of how we come to view others as objects worthy of sympathy as argued by Smith. Vision is central to moral judgment, both in Smith's argument and, as I show, in the episode itself, and engaging in moral reflection requires that individuals engage themselves in a project of seeing—and sympathizing—with others. My claim is not that the crew of the Enterprise are just bad Kantians; rather, my claim is that adherence to the principles of the Federation Charter is insufficient to motivate them to act on their duties.

I begin, in Section II, with a brief discussion of Sharon Krause's critique of rationalism in her book, *Civil Passions*, after which I note the Kantian qualities of the Federation, followed by a broad summary of the plot of the episode "I, Borg," and why I find Kantian analyses of it to be insufficient. Focusing especially on the figure of Picard and the choices he makes, I suggest that we can remedy this insufficiency by turning to Adam Smith. In Section III, I discuss the episode in detail, emphasizing the role of vision from both a cinematographic perspective (especially the way in which the camera is made to serve as a stand-in for the vision of particular persons) and plot perspective. I conclude, in Section IV, by briefly returning to Krause's argument, suggesting that Smithean vision lends itself to what James Griffin calls a "bottom up" approach to human rights.

I: FEDERATION AND BORG: ALIEN RIGHTS, KANTIAN DUTIES, AND SMITHEAN VISION

Before turning to the Kantian dimensions of Starfleet, I'll begin by noting that I take my bearings for much of what follows from Sharon Krause's *Civil Passions*, in which she remarks that

> The rationalist models of deliberation and norm justification that predominate in political theory today (as represented, for instance, in the work of John Rawls and Jürgen Habermas) suffer from a motivational deficit. The ideal of reason as a faculty that abstracts from sentiment, which undergirds impartiality on this view, disconnects the deliberating subject from the motivational sources of human agency, which are found in the affective attachments and desires from which subjects are asked to abstract. [5]

The problem with the rationalist model (and both Rawls and Habermas are Kantians), according to Krause, is that it seeks "to limit the contributions of affect to the realm of application, while norm justification itself is conceived as a function of a form or reason that transcends affective influences." [6] The problem with this approach, for Krause, is that "to insulate deliberation from affect is to disconnect it from the passions that motivate action." [7] My analysis of the episode highlights the affective dimensions of moral judgment and exemplifies Krause's critique of rationalism in cinematic form.

Let us begin with the Kantian provenance of the United Federation of Planets, and thus Starfleet. Its Kantian qualities are evident in two ways. First, at the level of collective governance, the Federation looks like a Kantian political system—a republic of republics. This becomes especially clear when we turn to Kant's essay, *Perpetual Peace: A Philosophical Sketch*, published in 1795. In that essay, Kant argues that achieving perpetual peace through "pacific federation"[8] requires that each member state be a republic, and defines a republic thus:

> A *republican constitution* is founded upon three principles: firstly, the principle of *freedom* for all members of a society (as men); secondly, the principle of the dependence of everyone upon a single common legislation (as subjects); and thirdly, the principle of legal *equality* for everyone (as citizens).[9]

The pacific federation, comprised of republics, is "a particular kind of league," and it seeks "to preserve and secure the *freedom* of each state in itself"; it would be "an *international state* (*civitas gentium*), which would necessarily continue to grow until it embraced all the peoples of the earth."[10]

In addition to republican governance and goals, the principles of the Federation Charter sound very Kantian, given their similarity to contemporary human rights discourse. Both Griffin and Habermas, among others, note the Kantian foundations for much contemporary human rights discourse. And there are good, and well-known, textual reasons within Kant's work to liken the Federation's principles in the Charter to his vision. Take, for instance, his account of the kingdom of ends in *Groundwork of the Metaphysics of Morals* (1785), a text cited by Habermas, among others, as foundational for human rights theory.[11] There, Kant writes:

> By a *kingdom* I understand a systematic union of various rational beings through common laws. Now since laws determine ends in terms of their universal validity, if we abstract from the personal differences of rational beings as well as from all the content of their private ends we shall be able to think of a whole of all ends in systematic connection (a whole both of rational beings as ends in themselves and of the ends of his own that each may set himself), that is, a kingdom of ends, which is possible in accordance with the above principles [i.e. "the principle of the autonomy of the will"].[12]

The status of rational beings as ends in themselves connects, in turn, to Kant's account of "the *dignity* of a rational being." Dignity is the quality intrinsic to humans as rational creatures: "What has a price can be replaced by something else as its *equivalent*; what on the other hand is raised above all price and therefore admits of no equivalent has a dignity."[13] Kant's account of freedom, in *The Metaphysics of Morals*, gives rise to a robust account of a core human right from which others may be derived:

> Freedom (independence from being constrained by another's choice), insofar as it can coexist with the freedom of every other in accordance with a universal law, is the only original right belonging to every man by virtue of his humanity.[14]

This "universalistic and individualistic conception of human dignity," argues Habermas, is precisely the core of Kant's account of human rights.[15] In effect, then, the Federation Charter transfers Kantian human rights discourse to the interstellar domain; as Judith Barad and Ed Robertson put it, "Because Kant was concerned with right conduct for all rational beings, not just humans, he left the door open for an ethical system that conveniently encompasses extraterrestrials as well."[16]

If the Federation approximates the ideal sketched out by Kant in *Perpetual Peace* and is rooted in principles akin to those found in the *Groundwork* and *The Metaphysics of Morals*, no entities are as hostile to the Federation's Kantian values as the Borg. Comprised of cybernetic organisms from a vast array of species, the Borg are not a species, per se. Rather, they are a collective consciousness, a "we" rather than a group made up of many "I's", and their pursuit of perfection through the assimilation of other species is their defining imperative. Not only is respect for the rights of sentient beings utterly alien to the Borgs' view of themselves and their place in the universe, but the Borg do not even conceive of themselves in an individuated way. Absent individuation and privileging the pursuit of perfection as assimilation, we can hardly expect the Borg to find themselves to be constrained by the dignity of persons or the value of autonomy. Indeed, the Borg are depicted as consistently acting aggressively toward the Federation, whether by attacking it or forcibly assimilating its members. Yet whatever else the Borg are, they are clearly rational beings, able to plan, calculate, and judge, among other capacities.

What happens, then, in the episode "I, Borg" (season 5, episode 23) when the deeply Kantian Federation—and its most Kantian being, Jean Luc Picard—finds itself in possession of an isolated Borg whom they can use to destroy the Borg collective? The plot may be summarized briefly: after transporting an isolated Borg drone back to the Enterprise, Picard is presented with the opportunity to defeat the Borg, once and for all. He can do this if he chooses to act against Kantian principles given that the Borg are, at least collectively, sentient. He can use the Borg drone to implant a devastating computer virus in the Borg collective computing mainframe, and this is what he decides to do. But over the course of the episode, he and the rest of the

Enterprise crew become uncomfortable with this plan as they come to see the Borg as an individual with rights.

On one level, as I've already suggested, we are presented simply with a clash between deontological and teleological ethics, with Kantian respect for persons winning out. Faced with a rational being who is not an "I" but a "we," the most Kantian human being in the Star Trek Universe—Captain Jean Luc Picard—makes a decision that would be incompatible with Kant's ethics. Perhaps he makes the initial decision because Hugh, when he is first brought to the Enterprise, does not refer to himself as an "I" but as a "we" (in keeping with Borg usage), and Picard realizes the error of his ways and implements his Kantian values once Hugh becomes individuated. That is, perhaps Piccard does not believe that the Borg is sentient in spite of the Borgs' collective rationality, but he comes to see Hugh as sentient once Hugh becomes individuated. In other words, as the episode progresses, Hugh ceases to be a "we" and becomes instead an "I," becoming an agent bearing rights. Once he is an agent bearing rights, it is imperative that these rights be respected. This is what I will term the "individuation creates obligation" explanation. The problem with this line of reasoning, however, is that the Federation Charter simply refers to "lifeforms," and does not differentiate this category according to different forms of consciousness.

Instead of the "individuation creates obligation" explanation, perhaps Picard simply engages in cold utilitarian logic from the get-go, seeking only to attain the goods of security and survival for the Federation at the cost of one being. In effect, he is rejecting Kantian ethics here not because of beliefs about individuation, but instead because of *realpolitik*: faced with a very different sort of enemy, he says that Starfleet has "no choice," and he is thus justified in using the Borg as a means to his ends. This is what I will term the "weak-willed Kantian" explanation. In the end, though, what matters is that Picard acts from duty; from a Kantian moral perspective, the episode has a happy ending because Picard acts rightly—even if in doing so he endangers the lives of millions of Federation citizens. As Barad and Robertson put it in *The Ethics of Star Trek*, "So long as our intention is pure, then our actions will always have true moral worth."[17] And because Picard has overcome his weakness of will, he comes to act on consistent Kantian principles.

Now, Picard's decision is rather contrived: he may save one innocent life by not using Hugh to introduce a deadly computer virus into the Borg's collective mainframe (it is not certain within the context of the episode that he will in fact save Hugh) at the likely cost of millions or billions more innocent lives. Beyond the fact that it is contrived, a Kantian reading of the episode is, as I have suggested, insufficient. After all, Kantian ethics may tell us that rights are to be respected, but it does not make us *desire* to respect them, per se—and it certainly doesn't motivate us to *care* for those who are individuals. It gives us principles, but it's not as clear how it engages with affect to motivate us to want to follow them.

This motivational problem becomes more pronounced when we focus on the figure of Captain Picard, whose initial choice to use the Borg as a means to his ends gives rise to the action of the episode. Picard, of all the humans on the Enterprise-D, has the strongest commitment to the principles of the United Federation of Planets, and as Challans puts it, "Picard stands as the bearer of Starfleet's conscience and an exemplar of moral autonomy"—a status that makes him, in several episodes, such an object of interest to Q. [18] Nor does it explain Picard's initial choice: did he forget his Kantian principles? Did emotion blind him given his prior traumatic history with the Borg? (Picard had been assimilated by the Borg.) Did he embrace utilitarianism—the consequences of sacrificing one Borg (individuated or not) outweighed any qualms about such a sacrifice—on a whim? If the problem were an excess of emotion, it would be odd that Picard comes to his senses in the end only because of his emotions (as I will show below). And it would be odd, too, if Picard simply opted for utilitarianism and forgot his Kantian principles. It is not clear to me, then, that a Kantian analysis is sufficient, contra the suggestion of Barad and Richards, especially when we focus on its action and its cinematography. A key motif in the cinematography is that the camera stands in as the eye of a spectator—that is, the camera sees the other actors as if it is the other actor(s) in the scene. Vision—seeing facial expressions, seeing emotions on display—is paramount to the episode's action and character development within the episode itself, whereby an individual as hostile to the Borg as Guinan comes to regard Hugh with sympathy. And vision is central not to Kant, but to his contemporary, the Scottish sentimentalist Adam Smith. So instead of reading the episode as the triumph of Kantian ethics over brutal utilitarian calculations, I will focus on it as embodying a particular form of moral psychology: the psychology of sympathy. Or, to put it in other terms, what makes it so easy for Piccard to make his initial decision to kill the Borg is the abstract quality of his moral principles as well as the motivational deficit he and the rest of the Enterprise crew face.

To return to the episode, then, the question may be formulated thus: What is it that allows each member of the crew to *act* on their Kantian principles? It is not the Kantian principles themselves, but instead vision—and a particular perspective—and sympathy. Now, it is well known that Smith's account of sympathy rests upon the faculty of imagination, a point he makes very early in the *Theory of Moral Sentiments* (henceforth *TMS*):

> As we have no immediate experience of what other men feel, we can form no idea of the manner in which they are affected, but by conceiving what we ourselves should feel in the like situation. [19]

Also well-established, especially by Charles L. Griswold, is the importance of vision to Smith's account of moral imagination. As Griswold remarks, "Our natural state is in society. Spectatorship is the condition for agency . . . and imagination is a condition for seeing oneself."[20]

Indeed, the priority of vision, both as a sense and as a metaphor for the pathways to moral imagination, is evident in the very first sentence of *TMS*:

> How selfish soever man may be supposed, there are evidently some principles in his nature, which interest him in the fortune of others, and render their happiness necessary to him, though he derives nothing from it except the pleasure of seeing it.[21]

His early—and very vivid—examples supporting this claim all involve vision:

> When we see a stroke aimed and just ready to fall upon the leg or arm of another person, we naturally shrink and draw back our own leg or our own arm; and when it does fall, we feel it in some measure, and are hurt by it as well as the sufferer. The mob, when they are gazing at a dancer on the slack rope, naturally writhe and twist and balance their own bodies. . . . Persons of delicate fibres and a weak constitution of body complain, that in looking on the sores and ulcers which are exposed by beggars in the streets, they are apt to feel an itching or uneasy sensation in the correspondent part of their own bodies. . . . Men of the most robust make, observe that in looking upon sore eyes they often feel a very sensible soreness in their own, which proceeds from the same reason; that organ being in the strongest man more delicate, than any other part of the body is in the weakest.[22]

The term "spectator," first introduced in I.1.1.4 and so central to Smith's account of both self-reflection and the judgment of others in the figure of the "impartial spectator," is itself rooted in vision and visual metaphors. The most obvious examples of the effects of sympathy, too, involve vision:

> Upon some occasions sympathy may seem to arise merely from the view of a certain emotion in another person. . . . Grief and joy, for example, strongly expressed in the look and gestures of any one, at once affect the spectator with some degree of a like painful or agreeable emotion. A smiling face is, to every body that sees it, a cheerful object; as a sorrowful countenance, on the other hand, is a melancholy one.[23]

To be sure, Smith clarifies that sympathy "does not arise so much from the view of the passion, as from that of the situation which excites it," adding that "We sometimes feel for another, a passion of which he himself seems to be altogether incapable," but these are special circumstances.[24] We can just as easily—and likely more readily—imagine when our sympathy is aroused from viewing the passion.

So central to our moral reasoning is spectatorship that society, Smith argues, is like a mirror, a point he makes by posing the hypothetical of a "human creature" growing up in isolation. Such a creature "could no more think of his own character, of the propriety or demerit of his own sentiments and conduct, of the beauty or deformity of his own mind, than of the beauty or deformity of his own face."[25] As Griswold remarks of this passage, "we cannot be a human individual without that connectedness resulting from recognition of one another as spectators."[26] Were such a person to be brought into society, he would have the mirror that allows him to engage in reflection: "It is placed in the countenance and behavior of those he lives with, which always mark when they enter into, and when they disapprove of his sentiments; and it is here that he first view the propriety and impropriety of his own passions, the beauty and deformity of his own mind."[27]

Vision is not without its flaws, a point Smith makes in III.3 ("Of the Influence and Authority of Conscience"). He writes, "As to the eye of the body, objects appear great or small, not so much according to their real dimensions, as according to the nearness or distance of their situation; so do they likewise to what may be called the natural eye of the mind: and we remedy the defects of both these organs pretty much in the same manner."[28] It is because of "habit and experience" that we understand that objects far from ourselves are not necessarily small, but simply look small.[29] So it is, says Smith, with "the selfish and original passions of human nature," which render "the loss or gain of a very small interest of our own . . . of vastly more importance . . . than the greatest concern of another with whom we have no particular connexion."[30] The (in)famous example of the Chinese earthquake illustrates this point:

> Let us suppose that the great empire of China, with all its myriads of inhabitants, was suddenly swallowed by an earthquake, and let us consider how a man of humanity in Europe, who had no sort of connexion with that part of the world, would be affected upon receiving intelligence of this dreadful calamity. He would . . . express very strongly his sorrow for the misfortune of that unhappy people, he would make many melancholy reflection upon the precariousness of human life, and the vanity of all the labours of man. . . . And when all this fine philosophy was over . . . he would pursue his business or his pleasure . . . with the same ease and tranquility, as if no such accident had happened. . . . If he was to lose his little finger to-morrow, he would not sleep to-night; but, provided he never saw them, he will snore with the most profound security over the ruin of a hundred millions of his brethren.[31]

Now, Smith does not approve of this way of reasoning, nor of the possibility that someone might trade 100 million unseen humans for the little finger; indeed, it is precisely the role of "conscience, the inhabitant of the breast, the man within, the great judge and arbiter of our conduct" who will check such selfishness—and that man within, incidentally, is the impartial spectator.[32] It is "the eye of this impartial spectator" that will correct such horrendous calculations on our part.[33] (Indeed, it is even the impartial spectator that is the origin of our moral rules, a point Smith makes in the chapter entitled "Of the Nature of Self-deceit, and of the Origin and Use of general Rules.") And this impartial spectator can only see if we can see, or at least have seen, ourselves in the eyes of others—and others with our own eyes. Engaging in moral judgment and acting upon our capacity for sympathy is very much a task for vision, and vision accomplishes precisely this task in the episode, as I show in the following section.

II: SEEING THE BORG WITH SYMPATHY

I noted above that a common visual motif in the episode's cinematography is the use of the camera as a stand-in for the actor observing another actor. We see at many points of the episode—and especially at points crucial for the unfolding of action and the development of character—the actors through each other's eyes. We see, as my summary and analysis will now show, their moral imaginations at play and the development and operation of their sympathies.

As the episode progresses, and as I briefly noted above, the Borg drone moves from being an "it" (in the words of no less a Kantian than Picard, and also by the Klingon security officer Lieutenant Worf, who urges that the Borg be killed immediately) to a "he" in the language of the Enterprise crew, just as the Borg drone sheds his "Designation" (3rd of 5) for a name—Hugh, as bestowed by his friend, Chief Engineer Geordi La Forge. That is to say, 3rd of 5 becomes individuated through his separation from the Borg collective and his interactions with the Enterprise crew. As a result, he sheds his identity as part of a collective consciousness and becomes aware of himself as an individual with his own plans and purposes. As the action unfolds we see this process occurring through the crew's own eyes—and through Hugh's eyes as well.

The action begins with the Enterprise picking up what they suspect is a distress call, leading them to beam an away team including Doctor Crusher, Lieutenant Worf, and Commander Riker, to the surface of a moon. There, they discover a starship wreck, which turns out to be a Borg vessel, and the lone survivor is a Borg drone. As Riker conveys to the Enterprise that they have made this discovery, the camera focuses on Picard, who stares ahead impassively. Initially, the only member of the crew to express any concern for the Borg drone is Beverly Crusher, the ship's doctor. Her sense of duty as a physician clearly informs her actions, and she prevails upon a reluctant

Picard who relents in the face of Crusher's urging, and orders the away team to beam up, Borg in tow.

Every individual on the Enterprise is, we may safely assume, familiar with the Federation Charter and the relevant rules and regulations governing the operations of Starfleet. And yet no one shows any concern for 3rd of 5 when he is discovered apart from Crusher, who explains her actions by reference to her duty as a physician. But it isn't just a lack of concern: it is active hostility—and subterfuge. Early in the episode, during an initial meeting with the officers, Picard floated the idea of trying to destroy the Borg collective through a novel weapon: the use of a computer virus implanted into 3rd of 5's cybernetic implants, a virus which would destroy the entirety of the Borg. When Picard subsequently lays out the plan in detail, he says it in the Borg's presence, quietly, looking straight ahead at the Borg, with the camera focusing on him, showing us Picard through the Borg's eyes.

One might respond here by saying that the Federation is at war with the Borg, and normal rules don't apply. Indeed, Picard himself says the rules are inapplicable when confronted by Doctor Crusher with the fact that he is advocating the destruction of a whole species (namely, the Borg). Kant, of course, denies just this reasoning in *Perpetual Peace*: "No state at war with another shall permit such acts of hostility as would make mutual confidence impossible during a future time of peace."[34] Whatever the Borg are, they are clearly lifeforms, and as such, Piccard's reasoning is incompatible with the Kantian principles found in the Federation Charter. Moreover, as Crusher points out, the Federation and the Borg are not, in fact, in a formal state of war, though Piccard notes that it is the Borg who are the aggressors, and that the Federation has no choice in the matter.

We may ask whether Picard is contradicting himself here. Setting aside the fact that there is no formal state of war between the Federation and the Borg, there are, in fact, rules in war. And the Borg are clearly lifeforms. The question, I submit, isn't whether Picard is contradicting himself here so much as *why*. He argues, when defending his proposed strategy, that the Borg are simply not individuals. They are, rather, a collective entity and, absent individuation, there are no Borg persons, if we understand personhood to entail individuation. Nor are there Borg civilians, as Riker points out, since they are a collective entity, with each of them being responsible for all of their actions. Yet as we have already seen, the terms "sentient" and "lifeform" are not specified as entailing individuation in the Federation Charter, and the Borg are clearly a lifeform.

In the first scene, following the meeting of the officers, Crusher states, after observing a clearly disoriented facial expression on 3rd of 5: that he seems frightened. While Crusher speaks, we see Hugh, looking down, his one exposed eye moving about uncertainly. Crusher, who has acted from duty as a medical officer from the beginning of the episode, is also the first to notice that the Borg experiences emotions. It is no accident, then, that just after Crusher's statement we encounter Picard and Guinan fencing in the ship's gymnasium and discussing the Borg. Guinan, it is worth noting, is an El-Aurian, a member of a species whose home world was destroyed by the Borg and whose surviving members live dispersed across the galaxy. Like Picard, who had been assimilated by the Borg earlier in the series ("The Best of Both Worlds, Parts I and II"), she has a particularly harsh stance toward the Borg, proving to Picard just how dangerous they are by pretending to be injured and, when Picard lets down his guard, batting down his épée and striking him. Her point is obvious: drop your guard at your own peril.

Guinan and Picard form a counter-movement to Crusher's sympathy for Hugh, and soon become a counter-movement to Geordi La Forge who, after Crusher, is the next member of the crew to form a bond with 3rd of 5. The ship's chief engineer, Geordi has been given the task of providing the drone with sustenance by supplying the drone with energy. Geordi is unable to see, and wears a prosthetic visor to allow him to do so; he sees with the aid of machinery, just as Hugh lives—and sees—with its assistance. While we cannot see Geordi's eyes, we see his face, and he is very expressive in both facial and bodily gesture. After he first provides the Borg with energy, the Borg tells Geordi, in typical Borg fashion, that he will be assimilated. In fact, it is Geordi who names 3rd of 5 "Hugh" while assisting Doctor Crusher with experiments that might lead to the destruction of the collective. He is thus present when Doctor Crusher observes that Hugh, who has always lived as part of the Borg collective and is now separated from it, feels alone. The look on Geordi's face shows that he is torn, and that he feels for Hugh. Geordi pauses, clearly uncomfortable, when Hugh asks what will be done with him when he and the doctor have finished testing him: he is uncomfortable about lying to the Borg about Picard's plan and the Borg's fate. Geordi subsequently describes his ambivalence to Guinan in Ten Forward, the social center of the vessel where she tends bar, explaining that Hugh seems to be little more than a child who is lonely. While he utters these words, we see Guinan's face through Geordi's eyes: she is expressing sheer disbelief. Met with Guinan's intransigence, he urges that she go and speak to the Borg.

Guinan relents and decides to visit Hugh in the brig, a visit that starts out quite frostily, with Guinan the focus of the camera, looking Hugh up and down and belittling him. And when Hugh tells her that resistance is futile—following her own statement of the phrase—Guinan contradicts him, noting that she herself was not assimilated. Hugh's response is unmistakably a question, and not a statement, as he reiterates her words. And when Guinan tells him that she no longer has a home, Hugh responds that she, too, must feel alone. The camera cuts to Guinan quickly, and she is silent; her face shows quite clearly that she has seen something in Hugh that has shaken her, and he drives home just how shocking a statement he has made, saying that he, too, feels alone. His words are met by Guinan, who we see from Hugh's vantage, with silence and a clear look of turmoil.

But it is in the next scene with Geordi that Hugh makes one of the most remarkable moves in his development, recognizing that he and Geordi have a friendship. This recognition stems from Geordi explaining to Hugh the concept of individuality, a concept Geordi explains by referring to himself as "I," not "we," and noting that being an individual involves his capacity for making choices. Geordi also makes clear that if he were to lose his individuality, he would prefer no longer to exist. Throughout Geordi's speech, the camera cuts between him and Hugh, but focuses on Geordi as he concludes. Geordi is here articulating the close connection between the capacity to choose and human dignity, illustrating just why it is so important that he *not* be assimilated. Beginning to grasp the concept of individuality as he observes Geordi, Hugh wonders whether Geordi is lonely; Geordi explains that he does feel lonely at times, and this is precisely why humans have friendships. And after explaining the concept of friendship to Hugh, Hugh recognizes that Geordi is his friend; when he does, Hugh is met with a silent gaze from Geordi who is clearly moved.

In the episode, we are seeing, to be sure, an "it" become a "he," a "we" become an "I," a non-individuated being become individuated. In this sense, he *is* beginning to be a person in the sense of individuation that Picard emphasized above. But we are also seeing the crew *see* him, and seeing him through their eyes, as a person—and we are being moved by his humanity. We see him through Crusher's eyes—alone, suffering, frightened; we see him through La Forge's eyes—a friend, little more than a lonely child; we see him through Guinan's eyes—empathizing with her, recognizing her mental state; and we see him through the eyes of Picard—an individual forming his own plans and purposes. And that perspective taking—directed by the camera's positioning and angle, literally and figuratively—redraws the topography of interaction from formal principles of justice to the dynamism and self-reflection of not just the characters, but to the viewers of the episode who are also moved to sympathy. For it is their experience of seeing Hugh that begins to draw them back from supporting Picard's decision. Geordi, for instance, in the scene following the one in which Hugh declares that they are friends, tells Picard that he has qualms about using Hugh to carry out Picard's plan Geordi is, in a sense, recognizing that Hugh is a person precisely because he has *seen* that he is a person, and is beginning to feel sympathy for him in the Smithean sense. Picard senses as much, and responds by denying the appropriateness of Geordi's response, likening Hugh to a laboratory animal.

Setting aside the strange image of the most Kantian human on the ship engaging in such brutal reasoning, Picard's comment underscores the fact that he is one of the few individuals in the earlier ready room conversation *not* to have spoken to Hugh, a point which is brought home by Guinan in the following scene. She notes that 3rd of 5 now has a name (Hugh), and says that he feels lonely. While she speaks, the camera focuses on Picard, who looks away, and who looks back only when Guinan pauses, affirming to Picard the impact of her having seen him herself. Picard restates his position, reminding Guinan that she had been strongly opposed to the Borg even being on the ship—he still refers to Hugh as an "it" while Guinan now refers to Hugh as a he. And when Guinan urges that he talk to Hugh, with Picard having told her first that he hadn't talked to him at all, Picard snaps, angrily stating that Hugh is a Borg, rejecting the category of personhood. Guinan's response is telling, as she implores that Picard actually go and see Hugh, face to face. For Guinan, Hugh is no longer a Borg, but something else. Guinan has *seen* something in Hugh that she did not expect to see and, having seen it, she recognizes that he is something very different from what she thought. Again, Picard's response is decidedly unsentimental with respect to the Borg; he denies that Hugh is no longer a Borg, and he denies that Hugh, because he is an adolescent, is somehow absolved of the Borg's collective guilt. Picard makes clear he intends to carry out his plan. The camera sees only Picard during this speech; we see him through Guinan's eyes. In the thrall of abstract rationalism, Picard cannot even begin to imagine that Hugh even has the status of an animal, let alone a person. But Guinan prevails upon him, and he has Hugh transported to his ready room.

What follows is a deeply moving dialogue between Picard, formerly Locutus of Borg during the period of his assimilation, and Hugh, formerly 3rd of 5. Hugh is brought to Picard's ready room by Worf, and we first encounter Picard in the scene pacing back and forth, alone, sighing and straightening himself up in preparation before Worf and Hugh enter. After reminding Hugh that his designation is 3rd of 5, he states, in reference to the Enterprise, that the ship and its crew will be eliminated. In effect, Picard is simply repeating to Hugh the statement that contains the Borg's imperative. But Hugh, slowly, tentatively, starts to argue against Locutus, with the camera moving back and forth between their faces. The tension of the scene heightens, with Hugh shaking his head at the prospect of Geordi being assimilated, emphasizing that Geordi would, in fact, prefer death to assimilation. And when Picard, speaking as Locutus, continues to press Hugh, Hugh calls Geordi his friend, and ultimately states that he will not cooperate with Locutus's efforts to assimilate the Enterprise, referring to himself in that crucial moment as "I." Hugh goes so far as to say to a clearly shocked Picard that he is no longer Borg, but is now Hugh. Hugh speaks those last lines about his new-found identity hesitantly, softly, but in the end, with determination, and as he says them, we see Picard, who straightens himself. It is clear that he has not just heard something from Hugh, but that he has *seen* in Hugh something has changed him. In this scene, we certainly hear dialogue between the characters, but we also see their faces and their body language through their own eyes: we see recognition on Picard's face through Hugh's eyes, just as we see the emotion in Hugh's face through Picard's eyes.

Now, in this scene, we might say that Hugh, the subject—the I—experiences his individuation and shows us that he can give himself commands, a recognition on his part that leads Picard to recognize that he is a subject. Faced with an individuated Borg drone, Picard, someone who ascribes to the Kantian values of Starfleet and the Federation, recognizes Hugh's personhood, sees that he is an end in himself, and realizes he can no longer use Hugh as a means to his own ends. Such a reading would be consistent with Kantian approaches to the episode, and in particular the "individuation creates obligation" view. But such a reading is, I suggest, not entirely sufficient when we think about the cinematography of the episode as a whole or this scene in particular. The cinematography of the scene shows us a Picard in the throes of recognition and a Hugh moved to defend a friend he loves; Hugh shows himself to be moved by sympathy and, seeing this, Picard, too, is moved.

Nor does Picard have recourse, when he subsequently explains his prior actions, to Kantian human rights or principles as he describes his change of heart. Instead, Picard says that he specifically chose not to see Hugh because he was set in his plan and did not want to experience any doubts. Having seen Hugh, though, Picard recognize him as a person, and thus as much an individual as any member of the crew. Picard recognizes Hugh as a lifeform bearing rights because he has spoken with him—and thus has *seen* him. As he begins to speak, he looks out the window into the emptiness of space, turning to and moving to sit at the table as he continues to speak, joining his officers. In explaining his recognition of Hugh as an individual, Picard states that he *chose not to see* Hugh because he realized just how powerful the experience of seeing him would be: it would show that he, in his plans and purposes, had failed to sympathize with another lifeform that seemed so very other. Had Picard seen the individuated Hugh, who elicited the sympathy of the Enterprise crew, earlier he might well have changed course earlier, too. But Picard chose *not* to see him precisely because he did not want to abandon the plan.

In the end, the crew offers Hugh a choice—they can return him to the crash site, and hence the collective, or they could take him in as a refugee. What they cannot do, though, is, as Crusher notes, wipe out his memory of the experience, for if they were to do so, they would destroy Hugh. At Hugh's insistence—and due to Hugh's desire to protect the crew, and especially Geordi, from Borg reprisal—he opts to be taken back to the crash site, where he is beamed up to a Borg vessel never to be heard from again. [35]

III: OF JUDGMENT, RULES, AND RIGHTS:
MOTIVATING THE DUTIFUL STARFLEET OFFICER

In moving from her critique of rationalism to her positive argument, centering on Hume, Krause suggests that Hume shares with a range of contemporary neo-Kantian scholars a commitment to both "the objectivity and the impartiality of judgment," but unlike them "the generalized standpoint in Hume grows out of, rather than abstracts from, the usual sources of human action and decision as they are found in affective attachments and desires."[36] If this is true of Hume, it is certainly true of Smith, and as Krause herself remarks, Smith's "elaborations of the Humean view, and his modifications to it, have struck many readers as a genuine improvement in moral sentiment theory."[37] That point aside, and more important for my argument, with Smith, as we have seen, it is the sheer power of the visual that is so striking. It is worth reminding ourselves that Picard admits that he chose not to speak with Hugh—and hence to see him—because he was committed to the plan, an admission that gives the lie to what he had earlier told Guinan when asked why he had yet to speak to Hugh: "I saw no need." Picard has to steel himself to turn and face Hugh in his ready room, and often looks away during the episode from those whose arguments or views he does not wish to move him in the episode. Picard's commitment to his decision, arrived at in the belief that Hugh was not a person, overrode the clear evidence that his crew had come to see Hugh differently. And it is not an appeal to *principle* that, in the end, motivates Picard to see Hugh; it is Guinan appealing to his conscience.

This is not to say, of course, that we are not met with a Kantian human rights regime in the Federation, or that Picard and the officers and enlisted personnel of Starfleet do not hold Kantian ideals. But it is to suggest that holding them and acting on them is not sufficient to explain the episode's complexity; acting *on* their principles requires sympathy and the ability to see. Acting *from* duty is possible, in the context of this episode, only because of the sentiments. To the extent that we encounter a commitment to human rights (or rather the rights of sentient beings) at the conclusion of the episode—and I do not wish to suggest we don't—it is closer to what Griffin calls a "bottom-up approach."[38] Whereas the "top-down approach" begins "with an overarching principle, or principles, or an authoritative decision procedure . . . from which human rights can then be derived," the bottom-up approach "starts with human rights as used in our actual social life by politicians, lawyers, social campaigners, as well as theorists of various sorts, and then sees what higher principles one must resort to in order to explain their moral weight."[39] *Actual social life*: the web of relationships, emotions, sentiments, and spectatorship that is the stuff of human interaction—the very things that allow the crew of the Enterprise to see and feel what they had, in general, been blinded to by reason alone.

NOTES

I wish to thank Helen Kinsella for comments on drafts of the chapter, Lori Kido Lopez for discussions regarding film studies, and the Institute for Research in the Humanities for research and office support during the summer of 2018.

1. See, most recently, Decker and Eberl, eds., *The Ultimate Star Trek and Philosophy: The Search for Socrates*.

2. "United Federation of Planets," fandom.com, http://memory-alpha.wikia.com/wiki/United_Federation_of_Planets#Membership.

3. "Charter of the United Federation of Planets," fandom.com, http://memory-alpha.wikia.com/wiki/Charter_of_the_United_Federation_of_Planets#Excerpt.

4. While it is beyond the scope and space of this paper, I would suggest that we can observe a similar dynamic in several other *TNG* episodes: "Allegiance" (season 3, episode 18); "The Wounded" (season 4, episode 12); "Darmok" (season 5, episode 1); "Inner Light (season 5, episode 25); "Face of the Enemy" (season 6, episode 14); and "Birthright," Parts I and II (season 6, episodes 16 and 17).

5. Krause, *Civil Passions*, 2.

6. Krause, *Civil Passions*, 2.

7. Krause, *Civil Passions*, 3.

8. Kant, *Perpetual Peace*, 104.

9. Kant, *Perpetual Peace*, 99.

10. Kant, *Perpetual Peace*, 104, 105.

11. Habermas, "The Concept of Human Dignity," 474.

12. Kant, *Groundwork*, 41.

13. Kant, *Groundwork*, 42.

14. Kant, *Metaphysics*, 3.

15. Habermas, "The Concept of Human Dignity," 475.

16. Barad and Robertson, *The Ethics of Star Trek*, 210.

17. Barad and Robertson, *The Ethics of Star Trek*, 213.

18. Challans, "The Enterprise of Military Ethics," 92.

19. Smith, *TMS*, 9.

20. Griswold, "Imagination: Morals, Science, and Arts," 36–37.

21. Smith, *TMS*, 9.

22. Smith, *TMS*, 10.

23. Smith, *TMS*, 11.

24. Smith, *TMS*, 12.

25. Smith, *TMS*, 110.

26. Griswold, *Adam Smith and the Virtues of Enlightenment*, 106.

27. Smith, *TMS*, 110.

28. Smith, *TMS*, 134–135.

29. Smith, *TMS*, 135.

30. Smith, *TMS*, 135.

31. Smith, *TMS*, 136.

32. Smith, *TMS*, 137.

33. Smith, *TMS*, 137.

34. Kant, *Perpetual Peace*, 96.

35. And he is never heard from again, until he would reappear in the episodes "Descent" and "Descent Part II" on a Borg vessel commanded by Data's evil twin brother, Lore, who had taken charge of the vessel that rescued Hugh and had gone into disarray after being affected by Hugh's individuality. In "Descent," it is worth noting, Picard is reprimanded by Fleet Admiral Nechayev for his choice, and she orders him to prioritize Federation citizens in the future. In defending his choice to Admiral Nechayev, Picard refers to his oath as a Starfleet officer.

36. Krause, *Civil Passions*, 12.

37. Krause, *Civil Passions*, 13.

38. Griffin, *On Human Rights*, 29.

39. Griffin, *On Human Rights*, 29.

WORKS CITED

Barad, Judith and Ed Robertson. *The Ethics of Star Trek*. New York: Harper Collins. 2000.

Challans, Tim. "The Enterprise of Military Ethics: Jean-Luc Picard as Starfleet's Conscience." In *Star Trek and Philosophy: The Wrath of Kant*, edited by Jason T. Eberl and Kevin S. Decker. Chicago: Open Court, 2008.

"Charter of the United Federation of Planets." Accessed June 5, 2018. http://memory-alpha. wikia.com/wiki/Charter_of_the_United_Federation_of_Planets#Excerpt .

Decker, Kevin S. and Jason T. Eberl, eds. *The Ultimate Star Trek and Philosophy: The Search for Socrates*. London: Wiley-Blackwell. 2016.

Griffin, James. *On Human Rights*. Oxford: Oxford University Press, 2008.

Griswold, Charles L. "Imagination: Morals, Science, and Arts." In *The Cambridge Companion to Adam Smith*, edited by Knud Haakonsen. Cambridge: Cambridge University Press, 2006.

Griswold, Charles L. *Adam Smith and the Virtues of Enlightenment*. Cambridge: Cambridge University Press, 1999.

Habermas, Jürgen. "The Concept of Human Dignity and the Realistic Utopia of Human Rights." *Metaphilosophy*. 41. 4. July 2010. 464–480.

"I, Borg" Transcript. Accessed June 5, 2018. http://www.chakoteya.net/NextGen/223.htm

Kant, Immanuel. *Groundwork of the Metaphysics of Morals*. Edited by Mary Gregor. Cambridge: Cambridge University Press, 1998.

———. *Perpetual Peace: A Philosophical Sketch*. In *Kant: Political Writings*. Edited by Hans Reiss. Cambridge: Cambridge University Press, 1991.

———. *The Metaphysics of Morals*. Edited by Mary Gregor. Cambridge: Cambridge University Press, 1996.

Krause, Sharon. *Civil Passions: Moral Sentiment and Democratic Deliberation*. Princeton: Princeton University Press, 2008.

Smith, Adam. *The Theory of Moral Sentiments*. Edited by D. D. Raphale and A. L. Macfie. Indianapolis: Liberty Fund. 1982.

"United Federation of Planets." Accessed June 5, 2018. http://memory-alpha.wikia.com/wiki/ United_Federation_of_Planets#Membership.

Chapter Nine

Knowledge of Death in Kazuo Ishiguro's *Never Let Me Go*

Constance C. T. Hunt

Kazuo Ishiguro, the 2017 Nobel Laureate in Literature, was born in Nagasaki, Japan, in 1954 and moved with his parents to England when he was five years old. All of his early life, education, and professional life were spent in England and since 1983 he has been a British citizen. He is the author of seven novels, a collection of short stories, screen plays, song lyrics, and other short fiction. Winning the 1989 Booker Prize for his perhaps best-known novel, *The Remains of the Day,* signaled the establishment of his reputation among both literary critics and the reading public. With the announcement that Kazuo Ishiguro had been awarded the 2017 Nobel Prize, there was renewed interest in and expanded public awareness of his work, reflected in increased book sales and the renewal of publishing contracts among global publishers.[1] For students of literature, it is always good news when a serious author like Ishiguro reaches an extensive, multi-national reading public.

Given the global reach of his writing, it is no surprise that Ishiguro's work has received wide-ranging scholarly attention. Some scholars have focused on the role of memory and forgetting which informs the narrative structure and character development in his novels. Other scholars have utilized psychological analysis to focus on the role of repression and displacement. Yet other scholars have situated his work within what they call the internationalist school of novelists, or "new world literature,"[2] in which they include writers such as Salman Rushdie and Hanif Kurieshi. These scholars argue that, despite his writing in English and having received his education in English schools, Ishiguro's birth in Japan, his situating two of his novels in Japan and one in Shanghai, and his extensive audience reached through translation, confirm this internationalist interpretation.[3] Ishiguro himself has commented, "I am a writer who wishes to write international novels. What is an 'international' novel? I believe it to be one, quite simply, that contains a vision of life that is of importance to people of varied backgrounds around the world. It may concern characters who jet across continents, but may just as easily be set firmly in one small locality."[4]

Interestingly, when asked in this same interview about the aim or goal of his writing, Ishiguro's emphasis is quite different than the scholarly perspectives referred to above. Instead, Ishiguro emphasizes the vision at the core of each work. He argues that what makes his novels internationally accessible is what he calls "universal" questions or issues. "[T]he next time I'm sitting down writing, if I want to continue to be interesting to all these people, I have to write things that are universal."[5] Despite the many insights provided by these scholarly approaches to his work, the extensive scholarship on Ishiguro's work has paid insufficient attention to the question of what these "universal" issues are. An excellent starting point for further inquiry into his reflections on such universal issues is Ishiguro's science fiction novel, *Never Let Me Go*.[6]

Set in 1990s Britain, *Never Let Me Go* (hereafter *NLMG*), is framed as the first-person memoir of a character named Kathy H. It presents an alternative history, or speculative fiction, of a society where bio-technological innovations have developed to the point that a class of human-like clones is well established. The society seems largely untroubled by this technology—a technology that allows the breeding of clones, whose organs will be harvested and transplanted into sick or aging non-clone humans in order to prolong their lives.

Since its publication in 2005, Ishiguro's novel has come to seem much less like science fiction or alternative history. The pace of bio-technological innovation has proceeded unchecked with cloning programs well-established in higher order mammals (such as dogs, cats, and horses) and legalization in Britain of three-person in vitro fertilization procedures. Human cloning, although illegal and as far we know not yet attempted, remains within close reach on the basis of currently utilized technology. Indeed, in late 2018, a Chinese scientist claimed to have modified the DNA of twin girls born in 2018, using Crispr technology.[7] The novel can be read as a consideration of the dilemmas associated with the rapid pace of bio-technological advancement. However, when interviewed about the novel, Ishiguro emphasized that he was not first and foremost exploring the implications of technological change. Rather, he underscored that he had long been preoccupied with writing, and indeed had drafted portions of, a novel about a group of students who had what he called a "strange fate."[8] He was primarily interested in considering what it would mean to know concretely that one's death was imminent, i.e., "about human beings against the rather bleak fact of our mortality."[9] Originally he considered setting the novel in a time period threatened by nuclear war but changed the setting after he heard a radio news report about bio-technological innovation.

This novel is his first, and so far his only, work employing the genre of science fiction. Within this genre, he chose to approach the setting as an alternative history because he claimed that he did not have the energy to create the myriad details of wholly new worlds: "I don't have the energy to imagine all those details—what cars or shops or cup holders will be like in the future. And I didn't want to write anything that could be mistaken for a 'prophecy.' I wanted my novel to be one in which any reader might find an echo of his or her own life."[10] Although the cloning revolution and the unchecked power of technology provide the crucial setting for the novel, Ishiguro's chief interest is to explore how the student-clones grapple with the knowledge of their imminent mortality. Human knowledge of death is the central, "universal" question at the core of the novel.

Throughout *NLMG*, there are numerous echoes of ideas raised in Plato's dialogues, especially those which focus on the death of Socrates depicted in the *Phaedo* as well as some key themes from *The Republic*. This chapter is in no way an attempt to explore in detail the arguments of either the *Phaedo* or *The Republic*; for that exploration there are exceptional works of scholarship already available.[11] Rather, the references in this chapter to key questions and ideas from *Phaedo* and *The Republic* opens up the deeper questions at the core of Ishiguro's novel and connects Ishiguro's work to the tradition of political philosophy and literature that aims to pursue universal questions. Although it is not possible to show that Ishiguro explicitly draws upon specific Platonic dialogues, there is evidence that Ishiguro is well acquainted with Plato's approach to moral reasoning and Plato's understanding of quintessentially human questions. In the previously cited *Paris Review* interview, when asked about authors who have influenced his work, Ishiguro identifies Plato, as an influence. After listing the novelists, Dostoevsky, Dickens, Austen, George Eliot, Charlotte Bronte, and Wilkie Collins, he adds and "I like Plato." Ishiguro continues,

> In most of his Socratic dialogues, what happens is, some guy is walking down the street who thinks he knows it all, and Socrates sits down with him and demolishes him. This might seem destructive, but the idea is that the nature of what is good is elusive. Sometimes people base their whole lives on a sincerely held belief that could be wrong. That's what my earlier books are about: people who think they know. But there is no Socrates. They are their own Socrates.
>
> There's a passage in one of Plato's dialogues in which Socrates says that idealistic people often become misanthropic when they are let down one or two times. Plato suggests it can be like that with the search for the meaning of the good. You shouldn't get disillusioned when you get knocked back. All

you've discovered is that the search is difficult, and you still have a duty to keep on searching. [12]

Ishiguro shares with Plato a similar preoccupation with examining the limits of moral reasoning and uncovering the illusions that regimes create and which human beings seem too readily to accept for themselves. In this 2008 interview, Ishiguro acknowledges that his earliest novels centered on the Platonic problem of self-deception, or inadequate understanding of the good. *NLMG* is among Ishiguro's later novels and contains both this first aspect and the second aspect that he claims to have learned from Plato: the resistance to misanthropy and the duty to keep on searching for the good. Ishiguro's examination of the "strange fate" of the student-clones and their grappling with their imminent death allows him to bring together both aspects of what he has learned from Plato.

Tracking Ishiguro's indebtedness to Plato in framing the questions of *NLMG* is clearest if one notices echoes between *NLMG* and certain passages from the dialogues. In *NLMG*, the first section contains numerous echoes to Plato's *Republic*, while the latter sections of Ishiguro's novel share a similar preoccupation as one finds in Plato's *Phaedo.* In the *Phaedo,* one of Socrates' disciples, Phaedo, recounts the day of Socrates' death at which he was present. He recalls that in the hours before Socrates' imminent death at the order of Athens, Socrates attempted to comfort his friends with the argument that his activity of pursuing philosophy was the best preparation for death. Socrates says to his friends, "the true philosophers practice dying and death is less terrible to them than to any other men." [13] The essay examines Ishiguro's similar exploration of the universal centrality of the question of knowledge of death and a shared sense of what a reflective attitude toward death might look like. Like Plato, Ishiguro in *NLMG* explores how the direct confrontation with the knowledge of death is crucial to an understanding of what is distinctively, and universally, human. Mapping the two insights that Ishiguro draws from Plato clarifies the deeper, universal questions of *NLMG.*

EDUCATION, ILLUSIONS, AND
THE DESIRE TO UNDERSTAND

The opening section of *NLMG* explores the problem of self-deception within an illusory world and in doing so contains two key echoes to Plato's *Republic.* The first echo to *The Republic* is the dramatic structure of exploring an ideal education directed by seemingly impartial "guardians" in order to structure a highly protected, illusory environment that does not permit rebellion or doubt and that hides deep deceptions. Secondly, in addition to the similar dramatic structure and role of guardians in both works, a second parallel occurs between the challenge to the illusions that occurs in the desire of

Ishiguro's student-clones to understand their situation and the desire to understand what Socrates suggests exists even among the chained prisoners in the image of the cave.

As a coming of age novel, *NLMG* centers on the student-clones' education and key moments of their passage from childhood to adulthood. Written as Kathy H.'s memoir, set in the present, the novel is structured into three parts: the first section roughly correspond to the clones' lives from birth to sixteen, during their time at Hailsham; the middle section to the period between sixteen and eighteen when they lived in the Cottages; and the final section to the period from eighteen until their late twenties, or early thirties in Kathy H.'s case. Kathy H.'s narrative moves back and forth between present and past throughout the novel. At the beginning of the novel, the reader does not yet know who, or rather what, Kathy H. and her friends are. Kathy H. uses without comment the bureaucratic language of the society to which she belongs to describe herself and others. Like the members of the best city in speech in Plato's *Republic*, everyone in the novel seems to accept their place in the society. She refers to herself as a "carer" and notes that she has been particularly good at caring for her assigned "donors." The reader is drawn into the enigma of the novel through this prism of euphemistic bureaucratic language, as if the reader were just another member of that society. Ishiguro develops this alternative history with understated language that typifies his measured, restrained style in approaching complex questions.

The education that Kathy H. describes at Hailsham has curriculum like that of a typical British public boarding school. She describes their studies in math and sciences, literature, history, and the arts. The students also regularly participate in sports on the playing fields directly attached to the school. For all the reader can tell in this early section, these children are being prepared to go to university and become upper middle-class professionals. The students themselves imagine that they will travel and work in various professions. Yet throughout this early education, the students are regularly reminded of their "specialness" and, in particular, their special responsibility to keep their bodies pristine and unblemished. They are required to go for weekly medical exams. The education, although similar to a standard curriculum, is intended to develop the students toward a predetermined goal, what Ishiguro had called a "strange fate." As in *The Republic*, the ideal education is structured to identify and sort the members of society into classes to maximize their capacities for the benefit of the society as a whole.

Similar to *The Republic*, Ishiguro invokes the title of guardians for those responsible for providing a defense against outside influences. Unlike in *The Republic*, the guardians in *NLMG* are also the architects of the ideal education, the role reserved for the philosopher-kings in *The Republic*. In *NLMG*, three guardians stand out in Kathy H.'s narrative: Miss Emily, the head of the school; Madame, a frequent visitor to the school; and Miss Lucy, a younger guardian. Miss Emily oversees the daily life of Hailsham and frequently leads lessons from geography to culture, health, and sex education. She intervenes when there are disputes among the students, and she oversees the other guardians. Madame's position in the school is more mysterious. She visits regularly and inspects the students' creative enterprises, their artwork, poetry, and short stories. She periodically selects students' work to take with her. For the students, the selection of their work becomes a point of significant pride when their work is chosen and consternation when their work is not selected. In addition to directing the students' early education, Miss Emily and Madame become pivotal to the narrative in the latter section of the novel. Miss Lucy, on the other hand, is a guardian only for a short time at Hailsham. The students recognize that Miss Lucy is not like the other guardians. There is a kind of uneasiness that simmers beneath the surface of her demeanor. In one instance, Kathy happens to see her crying in her office. Kathy says, "[I] watched her carefully whenever I could, not just from curiosity, but because I saw her as the likely source of important clues. And that's how it was, over the next year or two, I came to notice various odd little things she said or did that my friends missed altogether."[14] The guardians guide and oversee the education. Most of the recipients of the education are passive. Yet both *The Republic* and *NLMG* indicate that not all recipients of the education will be simply passive. In *NLMG,* key interactions with the guardians become pivotal to the students' challenging the limits of the illusory education.

The climactic scene of the first section of *NLMG* echoes crucial ideas from the cave image in *The Republic*. Although there are clues about the students' real destiny earlier in the novel, it is only at the end of the first section, that it is explicitly revealed that they are in fact clones, created and destined to be organ donors. In this scene Miss Lucy reveals to the students what their fate is. The students, now in their final year at Hailsham, had been chatting about the careers they might pursue. Some talked about being actors and possibly going to America to pursue the "best chance" at their acting careers. When Miss Lucy overheard them she interrupted them and said:

> The problem, as I see it, is that you've been told and not told. You've been told, but none of you really understand, and I dare say, some people are quite happy to leave it that way. But I'm not. If you're going to have decent lives, then you've got to know and know properly. None of you will go to America. . . . Your lives are set out for you. You'll become adults, then before your old, before you're even middle-aged, you'll start to donate your vital organs. That's what each of you was created to do. . . . You were brought into this world for a purpose, and your futures, all of them, have been decided. . . . You'll be leaving Hailsham before long, and it's not so far off, the day you'll be preparing for your first donations. You need to remember that. If you're to have decent lives, you have to know who you are and what lies ahead of you, every one of you.[15]

Like the students, the reader does not fully understand, until this moment, the "strange fate" of the students.

Despite the earlier clues suggested by the bureaucratic euphemisms she employs, Kathy H.'s narrative has been primarily about the evolving development of the children with their shifting friendships, jealousies, passions, and imaginative lives without any indication of their fate. The students, after hearing Miss Lucy's revelation, seem to agree that they had been "told and not told." They remembered making jokes about the donations and coming up with comical descriptions of unzipping themselves to hand over a kidney or a lung. Kathy H. recalled that the discussions about donations had often come up in the lessons about sex. The students knew from a very early age that they could not have children. However, when sex was discussed by the guardians, they emphasized that the students should be careful about their sexual partners, partly due to a concern about diseases but also because "sex affects emotions in ways you'd never expect."[16] The students knew but did not fully understand that their passions and desires would be subordinated to their ultimate fate as organ donors.

Two passages from the well-known cave image section in *The Republic* are especially relevant here for understanding Ishiguro's deeper meaning in the first section of *NLMG*. Socrates portrays the cave image as a metaphor for human beings' nature in its education or lack of education. Socrates describes a cave in which human beings are shackled and forced to observe shadows of puppets projected on the cave wall by a fire behind puppet-masters who are carrying the puppets. Remarkably, when describing the condition and capacity of the prisoners in the cave, Socrates says, "And what if the prison also had an echo from the side facing them? Whenever one of the men passing by happens to utter a sound, do you suppose that they [the prisoners] would believe that anything other than the passing shadow was uttering the sound?"[17] Socrates suggests that the prisoners' capacity to connect the only sounds that they hear with the only images that they see indicates that even with the limited and highly controlled information available to them the prisoners have an intrinsic capacity to understand the world as it presents itself to them. Even in their imprisoned condition, the prisoners draw upon a desire to connect the information that they do receive to create an explanation of the world around them; however, filled with illusions and flawed that explanation might be. The second relevant passage from the cave image takes this insight about the desire to understand into an even broader statement about the nature of education as such,

> [E]ducation is not what the professions of certain men assert it to be. They presumably assert that they put into the soul knowledge that isn't in it at all, as though they were putting sight into blind eyes. . . . But the present argument, on the other hand, indicates that the power is in the soul of each.[18]

Plato's cave prisoners and Ishiguro's student-clones both exhibit an intrinsic capacity to understand even within the highly constrained limits of their respective situations. The cave prisoners and student-clones both knit together disparate information in the attempt to explain the world around them. The illusory world they exist in is challenged only when a rebel escapes the confines of the cave or when Kathy H. and her closest friends are confronted with the revelation that Miss Lucy provides. Later in the novel, Kathy H. will take a further step in challenging the illusory world of the guardians' education. This desire to understand propels the student-clones both in the early section of the novel and even more strongly in the latter section of the novel.

Ishiguro's narrative seems to share the view that the desire to understand is innate to the student-clones. What especially stands out for the reader in Kathy H.'s recollection of their early days at Hailsham is the students' attempts to make sense of their circumstances and to speculate about the reasons for the various lessons and rituals that occur. Although they have incomplete information, the students continue to try to understand why certain things are happening and provide sometimes elaborate, flawed explanations for these occurrences. Even with the highly constructed, monitored education that the student-clones receive, they want to understand the world as it presents itself to them. The mistakes they make are similar in many ways to those made by the prisoners in the Platonic image of the cave. The student-clones are constantly trying to connect pieces of information and observations which may or may not actually belong together. They keep trying to make sense of their world, even when they realize that they have been "told and not told," that the evidence they have to rely on is incomplete. In Ishiguro's earlier novels, this wrestling with incomplete information that comes both from the regime and is self-generated results in an inability to break through a fundamental self-deception. Self-deception and an inability to escape this self-deception are the key dilemmas that inform those earlier novels. In *NLMG*, Ishiguro explores the first aspect of what he learned from Plato but also turns to the second aspect of what he observed in his reading of Plato, *i.e.*, the resistance to becoming misanthropic and the determination to pursue the search for the good, even in the face of the imminent death which awaits the clones.

FRIENDSHIP, LOVE, AND DEATH

The latter sections of the novel reflect the quiet, deep concern that emerges between Kathy H., Ruth, and Tommy in a portrayal of friendship and conversation that is similar to Plato's account of Socrates' final hours in the *Phaedo*. When faced with imminent death, neither Socrates nor Kathy H. and her friends resort to an embittered, accusatory misanthropy. Rather their final days, or hours in Socrates' case, are filled with a concern for the well-being of their friends. In that dialogue, Phaedo reports that Socrates discussed the character of philosophy and the immortality of the soul with those friends who visited him on his final day in the prison. In a warmly convivial, at times humorous, discussion, even while his legs grew numb from the hemlock he drank, Socrates engaged in conversation and inquiry with his friends. In particular, Socrates argues that, "the reason why I think a man who has really spent his life in philosophy is naturally of good courage and will attain the greatest blessings . . . [is] that those who are pursuing philosophy correctly study nothing but dying and being dead."[19] Faced with his imminent death, Socrates claims that he is the best prepared for death because his activity of pursuing wisdom has eliminated the illusions about this life. The student-clones are by no means philosophers; however, they develop a similar clarity of mind about the importance of friendship and a greater depth of human understanding as they move ever closer to their own mortality. Ishiguro seems to share with Plato the view that this courageous confrontation with imminent death reveals a deeply universal facet of one's humanity.

Throughout the novel, the triangle of friendship and love between Kathy, Ruth, and Tommy has been the primary driver of the narrative. In their early years at Hailsham and again at the Cottages, Kathy and Tommy have had an unusual degree of empathy toward each other. At various moments in the early parts of the novel, the reader expects that Kathy and Tommy will become a couple. But, in each of these moments Ruth interferes in any budding romance that might develop between Kathy H. and Tommy. When Kathy recognizes that she and Tommy will never become a couple at the Cottages, she immediately hastens her departure to begin her work as a carer. In the last section of the novel, set approximately five years after Kathy had left the Cottages, Kathy finds Ruth and then Tommy again. In this final section, the stages of the narrative uncover deeper insights into each protagonist's character. Ishiguro explores most emphatically how the knowledge of death affects the key protagonists and ultimately how their courage in the face of death allows them to uncover the final illusion that had been hidden about the purpose behind their education.

Kathy H.'s senior status as an experienced carer allows her to unofficially choose some of the donors whom she will support. When Kathy hears from another ex-Hailsham student that Ruth has had a difficult first donation, she finds Ruth and becomes her carer. Ruth tells Kathy that, since their time at the Cottages, she and Tommy had not kept in contact at all, and had, in fact, only stayed together out of convenience. Kathy agrees to contact Tommy's carer to arrange a day trip with the three of them to see a marooned boat. When they pick up Tommy, they quickly revert to their youthful characters: Kathy, the organizer and doer; Tommy, the ironic, tempestuous one; and Ruth, the schemer and talkative one. Kathy realizes that her feelings for

Tommy are unchanged: "My heart had done a little leap, because in a single stroke, with that little laugh of agreement, it felt as though Tommy and I had come close together again after all the years."[20] On their way back from seeing the marooned boat, Ruth confesses that she wants to put things right with, and for, Kathy and Tommy. Ruth says, "I'd like you to forgive me. . . . The main thing is that I kept you and Tommy apart. . . . It should have been you two. I'm not pretending I didn't always see that. Of course I did, . . . But I kept you apart. . . . Put right what I messed up for you."[21]

Ruth tells Kathy and Tommy that they should seek a "deferral." The deferral had been rumored about since they were at Hailsham and again while they were at the Cottages. It was said that certain couples, who could prove that they were really in love, could seek a limited reprieve of perhaps two or three years from their final donation. The remarkably clever Ruth has discovered Madame's address and gives it to Tommy insisting that he and Kathy seriously consider seeking the deferral. As Ruth faces her imminent death, the two things that drive her are her desire to make amends with her friends and to help her friends find a reprieve to live slightly longer in their love. When Ruth undergoes her second donation, she never regains full consciousness. Ruth's recognition of the love between her friends and her ability to use her cleverness to provide key information to them echoes Socrates' concern in the *Phaedo* to provide comfort to his friends. Had Socrates chosen to enflame his friends' hatred for the regime which condemned him or had he blamed his friends for their inability to free him, he would have left his friends filled with hatred and self-loathing. Both Socrates and Ruth choose comfort for and reconciliation with their friends rather than the misanthropic alternative. In particular, Ruth's act of friendship provides a sense of moral completion for her in the face of her mortality.

In the climactic scene of the novel, with Ruth's information about the location of Madame, Kathy H. and Tommy seek out the guardians to request a deferral. Kathy H. and Tommy's shared love, their courage, and their desire to understand, propel them toward this encounter with Madame and Miss Emily. Approximately a year after visiting the marooned boat, Kathy becomes Tommy's carer and lover. They immediately return to the easy, comfortable relationship that they had had as children at Hailsham, spending most afternoons together: "It was amazing really, the way the years seemed to melt away."[22] Kathy feels happiness at finally having this longed-for intimacy with Tommy, but they both feel a sadness that so much time had been lost before they had been able to come together. Initially they do not directly discuss seeking a deferral, but during her carer visits to other donors, Kathy makes a side trip to the town with the address that Ruth has provided where Kathy does see Madame at the address. When she finally acknowledges to Tommy that she has seen Madame, that Ruth had "got it right,"[23] they develop a plan to go to the town.

The details of the encounter with Madame and Miss Emily reveal important keys as to the status of the clones and the purpose of the illusory ideal education. When they arrive in the town, they see Madame almost immediately and follow her to her row house. After they tell her they are from Hailsham, Madame hesitantly invites them inside. Kathy explains that they have come to seek a deferral, but that they would not have bothered Madame if they were not really sure that they were in love. Madame's reaction is a combination of anger, sarcasm and pity: "Sure that you are in love? How can you know it? . . . So you are in love. Deeply in love. Is that what you are saying to me? . . . Why come to me?"[24] Tommy claimed that because she had reviewed their art, she would have a deeper knowledge of their inner character. Madame interjected, "of course . . . your art would reveal your inner selves! That's it, isn't it? Because your art will display your *souls!*"[25] Tommy and Kathy believe that Madame does have insight into their souls and that from this insight she will recognize that they are earnest, truthful, and capable of deep passion. Her response to them, however, is filled with suspicion, anger, and misdirection. Throughout their conversation, she keeps saying, "I go too far." For Madame, even speaking to them is against the rules, but listening to their request is completely outlandish. But there is something more behind her response. She is reflecting on the whole project that was Hailsham. When faced with Tommy and Kathy's request, she is confronted with the need to give an account of the purpose of their education. Her misdirection in the conversation is due in part to her reluctance to really address the topic, but also just outside the room where they are talking, Miss Emily is there in the house.

Miss Emily confirms that there is no deferral. She had heard students promulgating this rumor but always tried to stamp it out. Kathy pushes her to clarify: "Why did we do all of that [art] work in the first place? Why train us, encourage us, make us produce all of that? If we're just going to give donations anyway, then die, why all those lessons? Why all the books and discussions?"[26] Miss Emily answers them with a brief history of the project. In the first years of the rise of cloning, the cures that the technology produced overshadowed any reflection about the actual process of cloning. The public did not want to know where the organs came from; they only cared about prolonging their own lives or curing their children's diseases. The clones were hidden away in dismal warehoused conditions. If people did occasionally wonder about the clones, they convinced themselves that the clones were sub-human. With the efforts of the reformers, a few facilities, like Hailsham, developed through the financial support of private donors and limited public support of some politicians. While Hailsham existed, Miss Emily and Madame used the students' art to provide evidence to the donors of the clones' human capacities. "We took away your art because we thought it would reveal your souls. Or to put it more finely, we did it to *prove you had souls at all.*" Kathy and Tommy are surprised that this proof was necessary. Kathy replies, "Why did you have to prove a thing like that? Did someone think that we didn't have souls."[27] Kathy's question goes to the heart of the dilemma facing a society which accepts cloning. Such a society is unwilling to give up the cloning program, and therefore refuses to acknowledge the humanity of the clones. Even the reformers, Miss Emily and Marie-Claude exhibit disgust and hostility toward the clones. The guardians accept that the clones are fated to "donate" and "complete." The "humane" treatment that their reform efforts offered is on a par with the ethical treatment of livestock destined for human consumption. The reformers were more concerned with placating their conscience than with the fate of the clones. As Kathy and Tommy are leaving, Madame repeats, "You poor creatures."[28]

Are the clones human? Are Kathy and Tommy human? Do they have souls? Kathy and Tommy's courageous insistence on understanding their situation in the face of their death and the art of Ishiguro's novel requires the reader to grapple with these questions. Certainly, from the point of view of the self-interested, utilitarian society which uses the clones, the clones are not, or could not be human. They are designed for one purpose only: organ donation. Even the reformer-guardians accept the clones' fate. The reformer-guardians seem, in fact, to be the most thoroughly misanthropic in the end. Far from being a grim, ignoble tragedy, the friendship and love that emerges between the clones suggests a very different conclusion about the novel. As with Plato's presentation of Socrates' courage and desire to continue the conversation about the soul in the face of his death in the *Phaedo*, Ishiguro suggests that the callous cruelty of the student-clones' fate is mitigated by the clone-protagonists' courage in pursuing their understanding in the face of their own death. Their friendship, love, and courageous desire to understand seem to be quintessentially human capacities. Many readers of *NLMG* express a frustration that the student-clones do not rebel when they learn of their fate, but here Ishiguro's point seems most to resemble Plato's portrayal of Socrates in the *Phaedo*. Confronting their imminent death could provoke anger, hatred, and hostility, but the measured, reflective stance of Socrates, and Kathy H. and Tommy, suggests a deeper, unshrinking attitude toward imminent death.

CONCLUSION: KNOWLEDGE OF DEATH

Faced with the knowledge of their imminent death, Kathy, Tommy, and Ruth act in the most compassionate, human way possible. Ruth aims to make amends to her childhood friends for her jealousy and her manipulation of their feelings and relationship. If she and the others were beings who were simply shaped by a utilitarian fate, they would not care about anyone else. To the contrary, they all seem to relish the little time that they have to spend together before their deaths.

The second aspect of what Ishiguro argues he learned from Plato seems to be exhibited in Socrates' concern for his friends in the *Phaedo*, as well as the clones' rare capacity for camaraderie and fellowship. It is this friendship that binds them together. After Ruth's death, Kathy and Tommy spend their brief amount of time together, consummating their love, but also reading together, "stuff like *The Odyssey*,"[29] and just talking. Although Kathy and Tommy seek the deferral, they are not distraught when they discover it does not exist. As indicated above, they seek clarity and more understanding about their situation. When the reader might expect them to despair and become misanthropic, to the contrary, they, in a modest way, seek the truth as far as it is available to them. Their calm steadfastness in the face of their imminent death, especially Kathy's steadfastness, echoes the calm that Phaedo reports Socrates conveyed to his friends on his final day. When faced with his imminent death, Socrates surrounded himself with his friends and talked about philosophy and the immortality of the soul. Kathy, Tommy, and Ruth share that thoughtful desire of spending their remaining time with those whose presence they most enjoy and discussing the things that most please them. As mentioned earlier, Plato's insight that most people, when faced with adversity, become misanthropic was among those that most stood out to Ishiguro in his reading of Plato. Neither Kathy, Tommy, and Ruth, nor Socrates, become misanthropic in the face of their imminent death.

Many readers of the novel find it to be the most pessimistic and tragic of all Ishiguro's novels. When asked about this, Ishiguro has indicated that to the contrary he considers the novel his most positive: "I remember reading it back for the first time and concluding that it was my most cheerful novel to date."[30] The clones' dignity, humility, and strength in the face of their imminent death is the reason for Ishiguro's claim that the novel is his most optimistic and cheerful. The moral dignity of the clones—a dignity which gives them the strength to respond humanly to their condition—is contrasted with the deeply self-serving, utilitarian horizon of the society that has produced the clones—a society that has created a class of clones for the sole purpose of prolonging human life. This misguided project, which requires illusions and deep inhumanity is where the tragedy of the novel is found. The friendship of the clones in the face of their premature death is far from tragic.

In a remarkable passage in an interview where he discusses *NLMG*, Ishiguro remarks on how the "science fiction" setting of the novel enabled him to address the universal questions we have examined in this paper.

> Having clones as central characters made it very easy to allude to some of the oldest questions in literature; questions which in recent years have become a little awkward to raise in fiction. 'What does it mean to be human?' 'What is

the soul?' 'What is the purpose for which we've been created, and should we try to fulfil it?' In books from past eras—in Dostoevsky or Tolstoy, say—characters would debate these issues for 20 pages at a time and no one would complain. But in our present era, novelists have struggled to find an appropriate vocabulary—an appropriate tone, perhaps—to discuss these questions without sounding pompous or archaic. . . . It's a futuristic way of going ancient.[31]

In *NLMG*, Ishiguro depicts two answers or responses to the dilemma posed by the fact of death. Most human beings, he suggests, will respond to death by desperately clinging to life even if that requires the destruction of their capacity for human empathy. They will seek to create not only new technologies to prolong human life but construct social norms and illusions to justify this desperate effort. Only a very few will face death squarely and seek the company of friends in whatever time remains. The art of Ishiguro's novel leads the reader into a serious, universal reflection on the human response to and understanding of imminent death. Ishiguro employs the genre of speculative fiction in his exploration of the intrinsic desire for understanding even in highly constrained circumstances and of the clarity of understanding which the knowledge of imminent death brings.

The universal questions at the core of Ishiguro's novel are illuminated by tracing the two insights that Ishiguro claims to have understood from Plato. The first insight is that human beings have a persistent tendency toward self-deception and flawed understanding that is built upon illusions and incomplete understanding. Key passages from Plato's *Republic* exemplify this insight, which Ishiguro explores in the first part of *NLMG*. The second insight is that human beings should resist misanthropy, even in the face of the difficult pursuit of knowledge. Key passages from Plato's *Phaedo* exemplify this insight, which Ishiguro explores in the latter part of *NLMG*. While the genres they employ differ, Ishiguro seems to agree with Plato that these quintessentially human, universal questions form the core of any serious reflection in the pursuit of knowledge of human mortality.

NOTES

The author wishes to thank her generous and thoughtful colleagues in James Madison College at Michigan State University who have supported interdisciplinary studies in literature and political philosophy.

1. Heloise Wood, "Ishiguro's Nobel win leads to 20 global renewal deals," *The Bookseller.com*, October 10, 2017, https://www.thebookseller.com/news/ishiguros-nobel-win-leads-20-global-renewal-deals-649826.

2. David Damrosch, *What is World Literature?* (Princeton: Princeton University Press, 2003).

3. Wai-chew Sim, *Kazuo Ishiguro* (New York: Routledge, 2010).

4. Dylan Otto Krider, "Rooted in a Small Space: An Interview with Kazuo Ishiguro," *The Kenyon Review*, New Series, Vol. 20, No. 2 (Spring 1998): 146–154.

5. Krider, 154.
6. Kazuo Ishiguro, *Never Let Me Go* [*NLMG*] (New York: Vintage International Press, 2005).
7. Gina Kolata, et al. "Chinese Scientist Claims to Use Crispr to Make First Genetically Edited Babies," *New York Times*, November 26, 2018, https://www.nytimes.com/2018/11/26/health/gene-editing-babies-china.html.
8. "A Conversation with Kazuo Ishiguro about *Never Let Me Go*," https://www.bookbrowse.com/author_interviews/full/index.cfm/author_number/477/kazuo-ishiguro.
9. Kazuo Ishiguro, "The Art of Fiction No. 196," *Paris Review*, Issue 184 (Spring 2008).
10. Kazuo Ishiguro, "Future imperfect: Kazuo Ishiguro on how a radio discussion helped fill in the missing pieces of Never Let Me Go," *The Guardian*, March 25, 2006, https://www.theguardian.com/books/2006/mar/25/featuresreviews.guardianreview36.
11. Cf. Peter Ahrensdorf, *The Death of Socrates and the Life of Philosophy: An Interpretation of Plato's Phaedo* (Albany: State University of New York Press, 1995); Ronna Burger, *The "Phaedo": A Platonic Labyrinth* (New Haven: Yale University Press, 1985).
12. Ishiguro, "The Art of Fiction No. 196."
13. Plato, *Euthyphro. Apology. Crito. Phaedo. Phaedrus*, trans. Harold North Fowler, Loeb Classical Library 36 (Cambridge, MA: Harvard University Press, 1914), 67e2–5.
14. *NLMG*, 78.
15. *NLMG*, 81.
16. *NLMG*, 83.
17. Plato, *The Republic of Plato*, trans. Allan Bloom (New York: Basic Books, 1968), 515b.
18. Plato, *Republic*, 518b8–515c4.
19. Plato, *Phaedo*, 63e9–64a8.
20. *NLMG*, 222.
21. *NLMG*, 232.
22. *NLMG*, 238.
23. *NLMG*, 244.
24. *NLMG*, 252–253.
25. *NLMG*, 254.
26. *NLMG*, 259.
27. *NLMG*, 260.
28. *NLMG*, 272.
29. *NLMG*, 238.
30. Ishiguro, "Future imperfect."
31. Ishiguro, "Future imperfect."

BIBLIOGRAPHY

Ahrensdorf, Peter. *The Death of Socrates and the Life of Philosophy: An Interpretation of Plato's Phaedo*. Albany: State University of New York Press, 1995.
Burger, Ronna. *The "Phaedo": A Platonic Labyrinth*. New Haven: Yale University Press, 1985.
Damrosch, David. *What Is World Literature?* Princeton: Princeton University Press, 2003.
Ishiguro, Kazuo, *Never Let Me Go*. New York: Vintage International Press, 2005.
———. "The Art of Fiction No. 196." *Paris Review*, Issue 184 (Spring 2008).
Krider, Dylan Otto. "Rooted in a Small Space: An Interview with Kazuo Ishiguro." *The Kenyon Review*, New Series, Vol. 20, No. 2 (Spring, 1998): 146–154.
Plato. *Euthyphro. Apology. Crito. Phaedo. Phaedrus.* Translated by Harold North Fowler. Loeb Classical Library 36. Cambridge, MA: Harvard University Press, 1914.
———. *The Republic of Plato.* Translated by Allan Bloom. New York: Basic Books, 1968.
Sim, Wai-chew. *Kazuo Ishiguro*. New York: Routledge, 2010.

Chapter Ten

Founding a Posthuman Political Order in M. R. Carey's *The Girl with All the Gifts*

Erin A. Dolgoy and Kimberly Hurd Hale

As is often the case with science fiction stories, M. R. Carey's powerful novel *The Girl with All the Gifts* combines enduring myths with futuristic innovations, allowing readers to interrogate our understanding of the present and the possibilities of the future. Carey's titular protagonist, Melanie, is a young girl who possesses "all the gifts." Melanie embodies many of the characteristics typical of young girls across societies—she loves reading myths and writing stories, and she envisions herself simultaneously as a princess and as a warrior who rescues the princess. Yet Melanie does not live in our society, nor is she in fact a human being. Beginning twenty years after the effectual demise of human civilization, *The Girl with All the Gifts* depicts the apocalyptic end of humanity and introduces the nascent society established on the vestiges of the old. In her role as the founder of the new order, Melanie seeks to preserve the characteristics and culture that she loves about humanity, while making room for the new practices and values that are required by the posthumans of the future. Melanie, the unlikely founder of this new society, is the bridge between the human past and the posthuman future. In this chapter, we draw upon Aristotle's account of political society, Thomas Hobbes's and John Locke's discussions of the state of nature, and Niccolò Machiavelli's consideration of foundings and political necessity. In order to understand Melanie's actions and the reasons for her actions, we explore the relationship between necessity and justice in her transition from captive of the old society to founder of the new.

Carey's novel begins twenty years after *Ophiocordyceps*, a fungus prominent in the rainforests of South America, "jump[s] the species barrier," moving from ants to humans.[1] In its original form, the fungus overwrites the ant's central nervous system and then compels the infected ant to climb to a great height before causing the ant to explode, thereby disseminating the fungal spores over the largest possible area, increasing their opportunities to infect more hosts. Once the fungus mutates, becoming *Ophiocordyceps unilateralis*, it is able to infect humans[2] through their bodily fluids.[3] Infected humans become "hungries," slowly decomposing zombie-like creatures who compulsively seek and eat human flesh. Two decades after the fungal mutation, civilization as we know it has devolved: there are no formal governments; there are no systems of communication or trade; and there are no expectations of civility or safety. The few uninfected human beings who remain have either (1) devolved into "junkers"—nomadic humans who "don't build, or preserve . . . just stay alive" by brutal means[4]—or (2) retreated inside a British military base in order to seek a cure for the infection amid some semblance of the old order.

The novel's key characters are introduced at this military base. The ruthless Dr. Caroline Caldwell, the scientist responsible for finding a cure for the infection, is intent on returning *Homo sapiens* to the top of the evolutionary food chain. Militaristic sergeant Ed Parks maintains security at the base; he is less hopeful than is Caldwell that a cure can be found, but is nonetheless determined to preserve humanity for as long as possible. And Melanie's beloved teacher, Helen Justineau, is a psychologist charged with educating Melanie and her classmates in subjects ranging from Greek mythology to creative writing, in order to study their intellectual, psychological, and emotional behaviors. A liberal arts pedagogical effort seems incongruous in a post-apocalyptic environment, particularly since, like her classmates, Melanie is transported within her small world—"the cell, the corridor, the classroom, and the shower room"[5]—strapped (by her wrists, ankles, and neck) to a wheelchair designed to restrict her movement severely. The necessity of these precautions, however, becomes clear once Melanie's true nature is revealed. Neither she nor her classmates are *Homo sapiens*. These children, who look human, are symbiotes, second-generation hungries, infected by the fungus *in utero* and born to a "hungry" mother. Like a hungry, Melanie subsists entirely on protein and instinctually will attack and eat humans.[6] Unlike a typical hungry, however, Melanie manifests the genius-level intelligence and the capacity for emotional attachment that she inherits from her "human" side. Melanie understands her own ability to both reason and overcome her instincts. She is capable of foresight. Over the course of the novel, she learns that she is neither human nor hungry, but rather something entirely new; she is a hybrid. Melanie comes to accept the responsibilities that accompany her unique status.

Although Justineau and, eventually, Parks recognize Melanie as a sentient creature deserving of life and liberty,[7] Caldwell steadfastly maintains that once infection of any kind occurs, all vestiges of the human host are consumed by the parasite.[8] When the military base is attacked by junkers and hungries, Melanie and her former captors escape and seek refuge in London, where they encounter a tribe of feral hybrid children. Outside the security of the base, Melanie is no longer a captive, and the humans are no longer her jailers. Melanie then faces two harsh truths. First, the uninfected humans who remain on earth will never live peacefully with the hybrid children. Experimentation on, and vivisection of, the hybrids is considered necessary by the humans, as the hybrids' biochemistry represents the humans' best hope to find a cure for the fungal infection. Melanie believes that if the humans do find an antidote to the parasite, they will then, for their own self-defense and self-preservation, hunt the hybrid children and exterminate them. After she observes the group of feral hybrid children in the wilds of London, children who are capable of laying traps and hunting as a pack, Melanie comprehends the second truth: she will not be able to protect the uninfected humans whom she loves from either the fungus or attack, unless she can teach her fellow hybrids how to control their natural urges. This is an educational undertaking that, if achievable, will likely take years, during which time *Homo sapiens*, will be hunted and consumed, perhaps to extinction. Melanie predicts that both species will live in a constant state of war, struggling to survive and overcome their adversaries until their numbers dwindle, rendering the survivors unable to build permanent civilizations or preserve cultures, effectively eliminating rational life on earth. While she would prefer to allow both species to live in peace, she understands her choice. If she allows *Homo sapiens* to survive, she risks the genocide of her own species at the hand of *Homo sapiens*. If she chooses the extinction of *Homo sapiens*, she commits genocide and risks the eradication of all rational life on earth, but leaves open the possibility for the hybrid children to evolve and rebuild civilization. Melanie therefore decides to accelerate the spread of the fungal spores, ensuring that all remaining human beings are infected within a month, clearing the way for the rise of a hybrid society with her at its helm.[9] Once the spores are released, Melanie gathers the feral hybrid children to her. Justineau, the sole surviving human being, who must now live her life in hermetically sealed spaces, will continue to educate the hybrid children; she is charged by Melanie with passing on humanity's collective knowledge to the new species of posthumans.

This chapter examines both the necessity and the justice of Melanie's choice to force the acceleration of human evolution. We begin with a discussion of Aristotle's account of political community, followed by a consideration of two of the Enlightenment's most prominent formulations of the state of nature, presented in Thomas Hobbes's *Leviathan* and John Locke's *Second Treatise of Government*. We analyze the conditions under which human beings can be said to live in a pre-political society and the conditions which allow human beings to leave this state of nature. In the next section, in light of Niccolò Machiavelli's discussion of political founders, we examine Melanie's decision to release the fungal spores, thereby making the earth uninhabitable to *Homo sapiens*. We consider the ways in which Machiavelli's discussion of armed prophets applies to, and deviates from, Melanie's interactions with the feral children. The final section returns to Melanie's choice and the importance of the liberal arts for human flourishing (even if those who flourish may technically not be *Homo sapiens*).

APOCALYPSE NOW: RETURN TO THE STATE OF NATURE

The *Homo sapiens* on the military base maintain a mutually beneficial *de facto* social contract. Although there is no recognized national governing authority, the vestiges of the social contract seem to exist among the uninfected humans on the base. They recognize military rank; follow rules concerning how and when humans can communicate with the hybrid children; and attempt, to the best of their abilities, to protect one another from external threats of violence. The humans on the base understand themselves as the guardians of human civilization and are determined to save themselves from their two immediate threats: the hungries, incapable of rule, law, or self-mastery, who seek either to consume the humans or to turn *Homo sapiens* into hungries; and the junkers, who, according to the humans on the base, live in a state of nature (despite being capable of working together and undertaking projects). After the infection, the humans on the military base attempt to preserve human society, as it has been traditionally understood. In contrast to these humans, the junkers have chosen to revert to a brutal way of life. Although they live on the base, the hybrid children are not part of the *Homo sapiens*' social contract. In the most fundamental ways, the hybrid children who have been captured by the humans and imprisoned on the base are not part of the state of order there, and yet they are also not quite part of the state of nature outside the base.

After the base is overrun by junkers and hungries, Melanie, for the first time, has a sense of agency and freedom. As the only "civilized" hybrid to escape the military base, Melanie learns that she need not abide by the traditional rules governing moral or ethical behavior, as understood by her human companions. She is neither a citizen of British society, nor afforded the protection of "human rights" by those around her. She, by necessity, operates in a pre-political condition with regard to both the *Homo sapiens* (who reject her claims to personhood) and the feral hybrid children (who have no conception of a social contract). If some form of peaceful, sustainable treaty could be established between the two species, Melanie's choice to release the fungal spores would unquestionably deserve condemnation. Mutually beneficial peace, however, is impossible in the context of the novel. Neither side can be expected to respect the natural rights of the other; their relationship is one of predator and prey (although *Homo sapiens* and hybrid children would disagree on who is the hunter and who is the hunted). Given her political circumstances, Melanie cannot feasibly be bound to any political standards of right and wrong. She exists in the state of nature, and it is only by committing a crime of harsh necessity that she is able to survive and carve a space for the emergence of a new, just society, while, more importantly, controlling its development.

State of nature theory examines human beings at our most essential, stripped of the contrivances of institutions, education, and social norms. When the trappings of civil society are dispatched, we are able to see a version of the ways in which human beings might act, were no laws or customs in place to constrain our behavior. Once we are able to discern human nature in its most unsullied form, we can determine that civil government is a necessary remedy to the ills of the state of nature, and then begin to examine the types of regimes and the specific laws that are most effective in governing human society—an essential task of political science. After all, laws and customs that contradict some fundamental aspect of human nature are unlikely to lead to a happy, healthy, prosperous, or stable society. Our unencumbered knowledge about human nature can help us determine what we think is the best (or best possible) political order. Most classical and modern thinkers agree that the primary task of political philosophy is to determine the best regime. While classical thinkers use the city to reach the highest form of human potential, modern thinkers simply want to understand which type of city will conflict least with human nature and will, therefore, be most readily achievable.[10]

Plato and Aristotle both maintain that the city, including its laws and customs, is a part of human nature and that human beings need the city in order to express their essential humanity to the fullest. Some modern thinkers use the state of nature as the starting point for political philosophy, yet radically depart from these classical perspectives by identifying a conflict between human nature and politics. According to Plato and Aristotle, the purpose of a political community is not simply living, but living well.[11] Lawmakers, legislators, and political leaders are tasked with establishing political communities that cultivate virtue in the citizenry.[12] Aristotle understands "the city or political community" as the organization that provides for "the most authoritative good."[13] The political community, therefore, is that toward which all human beings strive, since human beings seek that which they believe is their good. We are each, as Aristotle understands us, "by nature a political animal."[14] Human beings exist, Aristotle explains, in order to achieve excellence, which is only possible as part of a political community. Our capacity to speak, human *logos*, is both a precondition for, and a consequence of, community.[15] We require speech in order to voice our reason, share our preferences, and provide our consent. While other animals are able to communicate their experiences of pleasure and pain, notions of virtue and justice are predicated on the human ability to express our rational concerns. It is only within a political community that we, as human beings striving to achieve excellence, are able to be part of a rational decision-making body. Human beings, Aristotle argues, naturally long to be part of a political community.

Melanie possesses these three distinct human qualities—the desire for community, the ability to communicate, and the capacity to reason. She is therefore capable of freely entering into a political community and determining the parameters of her social contract. Despite her human-ness, she is denied entry into the community of which she longs to be a part. While Justineau accepts the personhood of Melanie and the other hybrid children, Parks maintains that "[n]ot everyone who looks human is human;"[16] Melanie's reason and emotional capacity, according to Parks, do not qualify her for personhood, which he defines strictly as limited to *Homo sapiens*. Caldwell likewise has no compunction about experimenting on the hybrids, comparing their suffering to that of lab rats. Melanie is not, and believes she never will be, included in the social organization that governs the behavior of the humans on the base. She does not expect to belong to an enduring social contract of which Parks and Caldwell are a part.

Enlightenment political philosophy provides several accounts of the state of nature. The most relevant accounts to our consideration of Melanie are those of Thomas Hobbes and John Locke. An examination of these thinkers' conceptions of the state of nature is particularly useful in the context of *The Girl with All the Gifts*, as Melanie represents rational posthumans, a category of persons that have not yet come into being, but may eventually (perhaps even in the near future) challenge our current understanding of natural and civil rights. The state of nature provides us with an opportunity to speculate about what might happen to individuals like Melanie when they are outside the boundaries of "normal" conditions.

Hobbes's *Leviathan* presents a harsh view of the state of nature. Our natural condition, Hobbes avers, is one of radical equality; each human is equally capable of killing another person. All human beings, in the state of nature, regardless of relative intelligence and strength, have "equality of hope"[17] coupled with a single imperative: survival. Encompassed within this survival instinct is the natural right of self-defense and a natural law that mandates the seeking of peace.[18] Left to our own devices, Hobbes contends, all human beings become violent, since the best way to defend against an attack is to eliminate all possible attackers. Since the naturally weaker humans, when working in concert, are able to overpower a naturally stronger human, there is no natural supremacy in the state of nature. Radical equality and equivalent vulnerability cause human life in its natural state to be "solitary, poor, nasty, brutish, and short."[19] Hobbes explains that only once each individual surrenders to a common authority the right to prevent an attack, and thus enters into political life, can he or she ever relax enough to pursue other interests, such as philosophy, commerce, or art. Not all people will be content to relinquish their right to self-defense and accept the possibilities of peace, stability, and social order—after all, Hobbes argues, men lock their doors even in the most enlightened cities.[20] Some individuals will still crave power and dominion over their fellows, even within the bounds of a "peaceful" society.

Similarly to Hobbes, Locke views the state of nature as one of radical equality, wherein men have the liberty to "order their actions, and dispose of their possessions, and persons as they think fit."[21] Locke argues that in the absence of a ruling authority, the vast majority of human beings reasonably desire simply to be left alone.[22] Human beings acquire property by using their bodies and their labor to change the natural world, and they refrain from attacking other individuals whom they encounter. Preservation of property, including the body that one uses in labor, forms the basis of natural rights, according to Locke. This sort of radically individualized state of nature is not desirable in the long term, however. As a consequence of the inevitable tension between the acquisition of property by one person and self-preservation by another, the natural rights of multiple people are incompatible in a world of limited resources. When such a conflict occurs, for example in conditions of food scarcity, one person will inevitably violate the natural rights of another person. Since no common authority exists to arbitrate the conflict, each individual must seek to punish the transgressor.[23] One can easily understand how this condition may degenerate into chaos. A system must therefore be designed that both protects property and proportionally punishes violators of property rights. The appropriate arrangement, according to Locke, must take the form of a contractual political society.

In Carey's novel, the radical equality among human beings is evident in the interactions between the humans on the military base and the junkers. Objectively, the humans on the base are more powerful than the junkers: the military base is equipped with a fence, armored vehicles, weapons, and a security system. The junkers, however, are industrious. Despite their apparent comparative weaknesses, the junkers work together herding the hungries in order to topple the fence and overrun the base. As Hobbes suggests may happen, the increased strength of the humans on the military base does not guarantee their supremacy over the junkers. Biologically, the hybrid children are genetically superior to the humans on the military base and the junkers. The children are capable of living in an environment that is saturated by the *Ophiocordyceps unilateralis* and, therefore, toxic to *Homo sapiens*. The hybrids are not as vulnerable to physical discomfort as are human beings, as is evidenced on the base by the children's ability to sit chained to chairs for numerous hours each day. They do not possess a physical need for water in order to survive, or for varied foods in order to thrive—they only need to consume protein at regular intervals to maintain normal function.[24] Like that of the hungries, the children's saliva is poisonous to human beings, and they are instinctually driven to hunt their prey relentlessly. Yet, like the humans, the children are capable of higher-order reasoning, making tools, and hunting cooperatively. These genetic superiorities do not prevent the hybrid children from being hunted, captured, and killed by groups of humans working together. The hybrid children are vulnerable to the superior technology possessed by their human prey—technology that has allowed the humans to capture isolated feral children and imprison them on the base, and that could allow the humans to eliminate the small community of feral hybrids.

The state of nature represents humanity at its most natural. There are, of course, different definitions of "natural." Natural can mean pre-technological, if one takes a historical perspective. Or, the development of technology can be construed as a natural part of the human experience, since we use our nature-given reason to develop control over our environment. The state of nature therefore need not be primitive; in fact, it can be quite technologically advanced. As defined by both Hobbes and Locke, the key characteristics of a state of nature are threefold: the absence of a legitimate governing authority,[25] the unpredictability of interactions between human beings, and the omnipresent threat of violence. If these conditions are met, a person lives in the state of nature.

Melanie has always existed in a state of nature. While she is imprisoned on the base, she may be subject to a governing authority, but she certainly does not participate in either its selection or its governance. In fact, the established governing authority threatens her bodily autonomy and security. Although the hybrid children on the base are subject to some predictable routines, they are never certain at the beginning of each day whether their human caretakers are going to teach them Greek mythology, or send them to Caldwell's laboratory for vivisection. Melanie has never been part of a community of equals. Once Melanie, Caldwell, Parks, and Justineau escape the junker raid and are forced to flee the safety of the fences that surround the base, Melanie is free from the control of the humans, yet still remains in a state of nature. Justineau, Parks, and Caldwell experience a transition during the novel. While they are on the military base, a hierarchy remains intact, and cooperation exists among various other bases.[26] The hierarchy quickly devolves, however, when the base is overrun by junkers and hungries, forcing Melanie, Justineau, Parks, and Caldwell to flee. After their attempts to contact other military installations prove unsuccessful, they eventually accept the fact that they are on their own. The group travels to London, where the absolute collapse of prior forms of political, military, and social order is undeniable.

Carey repeatedly emphasizes that Melanie's life meets the second tenet of the state of nature: unpredictability with regard to human interaction. She will never be part of the human political community, since she is not *Homo sapiens*, and she will never be subject to the same social rules, behaviors, or respect that humans (at least theoretically) afford one another. She can never be sure whether a person she meets will treat her kindly, as does Justineau, or brutally, as does Caldwell. Melanie, therefore, exists outside the social rules of her human captors. As long as Melanie lives with the humans, she will never be regarded, at least by either Parks or Caldwell, as a political equal. As a consequence, she is as vulnerable, perhaps even more so, than an individual living solely in the state of nature, since the laws and rules that provide order on the base make her susceptible to constant threats of violence.

The third condition of the state of nature, the omnipresent threat of violence, is also readily apparent in the novel. The junkers are violent; according to the humans who have chosen to live on the base, junkers kill or enslave any uninfected person whom they encounter. The hungries are controlled by the fungus' compulsion to reproduce; numb to the passage of time, physical pain, or bodily decay, hungries relentlessly pursue, infect, and consume any human whom they detect. While those fleeing the base find brief moments of respite in their journey, the reader is acutely aware that any peace is short-lived.

Melanie understands herself to be in a war of all against all—she lives in Hobbes's state of nature. Every human, with the exception of Justineau, is viewed by Melanie as an enemy combatant and a threat to her own safety and the safety of the hybrid children. There is no possible future that includes *Homo sapiens* in which Melanie and the children are free.[27] Melanie's actions—including her release of the spores—are conducted under duress and can be understood as an exercise of her natural right to self-defense. It is Melanie who provides the best defense of her actions. Early in the novel, Melanie reflects on the reputation of Pandora, one of the Greek myths that Justineau teaches the students in class. Pandora, the first woman, is created by Zeus, the ruler of the Olympian gods, in order to wreak havoc on his enemies the Titans. Each of the Olympic gods gives Pandora a gift, which she keeps in a jar. Pandora, imbued with curiosity, is intended by her creator to open the jar and unleash the contents upon the world. Yet, "Melanie . . . didn't think it was right to blame Pandora for what happened."[28] Pandora is created to destroy the Titans; unleashing evil upon humankind is simply an unfortunate byproduct of fulfilling her purpose. Melanie, too, is designed by nature to destroy human beings. She and the hybrid children are adapted to the *Ophiocordyceps unilateralis* saturated environment. They are compelled to consume flesh, including human flesh. As a result of her education and experiences, Melanie also understands biology and is able to use complex human technologies. Ultimately, her captors make it possible for her to destroy them wholesale, rather than one at a time.

While *The Girl with All The Gifts* certainly depicts a state of nature (or perhaps states of nature), not all the characters regard this condition in the same way. As we note, the humans on the base are attempting to preserve the vestiges of their obsolete society. Unless Caldwell, or a scientist like her, is able to develop a cure, the death of *Homo sapiens* is inevitable. Yet, these human beings cling to the society into which they were born. The junkers have embraced the state of nature. They live in a perpetual state of chaos and uncertainty. While their reasons are never explained, the junkers have chosen to abandoned the trappings of civil society and have not attempted to preserve the illusions of safety, stability, or equality, as have the humans on the base; instead, they have reverted to a pre-civil condition. The hungries are no longer human, in any sense of the word. They have no tangible memories of life prior to infection; they exist as animals driven by instinct.

The hybrid children, however, are different from all other groups. These children have the ability to speak and reason; they also are able, as Melanie exemplifies, to overcome their desires for human flesh (although this need for self-mastery is irrelevant if there are no humans to consume). These hybrid children need a leader, one who is willing and able to protect them from the remaining *Homo sapiens* and from each other, and who will establish the rules and laws required to guide them into a peaceful, stable future. Unlike many founders, Melanie has no illusions about her choice to assume the mantle of leadership: if she does not rise to lead the hybrid children, someone else likely will.[29] While she has already wiped out the remaining *Homo sapiens* who could potentially oppose her, she will likely face new challenges once the hybrids develop complex language and reasoning skills. If Melanie is to control the development of hybrid society, she must act decisively.

MELANIE'S MACHIAVELLIAN TURN

Hobbes's and Locke's accounts of the state of nature are primarily concerned with the question of what makes political power legitimate, not with examining how political states actually come into being. Therefore, we argue, Melanie's actions are best viewed through the lens of Machiavelli's examination of political founders and foundings. Melanie must contend with the specific circumstances in which she lives, namely the remnants of our own civilization. While the political order—including the hierarchies, infrastructure, and practices—of *Homo sapiens* is in decay, there are still people who struggle to maintain the old order and to regain their supremacy by any means necessary. Dramatic political change, such as revolution or regime transformation, demands the overthrow of the existing political order, necessitating those who held power under the old regime to relinquish their efforts to retain that control. Melanie, as a consequence of her decisions to release all the fungal spores and to exterminate *Homo sapiens*, eliminates all possible adversaries who are attached to the old hierarchy, and makes room for the establishment of an entirely new order. She wipes out all the *Homo sapiens* who potentially might impede her rise. No humans remain to challenge her power, authority, or vision for the future. Melanie's Machiavellian calculations provide a framework in which to consider the implications of Machiavelli's understanding, as presented in *The Prince*, of the unpredictability and brutality of political change.

When founding a new political society, the presence of cultural memory among the citizens often necessitates violence to overcome the established order. Her new citizenry, comprised of both the feral children encountered in London and the possible survivors of the massacre at the base, have no experience of being ruled. Therefore, they have no such cultural memory harkening back to previous orders. However, any possible hybrid survivors from the base will have received a liberal arts education similar to that of Melanie, and will have been socialized similarly to human children. [30] As the reader sees early in the novel, the children on the base form alliances or become adversaries, such as Melanie's friend Anne, whose friendship is based on their proximity to each other, [31] or Melanie's enemy Kenny, who calls her names and mocks her weaknesses. Although the children have no experience of citizenship, they do display political natures.

Even before Melanie understands her true biological nature, she has established leadership qualities. In the beginning of the novel, Melanie expresses a desire to unite her fellows. She wants to teach sign language to the children on the base, so that they can communicate during the hours in which they are confined to their cells—an idea that even Justineau recognizes as imminently dangerous to their human captors. [32] Melanie understands her actions, especially her release of the spores, as being in the interests of her people (the hybrid children) and for the greater good of rational life on earth. She is a leader who finally determines to form her own people. As Machiavelli relates of Hiero of Syracuse, "he was of such virtue, even in private fortune, that he who wrote of him said 'that he lacked nothing of being a king, except a kingdom.'" [33] Melanie possesses this Machiavellian virtue of a political leader; she simply needs to choose her opportunity carefully, recognizing when circumstances dictate that she acts.

Most of the hybrid children are feral, meaning they are vulnerable to coordinated human attacks and the vicissitudes of nature. They have had no meaningful parental caregivers, no teachers, and no adult authority figures.

The hungries, incapable of being either ruled or tamed, die during the traumatic process of childbirth, leaving their offspring parentless. Moreover, all the first-generation hungries will eventually die, as uninfected food sources dwindle. The hybrid children are the only sentient beings with a chance to survive in the new environment; they will be left to build a new civilization, repopulating the earth with their own progeny and creating ways to harmonize their needs with their surroundings. Since the feral population of hybrid children has no language and no cultural history, Melanie has the opportunity to found a new civilization with them; the only cultural memory she must contend with is her own. She is able to control the development of language and the children's education, establishing unity. Much like how her own language acquisition and education was controlled on the base, the children will acquire only the knowledge that she chooses to disseminate.

Melanie first encounters the pack of hybrids while scouting for supplies in London. She is frightened by her first interaction with the feral children—aged four to perhaps fifteen; the naked, filthy children are armed with sticks and kitchen knives as they attempt to hunt rats for food. They do not appear to have names, nor do they have a language developed beyond grunts, squeaks, growls, facial expressions, and hand gestures. Yet, they are hunting in a pack and playing a game of sorts; they laugh and make faces.[34] One boy is the leader and protects the other children. Melanie understands her affinity to these feral children. Had she not been captured and taken to the base, she would likely be part of this macabre yet congenial picnic.[35] The feral children are pack animals: they hunt together; they communicate using gestures, clicks, whistles,[36] and subtle expressions;[37] they have ritualistic forms of dress and practice body modification, including filing their teeth;[38] and, when they work together, they are able to incapacitate and kill adult humans.[39] They are savage and wild, driven by their instincts. However, they are also loyal, have a sense of family or community, exhibit some type of hierarchy, and are able to hunt together, indicating that they seem to depend on each other for survival. Prior to encountering Melanie, however, the children are pre-political; they do not yet seem to engage in formal deliberation or reasoning. Their social organization seems to be premised on mere survival and physical supremacy. They have an inchoate ability to communicate, reflect a semblance of sociability, and seem capable of developing all the personal qualities, characteristics, and skills that Melanie has cultivated (absent her natural intelligence). With the proper guidance, attention, and education, each of these children will become capable of participating in a political society.[40]

Melanie understands that these children are vulnerable to the humans with whom she travels. She also understands that the feral children are more like her than different from her. She is unwilling to abandon her human companions to the mercy of the feral children, and she is also unwilling to allow Caldwell and Parks to subject the children to the same incarceration and experimentation to which she herself was once condemned. Her best choice, therefore, is to assume command of the hybrid pack and use her power to forge a new political order. Since the only authority that the hybrids currently respect is physical supremacy, she challenges the leader of the children to combat. Because the feral children exist in a primitive, tribal community, Melanie's victory represents a founding of "an altogether new principality," with a new, virtuous prince at its head.[41]

In the battle between Melanie and the leader of the feral children, Melanie tries to make herself appear like a monster from the Greek myths. She believes that the leader of the feral children must be physically beaten in order to save Parks and Justineau.[42] As Machiavelli teaches, armed prophets are successful, while unarmed prophets rarely install new orders.[43] Founders who succeed, Machiavelli suggests, possess both physical and spiritual authority. They are able to establish a relationship to a higher power. A founder who is able to appeal to the religiosity of the people or provide a divine impetus for his or her own actions can seduce those individuals who have faith. Melanie is not necessarily an armed prophet, since she does not invoke the gods directly. She does, however, depict herself as a figure from her beloved Greek mythology, making herself appear like a monster when she first interacts with the feral children. In so doing, she frightens the children. She is not a messenger of a higher power, but rather presents *herself* as the higher power. She is a more advanced, more knowledgeable, more capable being than the children whom she wants to lead. She uses technology and her knowledge of the psychology of mythmaking to overcome a physically stronger opponent. Ingenuity allows her to murder and supplant the leader of the feral children. Melanie exemplifies the type of *virtù*, both in her skill and her determination, that Machiavelli identifies as essential to political leadership. Although the children initially fear Melanie and run from her, at the end of the story she assembles her new tribe in a circle and prepares to educate them in the liberal arts.

Melanie's initial act of brutality is aligned with Machiavelli's exhortation that cruelty should be effectively utilized at the beginning of one's reign, but avoided thereafter.[44] A prince who begins his reign with an act of brutality and then softens his approach is likely to be regarded as merciful and liberal by the people, but a ruler who begins gently and then is forced to become cruel is likely to be forever hated. Melanie initially uses violence and fear to exhibit her superiority over the hybrid children, then offers them the chance to become more like her, educated and sophisticated members of a new civilization. Melanie understands that she has an opportunity to found a new political order. Fortune is, to some extent, in her favor. She also understands that favorable conditions do not guarantee success. Melanie must act decisively. She is not physically the largest hybrid child, and she is an outsider to the London pack. Melanie is able to take control of the children through trickery and manipulation—by applying her superior knowledge. If she successfully civilizes the children, however, this advantage will disappear. Moreover, if she does not initiate and control their education, a physically dominant hybrid may kill her. If Melanie does not seize her opportunity the first time that it is presented, another feral child may rise and take power.

There are similarities between Machiavelli's examples of individuals who have become princes by their own virtue—"Moses, Cyrus, Romulus, [and] Theseus,"[45]—and Melanie. Like her predecessors, Melanie has opportunity and fortune in her favor. In some respects, Melanie is much like Moses, who, Machiavelli explains, "find[s] the people of Israel in Egypt, enslaved and oppressed by the Egyptians, so that they would be disposed to follow him so as to get out of their servitude."[46] Had this opportunity not presented itself to Moses, he likely would have remained in the Egyptian court or toiled as a shepherd for his father-in-law. Moses's talent as a political revolutionary and lawgiver may have remained unrealized. Similarly, Melanie finds her own people "oppressed" by *Homo sapiens*, creating the conditions for the hybrid children to be liberated and civilized. Melanie is also akin to Romulus, whose exposure in his infancy establishes the conditions that allow him to become king of Rome. Melanie, too, is unintentionally exposed as a child. She is the offspring of a hungry mother who is physically and mentally incapable of caring for her child. Had Melanie not been abducted and educated by the humans on the base, if she survived she would likely be no different than the other feral children. Melanie recognizes and capitalizes on her opportunity.

Melanie, unlike most founders who have come before her, does not have to contend with the cultural memory of a conquered or colonized people. She is forming an entirely new principality, not conquering an existing society. After she releases the fungal spores, there are no *Homo sapiens* left on earth "who benefit[ted] from the old orders"; therefore, she has no established enemies.[47] She has learned "how not to be good," in a strictly moral sense, one of the primary tasks assigned by Machiavelli to his virtuous prince.[48] She understands necessity, as she reasons that the current natural conditions on earth will inevitably result in the deaths of all *Homo sapiens*; the environment has become poisonous, and *Homo sapiens* cannot survive. Murdering (or hastening the certain deaths of) all the remaining *Homo sapiens* is not just—it is genocide after all. However, saving her own life and the lives of the children like her (by preventing their murder by *Homo sapiens*) *is* perhaps part of justice. While neither Machiavelli nor Melanie believe that all ends justify all means, in this case, Melanie, in her role as Machiavellian prince(ss), reasons that the ends justify the means.[49] Melanie's choice—to hasten the inevitable deaths of all *Homo sapiens*—reveals the difficulty in establishing strict moral precepts, especially in politics.

Moral philosophy often uses Philippa Foot's "Trolley Problem" to capture the moral ambiguities in choices such as Melanie's: "[I]t may rather be supposed that he is the driver of a runaway tram [trolley] which he can only steer from one narrow track on to another; five men are working on one track and one man on the other; anyone on the track the tram enters is bound to be killed."[50] Foot's formulation asks us to consider whether or not it is ever moral to kill some individuals in order to save other individuals. Melanie's moral dilemma is further complicated: if she does not kill the *Homo sapiens*, she is likely to be killed herself. In order to preserve the civilization of her tormentors, Melanie is required to sacrifice her own life.

Almost all religious, legal, and ethical codes throughout history require that one not kill, with some strictly defined exceptions in each case. Melanie's choice to kill all the remaining *Homo sapiens* is plainly genocide. She effectively destroys all members—save Justineau—of a particular species. She eradicates human beings. While no *Homo sapiens* remain to judge or punish her crimes, Carey encourages his readers to consider whether or not the murders that she commits are justified. This is a difficult question to ponder. The *Homo sapiens* with whom she has interacted—with the exception of Justineau—have shown no signs that they respect her right to live. Melanie is protecting herself from grievous harm; as far as her experiences indicate, that harm is both immediate and inflicted by (almost) all members of the human species. As the effective leader of a new, posthuman species, Melanie lives in a constant state of war with humanity. She can never hope to enter into a social contract with *Homo sapiens*, as the relationship between *Homo sapiens* and hybrids is that of prey and predator. Though rational creatures may strive to overcome their natural violent impulses, the instinct of hybrids to feed on human flesh cannot be overcome before humanity is completely destroyed. The end of *Homo sapiens* as a species is inevitable; she simply hastens the process. Melanie's actions prevent a protracted war, which she believes the hybrids will eventually win, but will also destroy the beauty and wisdom of human culture.

PRESERVING THE LESSONS OF THE PAST: IN DEFENSE OF THE LIBERAL ARTS

Although Melanie believes that *Homo sapiens* cannot peacefully coexist with the new posthuman species of hybrids, she does not wholly reject humanity's legacy. Melanie's personality is deeply informed by the lessons that she has learned from her human teachers at the military base, particularly from Justineau. It does not matter to Melanie that Justineau's primary intent has been to measure the hybrid children's cognitive capacities in order to find a way to save *Homo sapiens*. Melanie, like Machiavelli, cares primarily about the outcome: Justineau has successfully imparted the lessons of a classical liberal arts education to her hybrid pupils. Melanie does not simply understand the value of love and friendship, she also understands the power of writing, storytelling, and myth-making. This education has given Melanie the tools to form a new community of hybrids, but, as liberal arts education is meant to do, it has also made her a better "person." As Parks explains, Melanie does not recognize that she is a monster. While she is on the base, Melanie is unaware that the *Homo sapiens'* world is over, and she does not understand that she is not human. It is only after she learns the truth about her nature and discovers the feral hybrids that she grasps the true state of her condition. Her anachronistic education "filled her head with all this unserviceable shit," despite the fact that she is supposed to die, one way or another.[51] By educating Melanie in the liberal arts, the human beings at the military base have shaped a creature capable of both ending humanity as a species and ensuring that human culture endures beyond that species' extinction. Melanie preserves the lessons of the liberal arts not only because they are a civilizing force, but also from her genuine desire to safeguard the stories that she loves.

As discussed earlier, Melanie's favorite myth is that of Pandora, who is given gifts by all the gods only to unleash havoc upon the world. Melanie is fascinated by Pandora, whom she views as being treated unfairly by Zeus. Pandora is created solely to produce the conditions for her jar of horrors to be opened; yet, she is condemned for fulfilling her life's purpose.[52] Melanie understandably identifies strongly with the mythical woman who is punished for failing to overcome her own nature. After Melanie saves Justineau by killing some of the junkers who have overrun the base, Justineau explains to Melanie that she should never be punished for who she is, justifying Melanie's murder of the junkers,[53] but also unwittingly providing the defense for Melanie's destruction of all the *Homo sapiens* (save Justineau who will spend the rest of her life in a hermetically sealed, mobile laboratory). Melanie does not want to hurt the human beings for whom she cares deeply, yet she must struggle to overcome the fungus' compulsion to feed on them.[54] As Melanie relates, even though she rationally understands that she should not bite humans (or open the jar), much like Pandora, "she's just been built so she has to, and she can't make herself stop."[55] Melanie is able to overcome this violent, primal aspect of her nature by drawing on her desire to protect her individual human companions, and on a more abstract, philosophical longing to be a good person worthy of Justineau's love. Melanie is motivated by admiration, love, and her desire to protect others. Her efforts surpass those of most human beings whose motivation to leave the state of nature is mere self-interest. In order to enter into a functional political society and gain the protection, stability, and civil rights afforded by that society, we must relinquish our unlimited natural rights and overcome our animalistic natures. We must become *capable* of political life, through study, discussion, and the practice of *self*-governance. Melanie is capable of participating in political life, she is practiced in study and discussion, and not only desires self-governance, but also seeks to establish a society that is *better* than the one that came before.

Of course, Pandora retains one gift after her jar is emptied upon the world: the gift of hope. Melanie likewise offers the hope of preserving rational life on earth. When Parks challenges her plan to accelerate the release of the fungal spores, effectively killing all remaining uninfected humans, Melanie explains that she is saddened by her choice, but that it is necessary. Her decision offers human culture a chance for redemption and continuation. She believes that the hybrid children will "be different. Like [her], and the rest of the kids in the class. They'll be the next people. The ones who make everything okay again."[56] Melanie realizes something that her human companions do not: by seeking to preserve the species in its current form, *Homo sapiens* will actually cause the permanent loss of "humanity." The network of military bases has been destroyed, and the only remaining uninfected humans are likely junkers, who, as discussed, are concerned solely with survival. They do not try to overcome their violent, animalistic urges, and they do not seek to preserve or enhance the collective cultural inheritance of humanity.

M. R. Carey, in *The Girl with All the Gifts*, reminds us that our humanness is not contingent on our biology. In fact, the most essential characteristics and qualities of human beings—love, friendship, desire, a longing for justice, rational thinking, and cultural memory—need not be found exclusively in *Homo sapiens*. In the future, evolution and human intervention may require us to reconsider what it means to be a human and what constitutes human culture. Melanie, by hastening the evolutionary process, shows us that we cannot choose the gifts we inherit, but we can choose how we use them. Melanie's actions, although not unambiguously just, are *necessary,* based on logical reasoning, to ensure her own survival and thus allow her a chance to preserve human excellence. Her treachery stems from her longing to create a better, more peaceful, more just world than the one into which she is born. Unfortunately, Melanie's re-founding of civilization requires that no *Homo sapiens* are left to appreciate the new order. Based on Melanie's experiences and her evaluation of our history, we would, of course, not only destroy her and her kind, but also any hope for the posthuman future.

NOTES

We would like to thank Frances Ratner and the editors of this volume, Steven Michels and Timothy McCranor, for their many suggestions and comments that have helped us to improve this chapter.

1. M. R. Carey, *The Girl with All the Gifts* (London: Orbit Books, 2014), 54.
2. Carey, *The Girl*, 54.
3. Carey, *The Girl*, 175.

4. Carey, *The Girl*, 215.

5. Carey, *The Girl*, 2.

6. Carey, *The Girl,* 12 and 83.

7. For an extended discussion of Melanie's personhood, as well as engagement with the relevant transhumanist literature, see Kimberly Hurd Hale and Erin A. Dolgoy's "Humanity in a Posthuman World: M. R. Carey's *The Girl with All the Gifts,*" *Utopian Studies* 29(3) (2018): 343–361.

8. Carey, *The Girl*, 38.

9. Carey, *The Girl*, 289.

10. There are, of course, exceptions to these formulations. Neither Plato nor Nietzsche are so easily categorized, for example.

11. Plato, *Apology of Socrates, in Four Texts on Socrates*, trans. Thomas G. West and Grace Starry West, 17a–42a (Ithaca: Cornell University Press, 1998); Aristotle, *Politics*, trans. Carnes Lord (Chicago: Chicago University Press, 2013), 1252b30.

12. Plato, *Republic*, trans. Allan Bloom (New York: Basic Books, 1991), Book IV.

13. Aristotle, *Politics*, 1252a4–6.

14. Aristotle, *Politics*, 1253a2.

15. Aristotle, *Politics*, 1253a8–15.

16. Carey, *The Girl*, 14.

17. Thomas Hobbes, *Leviathan*, ed. Edwin Curley (Indianapolis: Hackett Publishing Company, Inc., 1994), 75, I.13.3.

18. Hobbes, *Leviathan*, 79–81, I.14.1–7.

19. Hobbes, *Leviathan*, 76, I.13.9.

20. Hobbes, *Leviathan*, 77, I.13.10.

21. John Locke, *Second Treatise of Government*, in *Locke: Two Treatises of Government*, ed. Peter Laslett (Cambridge: Cambridge University Press, 1988), 269.

22. Locke, *Second Treatise*, 271.

23. Locke, *Second Treatise*, 274.

24. On the base, the children are fed a bowl of grubs once a week.

25. According to both thinkers, legitimacy is determined by a sovereign's willingness to abide by rule of law. Any type of regime can be legitimate, so long as the sovereign obeys his/her/its own laws.

26. Carey, *The Girl*, 3.

27. Carey, *The Girl*, 66.

28. Carey, *The Girl*, 11.

29. After they are forced to flee the base, Justineau tells Melanie about the spread of the infection and the collapse of human civilization. Melanie learns that unless capable people are in charge, tense situations often turn out very badly. Following the mutation of the fungus, had wiser humans been responsible for policy, the outcome may have been different. Melanie cannot risk the future of the hybrid children by allowing a leader less competent than she may be to arise. Carey, *The Girl*, 244–245.

30. The novel is not explicit about the fate of Melanie's classmates. Assuming the facility housing the children is successfully locked-down during the junker raid, the children should survive in stasis for a long period of time. Alternatively, they may have been killed by the horde of hungries used by the junkers to overwhelm the base's defenses.

31. Carey, *The Girl*, 6.

32. Carey, *The Girl,* 7 and 42–43.

33. Niccolò Machiavelli, *The Prince*, trans. Harvey C. Mansfield (Chicago: University of Chicago Press, 1998), 25. In footnote 5 of *The Prince*, Mansfield lists possible sources for this quotation: "Polybius, I 8, 16; VII 8; Livy XXIV 4; Justin, XXIII 4; I Samuel 18:8. Cf. the Dedicatory Letter to the *Discourses on Livy*."

34. Carey, *The Girl*, 317.

35. Carey, *The Girl*, 318.

36. Carey, *The Girl*, 384.

37. Carey, *The Girl*, 345.

38. Carey, *The Girl*, 390.

39. Carey, *The Girl*, 328–330.
40. Carey, *The Girl*, 365.
41. Machiavelli, *The Prince*, 22 (chapter VI).
42. Carey, *The Girl*, 392.
43. Machiavelli, *The Prince*, 22 (chapter VI).
44. Machiavelli, *The Prince*, 34–38 (chapter VIII). Machiavelli's discussion concerning the proper time for cruelty is somewhat tempered by his argument in *Discourses on Livy* (Book III, chapter 1), in which he claims that both republics and kingdoms must periodically be drawn toward the violence of their beginnings in order to renew themselves and avoid fatal deterioration. These two arguments can be reconciled through consideration of Melanie as both founder and ruler. She follows Machiavelli's recommendation in *The Prince*; presumably a future ruler will heed the warning in the *Discourses*. Niccolò Machiavelli, *Discourses on Livy*, trans. Harvey C. Mansfield and Nathan Tarcov (Chicago: University of Chicago Press, 1998).
45. Machiavelli, *The Prince*, 22 (chapter VI).
46. Machiavelli, *The Prince*, 23 (chapter VI).
47. Machiavelli, *The Prince*, 23 (chapter VI).
48. Machiavelli, *The Prince*, 61 (chapter XV).
49. The closest Machiavelli actually comes to saying this is in *The Prince*, 70–71 (chapter XVIII).
50. Philippa Foot, "The Problem of Abortion and the Doctrine of the Double Effect," *Oxford Review* 5 (1967): 1–5.
51. Carey, *The Girl*, 336.
52. Carey, *The Girl*, 83.
53. Carey, *The Girl*, 136.
54. Carey, *The Girl*, 15.
55. Carey, *The Girl*, 83.
56. Carey, *The Girl*, 399.

BIBLIOGRAPHY

Aeschylus. *The Eumenides*. In *Aeschylus I: Oresteia*, translated by David Grene and Richmond Lattimore, 131–175. Chicago: University of Chicago Press, 1953.

Aristotle. *Politics*. Translated by Carnes Lord, 2nd edition. Chicago: University of Chicago Press, 2013.

Carey, M. R. *The Girl with All the Gifts*. London: Orbit Books, 2014.

Foot, Philippa. "The Problem of Abortion and the Doctrine of the Double Effect." *Oxford Review* 5 (1967): 1–5.

Hale, Kimberly Hurd, and Erin A. Dolgoy. "Humanity in a Posthuman World: M. R. Carey's *The Girl with All the Gifts*." *Utopian Studies* 29(3) (2018): 343–361.

Hobbes, Thomas. *Leviathan*. Translated by Edwin Curley. Indianapolis: Hackett Publishing Company, Inc., 1994.

Locke, John. *Second Treatise of Government*. In *Locke: Two Treatises of Government*, edited by Peter Laslett, 265–428. Cambridge: Cambridge University Press, 1988.

Machiavelli, Niccolò. *Discourses on Livy*. Translated by Harvey C. Mansfield and Nathan Tarcov. Chicago: University of Chicago Press, 1998.

———. *The Prince*. Translated by Harvey C. Mansfield, 2nd edition. Chicago: University Of Chicago Press, 1998.

Pangle, Thomas L. "Interpretive Essay." In *The Laws of Plato*, translated by Thomas L. Pangle, 375–510. Chicago: University of Chicago Press, 1988.

Plato. *Apology of Socrates*. In *Four Texts on Socrates*, translated by Thomas G. West and Grace Starry West, 17a–42a. Ithaca: Cornell University Press, 1998.

———. *Laws*. Translated by Thomas L. Pangle. Chicago: University of Chicago Press, 1988.

———. *Republic*. Translated by Allan Bloom, 2nd edition. New York: Basic Books, 1991.

Rousseau, Jean-Jacques. *On the Social Contract*. In *Jean-Jacques Rousseau: The Basic Political Writings*, translated by Donald A. Cress, 141–235. Indianapolis: Hackett Publishing Company, 1987.

Chapter Eleven

Bacon, Transhumanism, and Reflections from the Black Mirror

David N. Whitney and Steven Michels

While many works of contemporary science fiction address the perennial questions of social and political life, few have done so with the popular appeal of the television series *Black Mirror*.[1] The show, created by Charlie Brooker for Channel 4 in Great Britain, first appeared in 2011 and was purchased by Netflix in 2015. After four seasons of three episodes each, the show returned for a stand-alone, interactive episode in late 2018 called *Black Mirror: Bandersnatch*, which required audiences to choose their own adventure and determine the plot and even the outcomes. The fifth season appeared in June 2019.

The show's vignette-style storytelling allows it to create a series of alternate and unconnected realities in which some technological innovation has altered how we live, love, and work. It is not wrong to call the show a twenty-first-century *Twilight Zone*. With a subtle reference to what our phones and computers look like when powered down, the name of the show also implies that these devices might reveal some dark truths about human nature and modern life. The episodes are unsettling and rarely leave the viewer with the feeling that the scenario presented within is mere fantasy. Because it is generally grounded in technology that appears realistic (if not now, then in the near future), it forces the viewer to confront fundamental issues of politics and existence related to our increasing control over nature.

To consider what the show has to say about science and social and political life, we return to where we started: early modernity and the scientism of Francis Bacon. Bacon's dogmatic emphasis on method (and the postulate that it can be utilized in all areas of knowledge), along with his reductionist account of man and his utopianism, leads to the reasonable claim that he is not only the founder of the new science (as he is often credited and rightly so), but also that he is also the originator of the belief that science can be used as a means to determine the values and structure of society, or what is called scientism.

We will examine the show in relation to Bacon (section one) and also to more contemporary transhumanistic thinkers (section two) who share many of Bacon's beliefs regarding science. We will also explore the political implications, often unstated, which these perspectives all seem to have in common, with particular focus on the utopianism of Bacon and the transhumanists. The final section considers the ethical implications of technology, with particular attention to the critiques of technology offered by Jean-Jacques Rousseau and Friedrich Nietzsche.

We now turn to two representative episodes ("The Entire History of You" and "San Junipero") that span the spectrum of pessimism and optimism offered by the show. Even though "San Junipero" ends on a decidedly happier note, it raises just as many concerns about the uncritical acceptance of technological advances as other episodes. *Black Mirror* presents us with challenges related to our increased control over nature. More to the point, it makes it difficult if not impossible to serve as a mere spectator. *Black Mirror* does more than reflect: it demands a response.

TWO IMAGES

"The Entire History of You," the third episode from the first season and written by Jesse Armstrong, strikes a familiar tone in the series. It offers us a glimpse into technology that already exists, albeit in a less sophisticated form: a device that records every moment of our lives. "The Grain" is a surgical implant, behind the ear, that allows users to record and "redo" videos of every moment of their lives.

The main character is a young lawyer, Liam Foxwell. The episode begins with him in a seemingly unsuccessful job interview, before heading to a dinner party. Since he arrived earlier than expected, Liam is able to catch a glimpse of his wife, Ffion, interacting with an old fling, Jonas. Liam immediately becomes suspicious due to her body language, the footage of which he rewatches numerous times while at the party. After returning home, the couple argue about the dinner party and Ffion's apparent affinity for Jonas. Ffion admits a history with Jonas but is not entirely forthcoming about the facts of their time together. Liam is able to redo a conversation from years ago to show Ffion is lying about the length of time the two were together.

While drinking through the night, Liam uses an advanced lip-reading feature to try to determine what was being said between Jonas and Ffion when he first arrived at the party. Disturbed by his suspicions, Liam drives to

Jonas's house in the morning. After confronting Jonas, Liam threatens him with a broken liquor bottle and demands that he erase the memory of the time he spent with his wife. During the encounter, Liam learns that his wife had rekindled her romance with Jonas about the time of his daughter's conception.

In the final scenes, Liam, having moved out, paces around his new place, and redos times with his wife and daughter before heading to the bathroom to remove his Grain with a razor blade. The episode ends with a cut to black and silence and, given that one complication of Grain removal is loss of sight, it is likely that Liam went blind.

"San Junipero," the fourth episode from the show's fourth season and the eleventh episode overall, strikes a much more optimistic tone than "Entire History" and indeed most other episodes in the series. The story, written by Brooker, surrounds two lead characters using technology to escape debilitating disease and old age. Technology has developed such that they can transfer consciousness from their physical bodies to a computer chip. The result is that they can create experiences, moving without restriction from time and place, even while they are infirm or unconscious. The larger question, which forms the crux of the episode, is whether to continue the journey after death. For the living, the use of the technology is limited to a handful of hours a week, but it can be used indefinitely after death, essentially offering immortality through "the cloud," referred to in the episode as "San Junipero."

The episode starts with Yorkie, one of the two lead characters, entering a club. Through an ad on a television outside, we learn that the year is 1987. Kelly, the other lead character, is introduced to the viewer via a conversation with Wes, a previous fling. In an effort to avoid engaging Wes further, Kelly strikes up a conversation with Yorkie, as if she is an old friend. While Yorkie has never danced before and has not had a drink in a long time, Kelly is the quintessential social butterfly, self-assured and ready to embrace the moment. A romantic spark becomes apparent early on, but Yorkie turns down an invitation back to Kelly's place as the night ends, citing her engagement.

Yorkie returns shortly thereafter and seeks out Kelly. Through their conversations in the club and after an intimate encounter at Kelly's, we find out Yorkie has never been in a romantic relationship, while Kelly was married. Yorkie reveals she is getting married next week, and later we find out her plans to pass over and become a full timer. In other words, her death is imminent.

Kelly insists on visiting Yorkie in real-life and with assistance from her caretaker is able to visit a quadriplegic Yorkie in the hospital. It turns out her engagement is to Greg, one of the caretakers at the facility. Greg agreed to marry Yorkie so that she could be euthanized. We find out that family consent is required and time (while living) is limited in San Junipero because "everyone would want to stay there." There are also strict regulations involving access to the system, as we find out when Kelly asks Greg to allow her a few minutes of access while she is visiting Yorkie in the hospital. Kelly uses the time to ask Yorkie to marry her. The two get married in the hospital room and Yorkie "passes over" shortly thereafter.

The final scenes are in San Junipero as Yorkie pleads with Kelly to change her mind and become a full timer. Kelly estimates that 80–85 percent of those in San Junipero are permanent residents of the virtual world. Kelly is only a tourist, however, and knows her time is limited. She simply wants to have fun while she still can and does not want to get attached given her limited time.

Yorkie's pitch is successful, as we see the two blissfully together as Belinda Carlisle's "Heaven is a Place on Earth" fittingly yet perhaps ironically plays in the background. We also get a glimpse inside TCKR systems where a machine is shown placing the data for Yorkie and Kelly into the system, which clearly has thousands, if not millions, of others. The immortality of the full timers in San Junipero is dependent on the proper functioning of the machines at TCKR systems, making the lyrics of the background song especially appropriate.

CONQUERING NATURE

Black Mirror offers a powerful vision of what science can do, sharing some similarities with Bacon, but also differing in some respects. Bacon, the first modern thinker to systematically address the relationship between science and society, was *the* partisan for the advancement of science in the early modern period. Although he cannot be credited with a particular scientific achievement, perhaps more importantly, he was in large part responsible for the adaptation of its method and had a sizable influence on Enlightenment thought.

For Bacon, the purpose of science and technology was "relief of man's estate"—that is, that empiricism and the scientific method would lead to new discoveries and inventions that would make life easier, productive, and happier, and also longer. He was an early proponent of the experimental method and argued that by understanding (and manipulating) nature, man could improve his condition. His *New Atlantis* boldly presented us with a scientific utopia in an age when science's value was not readily appreciated.[2] The benefits of science were not readily apparent to his contemporaries, and it was no small feat to convince them of its utility. Likening himself to Columbus, Bacon thought the experimental method could lead us into a new, better world.

The benefits of science, big and small, are certainly on display in every episode of *Black Mirror*. There are advantages of living with the Grain: for example, Liam is able to go over the end of a job interview to catch the vague and non-committal language said to him. In retrospect, the interview had not gone so well, giving Liam time to redo the entire interview and see how he can improve for next time. It also means that he can begin doing so immediately without waiting for the offer that will likely never come. The Grain would not give you another chance to make a first impression, but it would allow you to relive and reexamine those first impressions over and over again.

Apart from the significant professional advantages of living with the Grain, it also has minor interpersonal advantages, too. A Grain analyst notes how half of our memories could be false due to the ease with which memories can be corrupted. The Grain corrects for the inherent failure of the human brain to remember important information. Before entering the party, Liam uses his Grain to access previous encounters with the hosts of the party to remember important elements of their lives. Most importantly, it also makes it possible for Liam to learn that his wife is or was having an affair and indeed likely had a child with another man. He might have had his suspicions without the help of the Grain, but with it, he was able to replay elements of that evening and days past with perfect recall. He might very well have found out in another way, but the Grain made his powers of deduction concrete and unassailable.

The Grain goes a long way to overcoming one of mankind's flaws in a way that Bacon might endorse. Yet there are many disadvantages, some devastating, to living with such powerful technology, which Bacon did or could not anticipate. Indeed, one of the criticisms of modern, technological society is that we too easily become alienated from one another.[3] This is taken to another level in the episode, not because the people are any different than us, but because the technology allows for and even encourages it. At dinner, Jonas mentions his affinity for replays of past romantic encounters as a way to escape stale relationships. After Liam and Ffion's post-dinner party sparring, the couple has a curious kind of "make-up" sex, where they both use their Grains to access what are presumably previous encounters. They even position themselves to avoid having to look each other in their vacant stares. The fact that this behavior goes uncommented on by both of them suggests that it is a common occurrence, which is amusing given Liam's earlier ridicule of Jonas for how he treats his sexual past. Apart from the horror of having your lover get off on someone else, and the fact that videos still require interpretation and are therefore not entirely reliable, there is also the annoyance of being subjected to the mundane memories of others, as with one of the guests who finds it necessary to share details of a less-than-luxurious hotel room from a recent trip. Turning technology from an enhancement to a replacement is a sure sign of disenchantment. It is striking to see just how much the characters are not present because they are pouring over details of previous experiences.

At the same time, the Grain does little to assist with emotions, which is ultimately Liam's downfall. He has perfect recall, but when mixed with alcohol and lack of sleep, his jealousy overwhelms him. Some of Liam's anger undoubtedly related to the part of him that preferred not to have known about his wife's affair or that his daughter was not his own. He was angry enough at his wife to leave, but he was angry enough at the Grain to remove it and risk the physical consequences. Removing the Grain is arguably a rational act, but probably leaves him blind and will adversely affect the quality of his life going forward. He would have been better had he never adopted the technology. Even if he is able to forgive his wife and love her daughter as his own, the damage has been done. One chief characteristic of modern philosophy is its belief that rationality can replace virtue. But *Black Mirror* displays how technology does more harm than good without the self-control and restraint that virtue provides. [4]

Although alienation is most associated with Karl Marx, Rousseau is the earlier and more relevant thinker on the issue. Early in his *Second Discourse*, Rousseau blames technology for creating a gap between how we live in society today and our natural selves, who have the advantage of "constantly having all of one's strengths at one's disposal, of always being ready for any event, and always carrying oneself, so to speak, entirely with one." [5] Liam is dependent on the Grain and the sense of control that it seems to provide, when it is really making him erratic, dependent, and weak.

For Rousseau, reason is a source of alienation because it permits us to constantly think about the future. In the state of nature, we are by necessity preoccupied with physical needs and desires. Science and modernity afford us access to a kind of luxurious standard of living that would have hitherto been unimaginable. [6] The same principle is at work insofar as the only thing that Liam thinks about is the past, and he is burdened by his past self in an unhealthy way. Once Liam is unmoored from the natural limits of his brain, he cannot but help to do damage to his marriage and family. The break with our natural selves is the hard part, but it would seem to make the alienation and isolation in a social and political sense relatively simple to accomplish, if not inevitable.

The first philosopher to fully appreciate the consequences of the modern project was Nietzsche. In addition to warning against certain types of history or memories that can do damage to our ability to do great things, Nietzsche sees Bacon and other empiricists not as an advance of reason, but as "an *attack* on the philosophic spirit." [7] As he concludes, "It is not the victory of science that distinguishes our nineteenth century, but the victory of scientific method over science." [8] For Nietzsche, science is not an extension of human knowledge so much as it is a lowering of human potential. In that sense, the transhumanists are not transcending the limits nature has placed on humanity, but replacing life as a value and a goal with science and scientism. In that sense, it is not transhumanism, but anti-humanism.

This form of science is not hostile to religion, Nietzsche explains, but comes to rely on the discipline and simple morality that Christianity offers to give scientists a purpose beyond the devotion to their method. In its place, Nietzsche called for a science that did not have a flawed view of nature and human nature as its point of departure but was instead focused on the impulses and desires of human nature, in a way that resembles Rousseau.[9] Science in the service of life rather than itself would also leave room for, if not require, not only a philosophy worthy of the name, but also a real religion that could serve as the foundation for civilization.[10]

HEAVEN IS A PLACE ON EARTH

Bacon's vision of a scientific utopia in *New Atlantis*, while interesting, was nothing more than a fantastical dream to his contemporaries and, until the last century, was relegated to serving a modest role as inspiration for scientific societies (such as the Royal Society) or educational institutions. However, incredible scientific advances in the last few decades and an accelerating rate of growth in fields such as genetics, nanotechnology, and robotics have made some of Bacon's bolder predictions seem conservative. Transhumanism has emerged as a philosophical heir to Bacon's project and its proponents are arguing for a radical transformation of society in the same revolutionary spirit found in Bacon's philosophy.

Writing nearly five hundred years after Bacon, Zoltan Istvan, an avowed transhumanist, offers us a bold look at a not-so-distant future where transhumanists overcome seemingly insurmountable obstacles and literally transform the world. Consider Istvan's *The Transhumanist Wager* and note the striking similarities to Bacon's *New Atlantis*.

The revolutionary character of the work is readily apparent from the start as Istvan outlines the Three Laws of Transhumanism:

1. A transhumanist must safeguard one's own existence above all else.
2. A transhumanist must strive to achieve omnipotence as expediently as possible—so long as one's actions do not conflict with the First Law.
3. A transhumanist must safeguard value in the universe—so long as one's actions do not conflict with the First and Second Laws.[11]

Like Bacon, Istvan presents a utopian world transformed by science and technology. In both cases, the proponents of science represent a small minority of the population who separate themselves from the rest of the world in order to succeed (at least initially). Both nations possess strict codes of secrecy and closely guard their knowledge. They seek to control fate and conquer chance by learning the laws of nature, and a strong emphasis is placed on scientific education as a result.

Both philosophies embrace science as the way to overcome limitations of human nature that have plagued humanity. And since scientific knowledge depends on us, the only limitations we have are self-imposed. Therefore, the fact that we have not overcome death, for instance, is not necessarily because it is impossible. We simply have not gained the proper knowledge yet. Bacon would likely point to the incredible advances made in science and technology as proof of the efficacy of the experimental method he advocated, and transhumanists can point to the progress made over the last century as reasonable proof that their goals are attainable.

While there are numerous facets of transhumanism, Max More's definition adequately captures the spirit of the movement: "Transhumanism is a class of philosophies (such as extropian perspectives) of life that seek the continuation and acceleration of the evolution of intelligent life beyond its currently human form and human limitations by means of science and technology, guided by life-promoting principles and values."[12] More calls transhumanism a "life philosophy" and likens it to "complex worldviews such as secular humanism and Confucianism that have practical implications for our lives without basing themselves on any supernatural or physically transcendent belief."[13] He argues transhumanism takes the Enlightenment emphasis on humanism as a starting point but goes beyond mere "educational and cultural refinements" to improve human nature. In his view, transhumanism embraces the use of technology "to overcome limits imposed by our biological and genetic heritage."[14] The ultimate goal is to become "posthuman," which involves "exceeding the limitations that define the less desirable aspects of the human condition."[15] Diseases, aging, and inevitable death would be overcome, at the same time we would see an appreciable increase in cognitive abilities and a moderation and refinement of emotions.

Technology comes out in a better light in "San Junipero," which shows how technology does nothing but bring people together and extend life for as long as you want it. Extending life by moving consciousness to a digital form is consistent with transhumanism, if not Bacon's vision. Indeed, the process of moving consciousness to a digital form is simply known as "uploading" among transhumanists. Transhumanists who subscribe to functionalism would have no qualms about the prospect. According to More, "functionalism holds that a particular mental state or cognitive system is independent of any specific physical instantiation, but must always be physically instantiated at any time in *some* physical form."[16]

Uploading begs the question of what then we mean by life and how it is lived. We know physical pain can be taken out of the equation by the remark

Kelly makes to Yorkie on the rooftop. The hedonistic Quagmire seems to be filled with people who take physical pleasure as their only source of flourishing, but their excessive devotion to it might be related to their inability to really feel what they are experiencing.

Psychological pain is another matter. People in San Junipero clearly feel emotional pain. Yorkie, Kelly, and Wes all demonstrate significant emotional distress and long-term scarring. Kelly's husband turned down the opportunity to pass over to San Junipero, a decision Yorkie cannot comprehend. Later we find out the main reason was the loss of their daughter. The technology was unavailable to her so Kelly's husband did not think it was fair for him to use it. We can also question just how content Yorkie and especially Kelly will be as permanent residents in the long term. Kelly was adamant about not passing over due to her husband and daughter not doing so. Her relationship with Yorkie is new and exciting, but it might not be as permanent as the technology will allow.

One striking feature of San Junipero is just how much it resembles the "real world." This makes sense for those who suffer from debilitating diseases. In those cases, it is easy to imagine that relief from pain and the ability to do ordinary activities is what most would want. However, what about those who are not actively suffering from serious ailments? It is unclear how much agency we have in this version of the afterlife. In the afterlife, would we really want to be stuck in a replay of our everyday lives on earth indefinitely? As Nietzsche explains, the idea that your life would return eternally the same could either be thrilling or crushing depending on the life that you lived.[17]

While the technology employed in "San Junipero" is clearly consistent with transhumanist principles, the vision of a society that has overcome death is analogous to what Bacon shows us in *New Atlantis*. And like San Junipero, in spite of superficial appearances, there are good reasons to question whether the people in Bacon's tale are truly happy. As Dolgoy and Hale point out in the opening chapter to this volume, in spite of the repeated assertions to the contrary ("Happy are the people of Bensalem"), a closer look at the text reveals dark undertones. The scientists may have a genuine claim to happiness in the sense that they have the freedom to pursue scientific endeavors and are honored throughout the society. Meanwhile, average citizens are "free to enjoy the safety, security, prosperity, and fecundity of a technologically advanced society in exchange for their non-interference in the rule of Salomon's House."[18] They possess no ostensible political power and cannot leave the island. Procreation seems to be the greatest achievement for ordinary citizens, as evident by the Feast of the Family.

There are other questions that arise from the episode. We do know the use of the technology is strictly regulated thanks to Greg, but it is unclear how much involvement the government has aside from the familial consent law for euthanasia. Does the government also monitor the content? Is there a way out for those who have chosen to become full time residents? It is also unclear how many people have opted in to the system, but as with "Entire History," we have reason to believe that the decision to opt out is atypical. Perhaps the most important concerns are cost and access. Is TCKR one of many companies utilizing the technology or do they have a monopoly? Does everyone have the ability to be uploaded, or is it reserved for only those who could afford it?

In a society where everything is directed at scientific advances and mere fecundity is the honored as a virtue, it is not unreasonable to imagine ordinary citizens being "sacrificed" at the altar of science through experimentation. Even though death is not mentioned, there are fewer chambers for those who are healed than those who are sick. And given the celebration of fecundity within the society, the ban on traveling, widespread experimentation, and the limited size of the island, it is reasonable to assume that death may be much more common than is portrayed.[19] The utopias of Bensalem and San Junipero, seemingly happy on the surface, both point to significant problems.

"The Entire History of You" and the Grain also addresses the central platforms of transhumanism: enhancement. Enhancement refers to "a procedure that improves our functioning: any intervention which increases our capabilities for general flourishing."[20] Characteristics such as strength and agility, increased memory and intelligence, and resistance to diseases and aging all fit into the category. Ronald Bailey, echoing the proactionary principle outlined by More, argues for an aggressive pursuit of intellectual and physical enhancement.

More, much like Bacon, laments the lack of progress in certain areas of natural science, pointing to the general acceptance of the precautionary principle by policy makers. This can cause us to unduly focus on the worst-case scenarios and forego progress. In its place, More offers the "proactionary principle" on the assumption that inaction is often just as, if not more, dangerous as action.[21] Bailey suggests that enhancements will not only allow people the ability to better themselves physically, but also that they are likely to become more virtuous.[22] Drawing from Rawls's political liberalism, he argues transhumanism qualifies as a "reasonable comprehensive doctrine" and therefore deserves our tolerance.[23] The individual should be able to choose enhancement if he or she chooses. The Grain is not mandatory, but it is not entirely voluntary, since Ffion's baby has one. We also have to wonder if any activities may be limited, or banned altogether, for those who do not have a Grain. For example, Liam is required to show the security at the airport his last week of video. Although it would not be difficult to evade detection, we could easily see how having a Grain could be a requirement to get on a plane. The purpose of the Grain might be to "enhance" the recall of its users, but the end result could be a step toward political and social tyranny. It would also enable an entirely new form of spiritual and moral tyranny of the self, insofar as users allow the errors and misfortunes of the past to overwhelm their present and future opportunities and choices.

Moreover, there are also massive problems with being unable to wipe the slate clean, which progress sometimes requires. In accounting different forms of history, Nietzsche outlines a kind of history he calls "antiquarian," which deals with the immersion into the past, especially for academics. [24] The Grain turns everyone into unwitting academics and historians who are, as Nietzsche warns, burdened by the weight of the past. It can be beneficial in the sense that we can be inspired by or learn from the past, but it can also make us unduly deferential and unoriginal. Every kind of knowledge, scientific or otherwise, should be evaluated according to how it serves life, not how it serves itself.

Nietzsche is primarily referring to civilizations and peoples, but the lesson is truer for individuals. It is true, as the Grain analyst mentions at the party, about how much our memory deteriorates. What goes unsaid is how much of that deterioration is beneficial to wellness. The human brain is not a memory machine; it is a storytelling machine that spins narratives designed to make us understand the world and our place in it. What is psychosis other than stories that make us and our desires into villains. The inability to create such narratives might lead to a more empirical accurate and truthful life, but it would also be the makings of much misery.

There is the related issue of what the Grain would do to strong and creative people—Nietzsche's philosophers of the future, for example. Nietzsche's opposition to modern morality resulted from how, as he saw it, it ushered in an era of bad conscience and resentment against what had been understood to be natural and necessary passions. The Grain is not omnipotent, but it would possess a kind of omniscience that would invariably cause us to deny our will to power. In that sense, the Grain would not turn us into good people as much as it would make us feel like guilty Christians.

THE DANGEROUS DREAM

Bacon's unbounded optimism in the power of science led him to overlook the most pressing issues of human existence. The sobriety found in his earlier writings, in which he constantly warns against forgetting our mortal condition, gave way to an intoxicating dream in his final great work. There is a reason that the scientific paradise that was Bensalem was so isolated and kept insulated from the very things that have plagued every other society in history. Bacon substitutes his new science in the place of the natural philosophy of his predecessors but fails to adequately account for politics.

This is not to say that he ignores the subject altogether. Instead, it is simply subsumed under the umbrella of his new science:

> It may also be doubted (rather than objected) whether we are speaking of perfecting only Natural Philosophy by our method or also the other sciences, Logic, Ethics and Politics. We certainly mean all that we have said to apply to all of them, and just as common logic, which governs things by means of the syllogism, is applicable not only to the natural sciences but to all the sciences, so also our science, which proceeds by *induction*, covers all.[25]

In other words, the method is to be applied to every facet of knowledge, which is problematic for a number of reasons. For one thing, humans cannot (and should not) be subjected to experimentation in the same way the rest of the natural world can. Bacon essentially foresees no limit to man's ability to control his own fate through the domination of nature. He presents us with a technological society that seemingly knows neither death nor disorder—in other words, heaven on earth. The only precondition for this earthly salvation lies in the adoption of Bacon's new science. Humanity no longer needs fortune or divine intervention to pin our hopes on a bountiful afterlife; instead, we can manipulate nature to provide a seemingly endless array of earthly goods.

Bacon does not even list politics as one of the subjects that is studied in Solomon's House. It has a ruling body and regulations, but we are left to imagine its politics. The most basic responsibility of the regime seems to involve determining what discoveries are helpful or harmful. Bensalem is governed by science and scientists, but it is not for the sake of science or scientists. There is recognition of the need for policy making guided by "responsible and inclusive moral vision," but we are not given any insight as to how that is achieved.

Much of what is disturbing about *Black Mirror* is the way in which its characters feel like experiments for new untested technologies. It is also a litmus test for human nature. In the second season's "White Bear," also written by Brooker, a mysterious signal has turned most of humanity into aggressive voyeurs, while others are turned into hunters, who are lawless and violent, killing and stealing for sport. As one of the characters explains, "I guess they were always like that underneath; they just needed the rules to change and no one to intervene." In that sense, the show acts as a laboratory and turns its audience into research assistants.

In addition to the personal questions related to relationships and how much partners should or can know about one another, it also raises the question of freedom and civil liberties. Is there any way such a technology could be implemented without abuse from the government or private corporations? After arriving home from the party, Liam and Ffion quickly review the Grain of their baby to make sure the babysitter did her job properly. This is the first time we see a Grain accessed by a third party without the consent of the individual. This will happen again when Liam compels Jonas and Ffion to reveal their secret.

Not everyone in the society has one (we are told it is particularly unpopular with prostitutes), but it seems as if the vast majority of those in the society do embrace the technology. Indeed, everyone but Helen at the dinner party had one in, suggesting going without—she had hers removed—is a minority position. The first reaction of the other guests to this news is surprise, and the first question posed to her is whether it was a "political" decision. Helen says it was "gouged" from her eighteen months ago and probably sold on the black market since it was unencrypted.

As with Bacon and also transhumanism, much of the political implications are unexplored. And while there is not much in the episode about the governance of the society, we do see the technology being used by airport security, requiring everyone to play back their recent history before being allowed to proceed to board the plane. During the interview, Liam was also informed (rather casually) that his previous quarter would be examined by human resources through footage on his Grain, and when asked about it, he says there have been no deletions outside of the norm.

Many of the uses of the Grain within the episode are ostensibly designed to enhance security: the warning not to drive while impaired, airport security, and child care monitoring. Short of compulsion, surveillance, or subpoenas, there is also the everyday societal expectation that you will share aspects of your day on command, as when Liam was almost forced to redo his job interview after arriving at the party. Not surprisingly, it was Jonas who intervened and allowed Liam some semblance of privacy. Your days are not just recorded for you, but as Ffion and Jonas learn, they are also preserved for the scrutiny of others.

Bacon suggests the transition from his society to the one presented in *New Atlantis* will be relatively smooth and peaceful. Bacon assures us that "the danger of not trying and the danger of not succeeding are not equal since the former risks the loss of a great good, the latter of a little human effort." Unlike Bacon, Istvan embraces violence as a necessary requirement for the success of his movement. While he would prefer to see a peaceful transition, the odds of such an event occurring are remote. The attempts to change people's minds through persuasion and ordinary politics fail miserably in the story: violence and fear are the tools that ultimately bring success to the movement.

Black Mirror, like Bacon and the transhumanists, is also political in an indirect way. A couple of the episodes take on the issue of what technology and social media have done to electoral politics—the first episode ("The National Anthem") that involves a prime minister being blackmailed into having sex with a pig is the most prominent—but most of the episodes assume a political community of some kind and proceed to detail what life is like in it. For example, there could have been a violent upheaval in the world depicted in "Fifteen Million Merits," where everyone who is not needed for entertainment is used for energy—but since it is ultimately irrelevant to the story, it remains unsaid. Unlike the psychological torment and angst that is put on full display, any political revolutions that take place in the *Black Mirror* universe are private.

Given the spread of personal communications technology, the thrust of *Black Mirror* is primarily psychological and social, with political and economic questions looming in the background. With industrial technology, the impact was economic and social. What is more, Bacon and More likely spend so little attention on politics because they view political life as fundamentally an obstacle to the advancement of science. As such, there is not much to be learned from it, other than how to stop it from being an impediment to progress.

BACK TO THE FUTURE

While Bacon and transhumanists both make compelling cases as to the utility of science, they fail to offer sufficient guidance to navigate the political and ethical questions brought about by the technology that they champion. Bacon's experimental method is designed to explain phenomenal relations and how things work. Bacon explicitly denounces metaphysics and derides moral and ethical philosophy since it deals with the "proud knowledge of good and evil." It does not and cannot answer normative causes.

Black Mirror is far less optimistic about science and technology, but it is no more helpful in terms of guiding principles for social and political life. Where might we look for insight for how we might gain the benefits that science can bring, while also being mindful of the harm it can do when its agnostic force is left unchecked?

Religion might be an obvious answer. In his seminal *Democracy in America*, Alexis de Tocqueville claims religion as an essential institution in a democracy, which can help show citizens how to use their liberty in a virtuous way.[26] Were he writing today, he might say the same thing about religion and technology. Science is often pitted against religion, such that if the two perspectives are not able to live harmoniously, they might be able to balance one another, especially to the extent that religion can allow us to see ourselves and each other as more than a sum of our biological parts and impulses. Although it is mostly ignored by transhumanists and downplayed by Bacon, the recognition that individuals have inherent dignity can slow the reflexive embrace of technology that can result from reductionist perspectives.

San Junipero offers up a religion of sorts—or at least an approximation of the afterlife, which looks pretty good. It solves the question of what happens when we die: our consciousness is stored in a server that continues to run us as programs. There are certainly worse fates. But it does nothing to answer the question of whether immortality is *the right thing to do.*

Bacon's project can be interpreted as being consistent with Christian principles, even though part of that might have had more to do with the deference Bacon was affording religion, given the time of his writing. The history of Bensalem, after all, makes clear that the society's greatness derived from its science, not its religion. It is also strongly suggested that the scientists are responsible for the religion that is practiced on the island.

Toward the end of Book I of *Novum Organum,* Bacon anticipates a critique of his vision: "if anyone objects that the sciences and arts have been perverted to evil and luxury and such like, the objection should convince no one. . . . Just let man recover the right over nature which belongs to him by God's gift, and give it scope; *right reason* and *sound religion* will govern its use."[27] While this might be true, it must be asked *who* will exhibit right reason and *how* this can be assured, especially given the extent to which science and right reason can degrade non-scientific thinking. Bacon's attempt to reason away the difference is vague and unconvincing.

Conversely, Istvan firmly rejects all religion as nothing more than harmful superstition and as one of the primary obstacles to the realization of his vision. *The Transhumanist Wager* leaves no room for traditional religion and seems to suggest new principles of morality will naturally emerge once the revolution has occurred (without outlining what those principles might look like or how they will be formed). Istvan's story takes place well after the scientific revolution in a secularized Western world that has already been transformed by technology to an appreciable extent. Hostility to religion is no longer a disqualifying feature, and Istvan's work wholeheartedly embraces the antagonistic view of religion shared by "new atheists," such as Richard Dawkins, Christopher Hitchens, and Sam Harris.

It is clear that Bacon himself possesses a strong moral sense, as his project ultimately aims at the relief of man's estate and on charitable and beneficial inventions. For the most part, the same "good intentions" can be attributed to transhumanists. Yet Bacon and transhumanists both deride the moral philosophy of the classics and scholastics while failing to offer a suitable replacement. Science may be able to provide man with the power to control nature, but it does not tell him how to use that power. Bacon was prescient in his realization of the magnificent power that could be derived from science, and advances in medicine and technology have indeed helped to relieve man's estate. But natural science provides no guidance as to how we should use the power it gives us over nature. At the same time, the faith in science denigrates other institutions and ways of knowing that could be beneficial to individuals and society as a whole. Science is not only dangerous for what it can give us, but also for what it can take away.

Others have suggested the respect for individual rights and freedom offered by liberalism will be the panacea for the problems of collectivism or tyrannies related to technology.[28] The most obvious problem with this position is the fact liberalism is actually *declining* in the world as a whole—and not simply because liberal societies have already demonstrated a willingness to give up freedoms in the name of convenience or security.[29] Even in societies that have embraced science and allow for competition within the economic marketplace, corresponding political freedoms have not always followed. Perhaps no country exemplifies this better than China, with the recent implementation of a social credit system eerily similar to the disturbing "Nosedive" episode of *Black Mirror*, where everyone has the opportunity to rate everyone that they come into contact with.[30]

Apart from the challenges faced by technology, it is also an open question as to whether liberalism adequately accounts for the full amplitude of human nature. While the founders of liberalism can be credited with the natural rights tradition, they also took a narrow and rather dim view of humanity, which is not too different from what is on display in *Black Mirror*. Even if it is assumed that societies like Bensalem and San Junipero could come to exist, one still must wonder what would guide the decisions of the policy makers. The materialistic view of man, characteristic of modernity and consistent with liberalism, arguably undermines the dignity and value of human life. While liberalism certainly deserves credit for the spread of economic and political freedom, and for many of the advances in science and technology, there is also a litany of abuses at the hands of liberal societies—including weapons of mass destruction, eugenics, and discrimination of all kinds.[31] This is not to say liberalism does not have its merits, especially over shallow utilitarian approaches, but we should be cautious in our assumptions for what a political order based solely on individual rights can do writ large, especially when powerful technologies are added to the mix. This is what *Black Mirror* explores par excellence.

Education is and should be the preferred way to both realize and control the power of science. *Black Mirror*'s most explicit statement on education occurs in "Men against Fire," another Brooker episode, from the third season. The story tracks a solider (Stripe) who has been deployed to a foreign country to exterminate mutated humans, which are called "roaches." The roaches, we come to learn, are not actually mutants but only appear to be so due to a neural implant in the soldiers. In that sense, the education offered by the state is designed to serve the interest of the state, while doing great harm to the truth and the dignity of individuals on both sides of the border.

Without a program for a proper liberal education, it seems dubious that "right reason" will be exhibited, and yet right reason is also required to establish the conditions and the curriculum for such an education. This is why ancient political philosophers such as Plato and Aristotle went to great lengths to emphasize the importance of philosophic wisdom for political life and why the turn from a broad, liberal arts education to professionalism and job training is so harmful.

The fact that science has progressed as far as it has makes a satisfactory political science even more necessary. Our control over nature has vested us with great power. Yet political science in its current state is unable to offer much guidance for how to use that power. This is because of the deleterious effects of scientism. Too much emphasis has been put on the *method* used to acquire knowledge, while certain forms of knowledge, particularly ethical and political, are discounted completely unless they conform to the methodological expectations of positivistic science.[32] This type of attitude has all but erased normative philosophy from the curriculum of higher education, and the decline of moral philosophy can be traced to the same source.

Black Mirror may not give us answers to the questions, but it reminds us of the necessity of asking questions about what we value and what limits we should place on our freedom in order to remain free.

CONCLUSION

Several decades ago, Isaiah Berlin noted that the twentieth century would be remembered primarily for two things: the rise of political ideologies and the rapid advance of technology. Although the ideologies question has not been settled, with regard to technology, what was true of the last century could be even truer of the next.

It is apparent the transhumanist movement, as articulated by Istvan, owes much of its philosophical foundation to Francis Bacon. The most important difference is transhumanists are operating in a world that has already been transformed by science. The transhumanist movement suffers from the same fatal flaw as Bacon's philosophy in its failure to account for the potentially destructive effects of technology.

The exponential growth of technology has appreciably changed how we communicate with each other, how we view ourselves, and how we view technology itself. The genre of science fiction has generally explored the relationship between man and technology, but there is a particular urgency to contemporary works since we are on the verge of possessing the technologies portrayed.

As we near the end of the second decade of the twenty-first century, the prestige of science is virtually unquestioned and technological advancements are seen as natural and desirable. Assuming technology continues to progress exponentially, serious questions will have to be addressed as to the role of science within society. Some, like transhumanist Ray Kurzweil, see the merging of human and artificial intelligence as inevitable within the next few decades. While Kurzweil thinks the development will be decidedly positive for human civilization, recent history gives us good reasons to question such an optimistic viewpoint. It is worth noting the twentieth century, undoubtedly the most technologically advanced in human history, saw more people die at the hands of their own governments than in all of the wars in history combined. This is not to say that technology is the reason for those deaths, merely that our increased power over nature gives us the ability to do much greater harm (or good) than before.[33]

Technology gives man tremendous power and one must ask how power is to be used before celebration ensues. *Black Mirror* clearly demonstrates the potential dangers of this power. The transhumanist movement tends to suffer from the same flaw as Bacon's philosophy in its failure to account for the potentially destructive effects of technology. Finding the proper balance requires us to answer questions about human nature, the good, justice, and right order. Those questions constitute the proper domain of political science.

NOTES

The authors would like to thank Tim McCranor for his many helpful comments and suggestions. Portions of this chapter are adopted from David Whitney, "Salvation through Science? Bacon's *New Atlantis* and Transhumanism," VoegelinView, accessed February 17, 2019, https://voegelinview.com/salvation-science-bacons-new-atlantis-transhumanism/.

1. See also David N. Whitney, *Maladies of Modernity: Scientism and the Deformation of Political Order* (South Bend, IN: St. Augustine Press, 2019).

2. On the debate regarding whether *New Atlantis* is a finished work or not, see Jerry Weinberger, "Introduction," *New Atlantis* and *The Great Instauration*, ed. Jerry Weinberger (Wheeling, IL: Harlan Davidson, 1989), xii.

3. See Sherry Turkle, *Alone Together: Why Expect More from Technology and Less from Each Other* (New York, NY: Basic Books, 2017).

4. See Harvey Mansfield, "Rational Control," *The New Criterion*, September 2006.

5. Jean-Jacques Rousseau, *The Collected Writings of Rousseau*, ed. Roger D. Masters and Christopher Kelly, vol. 3, *Discourse on the Origins of Inequality (Second Discourse) Polemics, and Political Economy* (Hanover, NH: The University Press of New England, 1992), 21.

6. Rousseau, *Second Discourse*, 27.

7. Friedrich Nietzsche, *Beyond Good and Evil: Prelude to a Philosophy of the Future*, trans. Walter Kaufmann (New York, NY: Vintage Books, 1989), 189.

8. Friedrich Nietzsche, *The Will to Power*, trans. Walter Kaufmann and R. J. Hollingdale (New York, NY: Vintage Books, 1968), 261.

9. For more on Nietzsche's response to modernity, see Laurence Lampert, *Nietzsche and Modern Times: A Study of Bacon, Descartes, and Nietzsche* (New Haven, CT: Yale University Press, 1995).

10. See Steven Michels, "Nietzsche and the Religion of the Future," *Animus: The Canadian Journal of Philosophy and Humanities* 9 (2004): 52–72.

11. Zoltan Istvan, *The Transhumanist Wager* (St. Reno, NV: Futurity Imagine Media, LLC, 2013), 4.

12. Max More, "The Philosophy of Transhumanism," *The Transhumanist Reader: Classical and Contemporary Essays on the Science, Technology, and Philosophy of the Human Future*, eds. Max More and Natasha Vita-More (West Sussex: Wiley Blackwell, 2013), 4.

13. More, "The Philosophy of Transhumanism," 4.

14. More, "The Philosophy of Transhumanism," 4.

15. More, "The Philosophy of Transhumanism," 4.

16. More, "The Philosophy of Transhumanism," 7.

17. Friedrich Nietzsche, *Thus Spoke Zarathustra, The Portable Nietzsche*, ed. Walter Kaufmann (New York, NY: Penguin Press, 1982), 327–33.

18. See Dolgoy and Hale above, page 26.

19. See Dolgoy and Hale above, page 18.

20. Ronald Bailey, *"For Enhancing People," The Transhumanist Reader: Classical and Contemporary Essays on the Science, Technology, and Philosophy of the Human Future*, eds. Max More and Natasha Vita-More (West Sussex: Wiley Blackwell, 2013), 328.

21. See Max More, "The Proactionary Principle: Optimizing Technological Outcomes," *Transhumanist Reader*, 261.

22. Bailey, "Enhancing," 327.

23. Bailey, "Enhancing," 333.

24. Friedrich Nietzsche, "The Uses and Disadvantages of History for Life," *Untimely Mediations*, trans. R. J. Hollingdale (Cambridge: Cambridge University Press, 1997), 72–75.

25. Francis Bacon, *The New Organon* (Novum Organum), ed. Jardine and Silverthorne. (Cambridge: Cambridge University Press, 2000), 98.

26. Alexis de Tocqueville, *Democracy in America*, eds. Harvey C. Mansfield and Delba Winthrop (Chicago, IL: University of Chicago Press, 2002), 278–82.

27. Bacon, *Organon*, 101 (emphasis added).

28. Transhumanists such as Wrye Sententia, Ronald Bailey, Martine Rothblatt, and Patrick Hopkins all argue along these lines. Kimberly Hurd Hale has written extensively on problems of technology and society, argues we must renew our commitment to the values of classical liberalism. See *The Politics of Perfection: Technology and Creation in Literature and Film* (Lanham, MD: Lexington Books, 2016), 137.

29. According to Freedom House, freedom in the world has decreased each year for the past twelve years. "Freedom in the World 2018: Democracy in Crisis," accessed February 17, 2019, https://freedomhouse.org/report/freedom-world/freedom-world-2018.

30. As Adam Greenfield explains, "Every Chinese citizen receives a literal, numeric index of their trustworthiness and virtue, and this index unlocks, well, everything." Adam Greenfield, "China's Dystopian Tech Could be Contagious," *The Atlantic*, Feb. 14, 2018.

31. For a good summary of the eugenics movement's impact in the United States, see Trevor Burrus, "The United States Once Sterilized Tens of Thousands—Here's How the Supreme Court Allowed It," accessed February 17, 2019, https://www.cato.org/publications/commentary/united-states-once-sterilized-tens-thousands-heres-how-supreme-court-allowed .

32. On this point, see Eric Voegelin, *The New Science of Politics*, ed. Dante Germino (Chicago, IL: University of Chicago Press, 1952).

33. See R. J. Rummel, *Death by Government* (New Brunswick, NJ: Transaction Publishers, 1994), 24.

BIBLIOGRAPHY

Bacon, Francis. *The New Organon* (Novum Organum). Edited by Jardine and Silverthorne. Cambridge: Cambridge University Press, 2000.

Bailey, Ronald. "For Enhancing People." In *The Transhumanist Reader: Classical and Contemporary Essays on the Science, Technology, and Philosophy of the Human Future*, edited by Max More and Natasha Vita-More, 327–44. West Sussex: Wiley Blackwell, 2013.

Greenfield, Adam. "China's Dystopian Tech Could be Contagious." *The Atlantic*, Feb. 14, 2018.

Hale, Kimberly Hurd. *The Politics of Perfection: Technology and Creation in Literature and Film*. Lanham, MD: Lexington Books, 2016.

Istvan, Zoltan. *The Transhumanist Wager*. St. Reno, NV: Futurity Imagine Media, LLC, 2013.

Lampert, Laurence. *Nietzsche and Modern Times: A Study of Bacon, Descartes, and Nietzsche*. New Haven, CT: Yale University Press, 1995.

Mansfield, Harvey. "Rational Control." *The New Criterion*, September 2006.

Michels, Steven. "Nietzsche and the Religion of the Future." *Animus: The Canadian Journal of Philosophy and Humanities* 9 (2004): 52–72.

More, Max. "The Philosophy of Transhumanism." In *The Transhumanist Reader: Classical and Contemporary Essays on the Science, Technology, and Philosophy of the Human Future*, edited by Max More and Natasha Vita-More, 3–17. West Sussex: Wiley Blackwell, 2013.

———. "The Proactionary Principle: Optimizing Technological Outcomes." In *The Transhumanist Reader: Classical and Contemporary Essays on the Science, Technology, and Philosophy of the Human Future*, edited by Max More and Natasha Vita-More, 258–67. West Sussex: Wiley Blackwell, 2013.

Nietzsche, Friedrich. *Thus Spoke Zarathustra, The Portable Nietzsche*. Translated by Walter Kaufmann New York, NY: Penguin Press, 1982.

———. *Beyond Good and Evil: Prelude to a Philosophy of the Future*. Translated by Walter Kaufmann. New York, NY: Vintage Books, 1989.

———. *The Will to Power*. Translated by Walter Kaufmann and R. J. Hollingdale. New York, NY: Vintage Books, 1968.

———. "The Uses and Disadvantages of History for Life." In *Untimely Mediations*, trans. R. J. Hollingdale. Cambridge: Cambridge University Press, 1997.

Rousseau, Jean-Jacque. *Discourse on the Origins of Inequality (Second Discourse) Polemics, and Political Economy*. Volume 3, in *The Collected Writings of Rousseau*. Edited by Roger D. Masters and Christopher Kelly. 13 vols. Hanover, NH: The University Press of New England, 1992.

Rummel, R. J. *Death by Government*. New Brunswick, NJ: Transaction Publishers, 1994.

de Tocqueville Alexis. *Democracy in America*. Edited by Harvey C. Mansfield and Delba Winthrop. Chicago, IL: University of Chicago Press, 2002.

Turkle, Sherry. *Alone Together: Why Expect More from Technology and Less from Each Other*. New York, NY: Basic Books, 2017.

Voegelin, Eric. *The New Science of Politics*. Edited by Dante Germino. Chicago, IL: University of Chicago Press, 1952.

Weinberger, Jerry. "Introduction," *New Atlantis* and *The Great Instauration*. Edited by Jerry Weinberger, Wheeling, IL: Harlan Davidson, 1989.

Whitney, David N. *Maladies of Modernity: Scientism and the Deformation of Political Order*. South Bend, IN: St. Augustine Press, 2019.

Index

About the Contributors

Timothy McCranor is a doctoral student in the Political Science Department at Boston College.

Steven Michels, associate provost and professor of political science at Sacred Heart University, is the author of *Sinclair Lewis and American Democracy* (Lexington Books, 2017) and *The Case against Democracy* (Praeger, 2014).

Nicholas Anderson is a PhD candidate in political theory at Boston College. He holds a BA in liberal arts from St. John's College (2015). He is currently working on a dissertation on the role of hope in Kant's political philosophy.

Nivedita Bagchi received her PhD in political theory from the University of Virginia. She is the author of *Human Nature and Politics in Utopian and Anti-Utopian Fiction*. In addition, she has written, presented, and taught classes on *Casablanca*, the writings of Charlotte Perkins Gilman, and *The Lord of the Rings*. She is an associate professor of political theory at Millersville University of Pennsylvania.

Jeffrey J. S. Black is currently distinguished visiting professor of political science at the United States Air Force Academy. He is a member of the faculty of St. John's College, in Annapolis, Maryland, and Santa Fe, New Mexico.

Tobin L. Craig is associate professor of political theory and science policy at James Madison College, Michigan State University. His teaching and research focuses on the philosophic foundations and political implications of modern science.

Erin A. Dolgoy teaches courses in American politics, political theory, and interdisciplinary humanities at Rhodes College as assistant professor of political science. Her work has been published in *Perspectives on Political Science*, *Utopian Studies* (with Kimberly Hurd Hale). She is co-editor (with Kimberly Hurd Hale and Bruce Peabody) of *Short Stories and Political Philosophy: Power, Prose, and Persuasion* (Lexington Books, 2019).

Kimberly Hurd Hale is assistant professor of politics at Coastal Carolina University. She is author of *Francis Bacon's* New Atlantis *in the Foundation of Modern Political Thought* (Lexington Books, 2013), *The Politics of Perfection: Technology and Creation in Literature and Film* (Lexington Books, 2016), and co-editor (with Erin A. Dolgoy and Bruce Peabody) of *Short Stories and Political Philosophy: Power, Prose, and Persuasion* (Lexington Books, 2019).

Constance C. T. Hunt is an associate professor at James Madison College at Michigan State University, East Lansing, MI, huntc@msu.edu.

Daniel J. Kapust is professor of political science at UW-Madison, where he directs the Center for Early Modern Studies and the Political Economy, Philosophy, and Politics program. He works primarily on the history of political thought and has published books and articles on figures including Cicero, Sallust, Tacitus, Livy, Machiavelli, Hobbes, and Adam Smith.

Damien K. Picariello is assistant professor of political science at the University of South Carolina–Sumter. He is the editor of *Politics in Gotham: The Batman Universe and Political Thought*, available in paperback in the spring of 2020.

Danielle Sottosanti is a postdoctoral teaching fellow at Fordham University, where she has taught classes on post-apocalyptic fiction, innocence, and writing. Her research interests include medieval romance, post-apocalyptic literature, religious conversion, and race in medieval literature.

David Whitney is an associate professor of political science at Nicholls State University in Louisiana. He is author of *Maladies of Modernity: Scientism and the Deformation of Political Order* (2019).

Paul T. Wilford is assistant professor of political science at Boston College. He writes primarily on Kant and Hegel. He is co-editor of *Athens, Arden,*

Jerusalem (Lexington Books, 2017) and *Kant and the Possibility of Progress* (2020).

www.ingramcontent.com/pod-product-compliance
Lightning Source LLC
Chambersburg PA
CBHW022308280326
41932CB00010B/1023